# Microcomputer Models for Management Decision-Making

## Software and Text

# Microcomputer Models for Management Decision-Making

Software and Text

**Terry L. Dennis**
Rochester Institute of Technology

**Laurie B. Dennis**

West Publishing Company
St. Paul ■ New York ■ Los Angeles ■ San Francisco

| | |
|---|---|
| *Copyediting* | Kim Bornhoft |
| *Interior Design* | David Corona Design Associates |
| *Indexing* | Nancy Little |
| *Composition* | G&S Typesetters, Inc. |
| *Cover art* | San Francisco Skyline, © Steve Proehl, The Image Bank/Minneapolis |

**Equipment Needs:** These programs can be run on an IBM PC or XT or PS/2 or many of the IBM compatibles. The minimum required equipment includes: IBM PC, 256K memory, one double-sided disk drive, DOS version 2.0 or higher (3.0 or 3.1 requires 320K of memory) and a printer (optional).

IBM is a registered trademark of International Business Machines Corporation.
The use of trademarks or other designations is for reference purposes only.

(5¼)   95  94  93  92  91  90  89  88      8  7  6  5  4  3  2  1
(3½)   95  94  93  92  91  90  89  88      8  7  6  5  4  3  2  1

Library of Congress Cataloging-in-Publication Data

Dennis, Terry L.
  Microcomputer models for management decision-making / Terry L.
Dennis, Laurie B. Dennis.—2nd ed.
    p.  cm.
  Bibliography: p.
  Includes index.
  ISBN 0-314-64954-9
  **ISBN** 0–314–38549–5
  1. Management science—Computer programs.  I. Dennis, Laurie B.
II. Title.
T56.24.D46  1988                87-29506
658.4′03—dc19                       CIP

# Dedication

---

*To our parents*
Don and Mary
Ken and Margaret

# Contents

## Chapter 2   Tutorial

## Chapter 3  Linear Programming

## Chapter 4   Integer Linear Programming                                              77

## Chapter 5   Goal Programming                                                       107

## Chapter 6   Transportation                                                         125

# Preface

In the preface to the first edition of this book, we wrote of the not too distant past, when learning to use the quantitative tools of management science usually required students to spend inordinate amounts of time number crunching. We wrote that in too many instances, so much time was spent on teaching and learning the mechanics of the algorithm and performing calculations that problem solving and decision-making (ideally, the real objectives of the course) became secondary. Time spent on teaching or reviewing computational procedures was time taken from other important topics, such as problem formulation and analysis and interpretation of results. Moreover, the emphasis on computational procedures created an artificial situation in the classroom. Once a model had been taught and the test given, it was often discarded and not mentioned or used again ("If this is the third exam, this must be a Markov problem").

We continue to feel that a change is taking place in the classroom and in textbooks. As a result of the increased availability of time-sharing computer terminals and the ubiquitous presence of the microcomputer, the computer is increasingly being used to take the drudge work out of using management science models. Computers are being used by students and faculty to do the number crunching, just as they are being used to do so in the real world. Teachers, texts, and students can now concentrate on using these models to solve problems.

In just the short time between editions, we have seen evidence that this change is not just our gut feeling, or happening in only a few isolated situations. We see the result of this change in the proliferation of solution software, in the interest shown in papers and articles that deal with using computer models to teach MS/OR, in attempts to review and set standards for such software, and most importantly in the September 11, 1986, Final Report of the TIMS Education Committee ("Proposed Model Framework for a First Course on Operations Research/Management Science"), which states "it is expected that the students will be asked to perform analysis using software packages." More and more students are being encouraged to take advantage of computer solutions to MS models. We are being given the opportunity to move on to the next plateau: teaching and learning how to solve problems, defining, delineating and formulating a real situation into its component parts, and selecting the models which will best solve that problem.

We think that the second edition of this book will continue to help us move in that direction. We feel that the models in this book will give students the opportunity to become more familiar with the kinds of computer-based solutions they will be using in business after graduation. It will also relieve them of the tedious computational burden and frequent mathematical errors associated with these models and allow them to concentrate on the problem formulation and solution analysis. However, it is still intended as an instructional tool. To that end, we have

   made data entry in these models as easy as possible by including a new tabular spreadsheet entry format for several of the models, consistent with typical textbook format,

   included an easy-to-use error correction routine,

   provided a way to make modifications or do postoptimality analysis without having to reenter all of the data,

   formatted the output to look like the output shown with the textbook algorithms,

   made the programs extremely tolerant of common errors (they are very user-friendly),

   enabled the user to send output to either a printer or a disk file (or both) after the problem has been solved,

   and have given the user the opportunity to save problems to a disk file for later use or modification.

The new edition contains three new programs: ILP, which will solve ILP, MILP, and 0,1 problems; Goal Programming, which will solve weighted multipriority problems; and Computer Simulation, which includes Monte Carlo simulation, an inventory simulation and a time-dependent queuing simulation. The models have all been tested by reviewers and students.

We emphasize in the first chapter that this book is intended as a supplement to a management science textbook. We also believe, however, that under the right circumstances, in the right classroom, with the right instructor, it can be used as a stand-alone text. However, using this book alone requires a certain level of understanding or knowledge of these models by the user. This can be true in a graduate class or an advanced seminar. In this case the emphasis can assuredly be on problem solving using these models. For instructors using this book as a supplement to a traditional text, we have included a table at the end of this preface which relates this book to several popular texts. (Several of the texts are due to come out in new editions soon, so you may want to check the edition number before using the table.)

The programs were all written in BASIC and compiled to increase their running speed. To the best of our knowledge, the programs run on all IBM PC/XT compatible microcomputers (and the new System 2 computers as well).

We would like to take this opportunity to thank Patrick J. Fitzgerald, Dick Fenton, Nancy Hill-Whilton, Denise Bayco, Jean Cook, and Lucinda Gatch of West Publishing Company, Susan L. Reiland, James A. Pope, James Patterson, Tim McGrath, Sanjieve Phukan and all of the other individuals involved in the review of this text and the models.

## Topical Cross-References to Other Texts

End of Chapter Questions from the following books and others can be answered using the models in the corresponding chapters in this book.

| Dennis & Dennis | AS&W Int MS | AS&W Qnt Mtds | HIler & Lbmn | Cook & Russ | Davis & McKwn | Eppen & Gould | Lee Moore Taylr | Turban & Mered | Taha | Lapin |
|---|---|---|---|---|---|---|---|---|---|---|
| 3 LP | 3–6 | 9–12 | 3–6 | 4–5 | 4–5 | 5–6 | 2–4 | 5–6 | 2–4 | 9–14 |
| 4 ILP | 8 | 14 | 13 | 9 | 9 | 8 | 14 | 6B | 8 | 16 |
| 5 Goal Prog | 6 | — | 8 | 9 | 8 | 19 | 13 | 6 | — | — |
| 6 Trans | 7 | 13 | 7 | 6 | 7 | 7 | 5 | 7 | 5 | 15 |
| 7 Assign | 7 | 13 | 7 | 6 | 7 | 7 | 5 | 7 | 5 | 15 |
| 8 Networks | 9 | — | 10 | 7 | 7 | 9 | 6 | 8 | 6 | — |
| 9 PERT | 10 | 15 | 10 | 8 | 6 | 10 | 6 | 8 | 12 | 17 |
| 10 Forecast | 15 | 7 | 19 | 13 | — | 18 | — | 15 | — | 4 |
| 11 Simulatn | 12 | — | 23 | 15 | 14 | 14 | 11 | 14 | 17 | — |
| 12 Det Inv | 11 | 16 | 18 | 16 | 11 | 11 | 7 | 12 | 13 | 7 |
| 13 Prob Inv | 11 | 16 | 18 | 16 | — | 12 | 7 | 12 | 13 | 8 |
| 14 Dec Thry | 16 | 4 | 22 | 12 | 12 | 15 | 8 | 3–4 | 11 | 5,6,21 |
| 15 Queuing | 13 | 18 | 16 | 14 | 13 | 13 | 10 | 13 | 15,16 | 18 |
| 16 Markov | 14 | — | 15 | 17 | 15 | 16 | 9 | 10 | 14 | 27 |

### Books used in this table:

Anderson, David R., Dennis J. Sweeney, and Thomas A. Williams. *An Introduction to Management Science*, 4th ed. St. Paul: West Publishing Company, 1985.

Anderson, David R., Dennis J. Sweeney, and Thomas A. Williams. *Quantitative Methods for Business*, 3rd ed. St. Paul: West Publishing Company, 1986.

Cook, Thomas M., and Robert A. Russell. *Introduction to Management Science*, 3rd ed. Englewood Cliffs, New Jersey: Prentice-Hall, 1985.

Davis, K. Roscoe, and Patrick G. McKeown. *Quantitative Models for Management*, 2nd ed. Boston: Kent Publishing Company, 1984.

Eppen, G. D., and F. J. Gould. *Introductory Management Science*. Englewood Cliffs, New Jersey: Prentice-Hall, 1984.

Hillier, Frederick S., and Gerald J. Lieberman. *Introduction to Operations Research*, 4th ed. Oakland, California: Holden-Day, Inc., 1986.

Lapin, Lawrence L. *Quantitative Methods for Business Decisions with Cases*, 3rd ed. San Diego: Harcourt Brace Jovanovich, Inc., 1985.

Lee, Sang M., Laurence J. Moore, and Bernard W. Taylor III. *Management Science*, 2nd ed. Dubuque, Iowa: Wm. C. Brown Publishers, 1985.

Taha, Hamdy A. *Operations Research*, 4th ed. New York: Macmillan Publishing Company, 1987.

Turban, Efraim, and Jack R. Meredith. *Fundamentals of Management Science*, 3rd ed. Plano, Texas: Business Publications, Inc., 1985.

# Chapter 1

# Introduction

**M**anagement Science has generally been defined as the application of scientific methodology—scientific procedures, techniques, tools—to managerial problems in order to better develop and evaluate solutions. It provides a strategy or framework for approaching problem solving in a logical, consistent, and systematic manner. Model building or the use of models is a key *tool* in this approach. Moreover, the use of computers and computer solutions for these models is increasingly recognized as a fundamental characteristic of management science. Computers offer a fast, accurate, flexible, and relatively inexpensive means of solving problems.

This book and the accompanying disks of microcomputer models are intended to supplement a management science, operations research, or quantitative methods textbook. They can also be used independently by someone with prior experience in this area to solve small to moderate-sized problems; however, the models are not designed solely for applications problems. The size of the problem that can be solved by each program is limited, but the programs should be more than adequate for classroom examples and problems.

The book serves as a guide to the models and the programs on the disk. It contains useful information about the limitations of each program, for example, the size of the problem which can be run. Moreover, it can be used both as a tutorial and as a quick reference handbook for the disks. In general, reading the book before proceeding to the models will save you time and errors.

## 1.1 Organization of the Book

We have designed the book with both the first-time and the sophisticated computer user in mind. Obviously, such user needs differ, and it is extremely difficult (if not impossible) to be all things to all users. We have organized the book so that it can be used as both a tutorial, with step-by-step instruction, and as a quick reference, with easy-to-find answers to specific questions.

This chapter provides an overview of the programs and presents a detailed description of those parts of the programs that are common to all the models, such as error correction and Ending Menu. It also includes a discussion of the things you need to know in order to use the programs: special keys; user cautions; entry conventions, restrictions; error messages; etc. This chapter is *essential* reading for getting started and can be used later for quick reference.

Chapter two is a tutorial. It provides a step-by-step guide to the solution of a linear programming problem, a transportation problem, and an EOQ inventory problem. Chapter two demonstrates in detail such things as: how to use the menus for model selection; entering data from prompted input and as tabular input; correcting errors; and using the Ending Menu to print problem output, save the problem to a disk file, and to modify data and run the problem again. It is especially valuable for the first-time user.

Chapters three through sixteen are the individual model chapters and each of them can stand alone. Because the computer programs are designed for ease of use, and because the programs are all of similar design, there is, of necessity, a great deal of repetition from chapter to chapter. This can be comforting for the new user because the repetition reinforces what has already been learned. For the sophisticated user, and as the new user becomes more familiar with the programs and the computer, the repetition can be cumbersome and annoying. Therefore, each chapter is designed for use both as a quick reference (to look up specific details, restrictions, and requirements of that particular program), and as a detailed description of how to use the program. However, those parts of the programs that are common to all, like error correction or the Ending Menu, are *not* detailed in each chapter.

The programs and this book function jointly as an instructional tool. We emphasize ease of use by making data entry as easy as possible and, as much as possible, consistent with the problem format found in most textbooks today. The programs are tolerant of common errors and the errors are easy to correct. This means the programs are good at error trapping and are user friendly (although some erroneous entries may not be caught). It is possible to make modifications in the data and run the problem again without having to reenter all the data. There is also the capability of storing a problem to disk for later retrieval. Moreover, we attempt to make the programs as consistent throughout as possible; therefore, when you have learned to use one program, you have really learned to use them all. Obviously, the input or data entry is model specific, but the manner in which this data is entered, corrected, and output is consistent.

## 1.2 The ENTER/RETURN Key

Before proceeding, we should mention a special convention used in this book and on the monitor screen. Computer keyboards, like typewriters, have a carriage return key. Sometimes this key is referred to as the RETURN key and sometimes as the ENTER key. The standard IBM PC manual calls it the ENTER key, and the key itself has the ⏎ symbol on it. For consistency, we will use ⟨RET⟩ when referring to this key. In general:

- All responses (highlighted menu selections or choices, for example, (YES/NO), and prompted questions requiring a response) must always be followed by ⟨RET⟩ to complete the entry.

- On entries of more than 80 characters (the width of the screen), ⟨RET⟩ is not pressed until the entry has been completed. When you reach the right-hand edge of the screen, just continue typing. Your entry will automatically wrap to the next line. Free form linear programming entries may be approximately 750 characters long (about nine lines on the screen), although the tabular entry method will probably be easier to use for problems this large.

## 1.3 Installation and Setup

### Required Equipment

These models are designed to run on an IBM PC, XT, AT or PS/2 or on IBM compatible microcomputers using DOS 2.0 or higher. If you are using DOS 2.0 or DOS 2.1, the microcomputer should have at least 256K of memory (RAM). If you are using DOS 3.0 or 3.1, however, you will need at least 320K of memory (RAM) because these versions of DOS occupy a larger portion of the computer's memory, leaving less space for the programs. DOS 3.2 and DOS 3.3 are even larger and will require about 512K of memory.

### Installing DOS on Your Dennis & Dennis Models Disk(s)

DOS (disk operation system) is not on the disk(s) you received with this book. This means that if you place your Dennis & Dennis disk (#1) into your computer and turn it on, the computer will not boot (start up) properly. It is not necessary to install DOS on your disk. To use the disk without installing DOS, boot the computer with a DOS disk and then replace it with the Dennis & Dennis disk (#1). However, having DOS on the disk makes it more convenient to use the disk(s). If you have the 5¼ inch D&D disks, you should install DOS version 2.0, 2.1, 3.0 or 3.1 on disk #1. If you have the 3½ inch disk, you should install DOS 3.2 or 3.3 on the disk.

### Making Your D&D Models Disk Self-Booting

Using a Computer with 2 Floppy Drives (A and B)

To make your 5¼ inch D&D disk (#1) or your 3½ inch D&D disk self-booting with two disk drives (A and B), place the DOS disk in drive A and turn the computer on. When prompted for the date and time, press ⟨RET⟩. When you have the DOS prompt ( A⟩ ), place the D&D models disk #1 in drive B and type

        B:INSTALL

and press ⟨RET⟩. There is no space between the B: and the word INSTALL. This will run the installation program, transferring DOS and the COMMAND.COM file onto your D&D disk.

Using a Computer with 1 Hard Drive and a Floppy Drive (C and A)

If your DOS files are on a hard disk (drive C), boot the computer. When you have the DOS prompt ( C⟩ ), place the D&D models disk #1 in drive A and type

        A:CINSTALL

and press ⟨RET⟩. The installation program uses the SYS.COM and COMMAND.COM files to install DOS, so they must be in the default directory on the C drive.

When you are told the installation procedure is complete, remove the DOS disk from drive A and put it away. Your D&D disk should now be self-booting. (If you are using a computer with a hard-disk, you should type A: and press ⟨RET⟩ to change the default drive to drive A before proceeding.) Place the D&D disk (#1) in drive A, type

        START

and press ⟨RET⟩. You should see the D&D title screen. You should then be prompted to enter your name. Type your first name, a space, your last name and press ⟨RET⟩. You will then see a second title screen appear briefly followed by the Main Menu. At this point, you can select a model to run or return to DOS.

Once you have made your D&D models disk #1 self-booting, you should never have to do it again. Since disk #2 is *not self-booting* (nor can you make it so), *you must always boot from disk #1*.

### Formatting a Blank Disk

If you wish to store programs you have run on a disk or if you wish to send problem results to a disk for later printing, you must format a separate disk before you can use it. The following procedure must be followed to format a blank (new) disk. *CAUTION: Do NOT format either of your D&D models disks.*

1. Place the DOS disk in drive A and turn the computer on. (On computers which boot from a hard disk, it may not be necessary to place a DOS disk in drive A.) Press the ⟨RET⟩ key when prompted for the date and time. When the DOS prompt A⟩ (or C⟩ ) appears, type

       FORMAT B:

   and hit ⟨RET⟩.

2. When instructed to do so, place a new disk (*not one of the D&D disks*) in drive B and hit the ⟨RET⟩ key. You will see the message

       Formatting . . .

   followed by the message

       Format complete

       Format another (Y/N)?

3. Press the "N" key and remove both disks. Label the storage disk. This disk can now be used to store programs that you wish to rerun or modify and run again at a later date, or program results that you may want to print at some other time.

### Installing a Serial Printer

The programs on the models disks will automatically send the printed output to a parallel printer when instructed to print, if a printer is attached to your computer. (The program assumes the printer is attached to printer port #1, identified as LPT1:.) If your printer is a serial printer, you will have to give the computer special commands before running the D&D models. To do so, place a copy of your DOS disk in drive A and at the DOS prompt, type

       MODE LPT1:=COM1

You can then replace the DOS disk with the D&D models disk #1 and type **START** to begin running the programs. Do not re-boot the computer. If a serial printer does not work properly using this procedure, it may be necessary to use the DOS MODE command to properly set the serial interface before entering the MODE LPT1:=COM1 command. Check your DOS manual (MODE command, "For Asynchronous Communications Adapter" option) for further instructions. If you are continually using a computer with a serial printer, you may want to create an AUTOEXEC.BAT batch file on the D&D models disk #1 which will automatically execute the necessary MODE commands and the START command. Again, check your DOS manual for instructions.

## 1.4  Program Features

The programs on these disks are all menu driven. To select a particular program, make data entries, print output, rerun the program, exit, you must first make a choice from a menu. When you boot the computer and start the programs on models disk #1, you will see a title screen followed by the D&D Main Menu. The Main Menu is your access to the model programs. Because the models require information input from the Main Menu on disk #1 to run successfully, *you must always begin there.*

### The Main Menu

Place your self-booting D&D models disk #1 in drive A and turn the computer on. You will be prompted to enter the date (month/day/year, for example, 7/14/88). When you hit the ⟨RET⟩ key, the Models title should appear briefly followed by the Main Menu, which is shown in Figure 1.1.

To select a model program to run from the Main Menu, use the up ↑ or down ↓ arrow keys to highlight the model you wish to run. The name of the highlighted program will also appear in the "selected" box below the menu. Once you have selected the model you want, hit the ⟨RET⟩ key to confirm your choice. If the model you have selected is on disk #1 (Linear Programming to Assignment), the disk drive should whir as the selected program is read from the disk, and the title screen for that program should appear briefly on the screen, followed by one of two program menus. If the model you have selected is on disk #2 (Network to Markov), you will be instructed to insert disk #2 in the disk drive and to press ⟨RET⟩ to continue. Once you have done so, the program will load and begin running. Table 1.1 shows the list of the programs on each disk.

```
┌────────────────────────────────────────────────────────────────┐
│  ┤ MICROCOMPUTER MODELS FOR MANAGEMENT DECISION MAKING ├        │
│   ┌──────────────────────────────────────────────────┐          │
│   │              Linear Programming                   │          │
│   │              Integer Programming                  │          │
│   │              Goal Programming                     │          │
│   │              Transportation Model                 │          │
│   │              Assignment Model                     │          │
│   │              Network Flow Models                  │          │
│   │              PERT Networks                        │          │
│   │              Simulation                           │          │
│   │              Forecasting                          │          │
│   │              Deterministic Inventory              │          │
│   │              Probabilistic Inventory              │          │
│   │              Decision Theory                      │          │
│   │              Queuing Models                       │          │
│   │              Markov Analysis                      │          │
│   │              Quit and Return to DOS               │          │
│   └──────────────────────────────────────────────────┘          │
│                        ┌──────────────────────────────┐         │
│  Model Selected ->     │    Linear Programming         │         │
│                        └──────────────────────────────┘         │
│      Use the Up and Down arrow keys to make your choice          │
│      Then hit the Enter <RET> key ( ◄┘ )                         │
└────────────────────────────────────────────────────────────────┘
```

**Figure 1.1**     Main Menu Screen

**Table 1.1**
List of Programs

| DISK #1 | DISK #2 |
|---|---|
| Linear Programming | Network Models |
| Integer Programming | PERT/CPM |
| Goal Programming | Forecasting |
| Transportation Model | Deterministic Inventory |
| Assignment Model | Probabilistic Inventory |
| | Simulation |
| | Decision Theory |
| | Queuing Models |
| | Markov |

### Subprogram or Data Entry Menus

Most programs will have a secondary or subprogram model selection menu since the program can be used to solve different types of problems. For example, the network flow models program will solve shortest route, maximal flow, and minimal spanning tree types of problems; the deterministic inventory models program will solve EOQ, production lot size, EOQ with backorders, or quantity discount types of problems. This second menu, the model selection menu, allows you to select the type of problem (subproblem) that you wish to solve. One of the choices in this menu will always be Problem from Disk File, which allows you to retrieve a problem that was saved previously. Since the type of problem is included as part of the data saved on the disk, this choice will automatically include the selection of one of the subprogram choices.

Some programs, such as the linear programming, transportation, or assignment programs, have only one solution procedure. These programs will usually begin with a data entry menu, which gives you the choice of entering the data from either the keyboard or a disk file. The linear programming menu is somewhat specialized in that it gives you the choice of entering the data from the keyboard in either a free form or tabular entry version, or from a disk file.

Following this second menu, which will be either the model selection menu or the data entry menu dependent on the program being run, you will be expected to enter the data necessary to solve the problem. This keyboard entry procedure will take one of two forms (and some models will use both). The first form is prompted input. You will be prompted to enter each data item, for example, "HOW MANY VARIABLES ARE THERE ?". You respond by typing in the appropriate response and pressing the ⟨RET⟩ key. The second type of data entry is a tabular entry form. You will be given a blank table and expected to fill in the appropriate entries. With the tabular entry format, you can type in each entry and complete it by pressing either the ⟨RET⟩ key or one of the arrow keys on the numeric keypad. You continue in this fashion until all of the necessary entries have been made.

### Problem from Disk File

Entering a problem from a disk file can be done only *after* a problem has first been entered and then saved to a disk file. Assuming such a disk file exists, select the "Problem from Disk File" from the menu and hit ⟨RET⟩. The program will then prompt

```
Enter the filename beginning with the disk drive designation.
d:xxxxxxxx   or   d:\ssssss\xxxxxxxx   Do not enter a file suffix.
   (where d = disk drive and ssssss is an existing subdirectory)

WHAT IS THE FILE NAME ?
```

If your data was in a file named MYFILE on your storage disk in drive B, you would type B:MYFILE and press ⟨RET⟩. The data would then be read from that file and displayed on the screen. At that point, you could accept the data as correct and proceed to the solution, or you could modify it (as discussed in the next section) and then proceed.

## Correcting Mistakes

If you make a mistake when typing a data entry, and catch it before pressing the ⟨RET⟩ key, you can correct it by using the backspace/erase key (←) located above the ⟨RET⟩ key. This key permits you to back up and delete your entry character by character. You cannot use this key to correct mistakes once you have pressed the ⟨RET⟩ key, but if and when this occurs, all is not lost.

### Prompted Entry Mistakes

At the completion of the last entry of a program relying upon prompted input, the program will summarize all of your inputs on the screen under the heading "HERE IS WHAT YOU ENTERED:". Each entry will be numbered, and at the end of the summary you will be asked, "DO YOU WANT TO MODIFY THE DATA ? (YES/NO)". This is your chance to check the data to make sure you did not make any entry mistakes. If there are no mistakes, simply press ⟨RET⟩ (since NO is the default choice). The **default** choice is the choice highlighted when the menu or prompt appears. If you did make a mistake, however, select YES by pressing the left arrow key or the "Y" key and press ⟨RET⟩. You will be prompted, "WHAT LINE DO YOU WISH TO CHANGE ?". Enter the number of the line preceding the erroneous data and, after the prompt appears, enter the correct value. As you make each change, the "HERE IS . . ." screen will automatically refresh itself with the new value, allowing you the opportunity to make another correction if necessary. This procedure allows you to continue making corrections, one at a time, until all the data are correct. At that time, you respond "NO" to the prompt "DO YOU WANT TO MODIFY THE DATA ?" and continue with the problem. Figure 1.2 shows the "HERE IS . . ." screen for an EOQ problem.

**Figure 1.2**
"HERE IS WHAT YOU ENTERED:" Screen

```
HERE IS WHAT YOU ENTERED:

(1) ANNUAL DEMAND               6000
(2) COST OF PLACING AN ORDER    $ 45
(3) CARRYING COST               $ 2.35
(4) NUMBER OF DAYS PER YEAR     260
(5) LEAD TIME IN DAYS           3

DO YOU WANT TO MODIFY THE DATA ? (YES/NO)
```

Assume that you made a mistake when entering the annual demand, and that you actually meant to enter 8000. Press the right arrow key to highlight "YES" and press ⟨RET⟩, then respond to the prompts as shown in Figure 1.3. When asked "WHICH LINE DO YOU WISH TO CHANGE ?", enter **1**, which corresponds to annual demand, and press ⟨RET⟩. You will then be given the opportunity to enter a new value, "ANNUAL DEMAND ?". Enter the correct figure, **8000**, and press ⟨RET⟩. The screen will clear and the "HERE IS . . ." screen will reappear with the corrected annual demand figure. If you made additional mistakes, correct them, one at a time, using the same procedure. Once all mistakes are corrected, simply respond "NO" to the "DO YOU WANT TO MODIFY THE DATA ?" prompt.

**Figure 1.3**
Modification of
Data

```
HERE IS WHAT YOU ENTERED:

(1)  ANNUAL DEMAND                  6000
(2)  COST OF PLACING AN ORDER       $ 45
(3)  CARRYING COST                  $ 2.35
(4)  NUMBER OF DAYS PER YEAR        260
(5)  LEAD TIME IN DAYS              3

DO YOU WANT TO MODIFY THE DATA ? (YES/NO)

WHICH LINE DO YOU WISH TO CHANGE ? 1

ENTER THE CORRECT VALUE BELOW:

ANNUAL DEMAND ? 8000

(new screen at this point)

HERE IS WHAT YOU ENTERED:

(1)  ANNUAL DEMAND                  8000
(2)  COST OF PLACING AN ORDER       $ 45
(3)  CARRYING COST                  $ 2.35
(4)  NUMBER OF DAYS PER YEAR        260
(5)  LEAD TIME IN DAYS              3

DO YOU WANT TO MODIFY THE DATA ? (YES/NO)
```

Tabular Entry Mistakes

When you are using a program that uses a tabular input procedure, there is no "HERE IS . . ." input summary. The table or tableau remains on the screen, allowing you to inspect it and make corrections as necessary before proceeding. After you have made all of the entries, check them for accuracy and correct any mistakes. The cursor movement keys (the arrow keys and the [Home], [End], [PgUp] and [PgDn] keys, as discussed in this chapter) allow you to move to any entry location. Once you have moved the cursor to the erroneous entry, simply reenter the correct value. You may then move to another location to correct another entry. When all corrections have been made, you accept the entries using the [F9] key.

Tabular inputs usually require that the type of problem, for example, MAX or MIN, the number of rows, and the number of columns be entered as prompted input before the tableau appears. The function keys can be used to correct mistakes in these entries. The [F3] key reverses the type of problem (MAX to MIN or MIN to MAX), the [F5] key deletes a row (checking first to make sure that is your intent), the [F6] key adds a row, the [F7] key deletes a column (again checking first), and the [F8] key adds a column. Of course, if you add a row or column, you will then have to enter the appropriate values into that row or column.

In tabular input, once you have verified the entries as correct, you press the [F9] function key to accept them, and then proceed to the solution of the problem. Pressing this key is exactly the same as selecting the "NO" response to the "DO YOU WANT TO MODIFY THE DATA ?" prompt at the end of the prompted input summary. Figure 1.4 shows a tabular input for a transportation problem with three rows and four columns.

**Figure 1.4**
Tabular Entry
Format

[MIN] ENTER TABLEAU VALUES:

|  | D1 | D2 | D3 | D4 | SUPPLY |
|---|---|---|---|---|---|
| S1 | 14 | 13 | 18 | 16 | 150 |
| S2 | 12 | 18 | 20 | 13 | 150 |
| S3 | 16 | 14 | 19 | 15 | 150 |
| DEMAND | 100 | 100 | 100 | 100 | |

Use Arrow keys, [Home], [End], [PgUp], [PgDn] to make entries.
[F3] Reverse MAX and MIN,      [F5] Delete Row,      [F6] Add Row
[F9] to accept entries,      [F7] Delete Column,      [F8] Add Column

Once you have accepted the input as correct, the program will calculate the solution to the problem (with the exception of the linear programming model, which first prompts for some additional inputs).

If, for some reason, you accept incorrect values, either by responding "NO" in prompted input or pressing the [F9] key in tabular input, all is not lost. You can usually solve the problem with the incorrect data, disregarding the output, and then, when you reach the Ending Menu, select the "Modify Data and Run Again" choice. This choice returns you to either the "HERE IS . . ." input summary or tableau screen. At this point, you can modify the data and solve the problem again.

### Summary—Correcting Mistakes

If you make a mistake when typing an entry and notice it before you press ⟨RET⟩, use the backspace/erase key to backup and correct your entry.

Prompted Input

1. Check the inputs at the "HERE IS . . . " input summary. If you find a mistake, select "YES" in response to the "DO YOU WANT TO MODIFY THE DATA ?" prompt.
2. Enter the line number on which the mistake appears and press ⟨RET⟩. If there is more than one mistake, correct one at a time.
3. Enter the correct value when prompted to do so and press ⟨RET⟩.
4. You will return to step 1. If all the entries are correct, press ⟨RET⟩ while the "NO" response is highlighted.

Tabular Input

1. After completing your entries, but before pressing the [F9] key, check the entries for accuracy. If you find no mistakes, press the [F9] key; if you do find mistakes, proceed to steps 2–5.
2. If the mistake is in a tabular entry, use the special keys to move the cursor to the entry and reenter the correct value.
3. If the mistake is in the number of rows or columns, use the appropriate function key to add or delete a row or column. When adding, fill in the new row or column.
4. If the mistake is in the type of problem (found in square brackets in the upper left-hand corner of the screen), use the [F3] key to change it.
5. Return to step 1 and repeat the process until all mistakes have been corrected.

### Program Solution/Output

At this point in the program, you will see the program solution, or if the solution is too extensive to fit on one screen, you will see part of the solution followed by the instruction to "Press any key to continue." The actual output will vary from program to program and will be discussed specifically in each chapter.

### Ending Menu

Following the solution to the problem, you will see an Ending Menu. The Ending Menu is exactly the same for all models. It is shown in Figure 1.5.

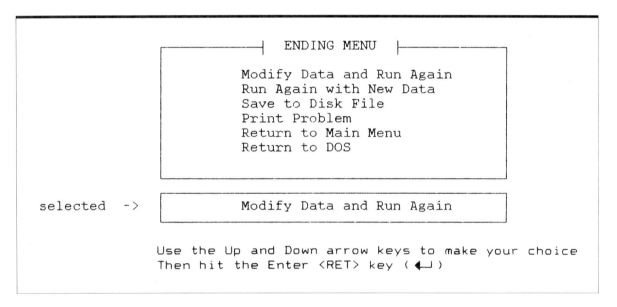

ENDING MENU

Modify Data and Run Again
Run Again with New Data
Save to Disk File
Print Problem
Return to Main Menu
Return to DOS

selected  ->   Modify Data and Run Again

Use the Up and Down arrow keys to make your choice
Then hit the Enter <RET> key ( ◂┘ )

**Figure 1.5**      Ending Menu

"Modify Data and Run Again," returns you to the data summary ("HERE IS . . .") or completed tableau. This allows you to modify the data and solve the problem again. This choice can be used to perform **postoptimality analysis**, modifying the data and determining the sensitivity of the model to these changes.

"Run Again with New Data," clears all current data entries and returns you to the beginning of the data entry section of the program. This allows you to run another problem of the same type without having to exit and then reenter the program.

"Save to Disk File," allows you to save the data used in the problem you just completed to a disk file. When you choose this option, you will be prompted

Enter the filename beginning with the disk drive designation.
d:xxxxxxxx   or   d:\ssssss\xxxxxxxx   Do not enter a file suffix.
   (where d = disk drive and ssssss is an existing subdirectory)

WHAT IS THE FILE NAME ?

If you wished to save the data in a file named PROBLEM1 on your storage disk in drive B, you would type **B:PROBLEM1** and press ⟨RET⟩. Legitimate file names must use the letters of the alphabet (A–Z) or digits (0–9) and be no more than eight (8) characters in length (not counting the drive designation). Once the data are saved, you will be returned to the Ending Menu.

"Print Problem," allows you to print a summary of the problem input and the problem output. You will be given the choice of printing to either a disk file or a printer. Selecting the printer will send the output to a printer, provided one is connected to your computer and turned on. *Caution*: if you attempt to send output to a printer when your computer is not connected to one, you are going to wait a *very* long time for the program to resume. (See the section on Terminating a Program should this ever happen.) If you select disk file as the printing option, you will be asked to enter a file name. The output will then be written, as a DOS text file, to the disk specified. This option is best when you may want to print the output at a later time. When the output has been printed, you will be returned to the Ending Menu.

Output files can be printed without entering the D&D models programs. At the DOS prompt, use either the DOS PRINT command, that is, at the DOS prompt, type

    PRINT B:MYFILE

or, if the PRINT.COM file is not available, simply type

    TYPE B:MYFILE>PRN:

This will redirect the output from the screen to a parallel printer. (If you are using a serial printer, enter **COM1:** instead of PRN:.)

"Return to Main Menu," exits the program and returns to the Main Menu. Use this option when you are finished with a model, but wish to run another program using a different model. (Subprograms, that is, different variations of the same model, can be run through the second option, Run Again with New Data.)

Both disk #1 and disk #2 contain a Main Menu. You may, therefore, return to the Main Menu with either disk in the disk drive. If the model you wish to run is on the other disk, you will be instructed to switch disks.

"Return to DOS," exits the D&D models completely, returning to the DOS prompt.

## 1.5   Chapter Design

The specific model chapters, Chapters three through sixteen, are designed to be consistent. Each chapter includes an introduction to the model, an overview of the program and the model variations it will solve, a fairly extensive discussion of the program input and output, a quick summary of program requirements and restrictions, and example problems to demonstrate how the program works. Specifically, each chapter includes:

1. *A brief introduction to and overview of the model being presented.* This serves as a bridge to the textbook being used in the course.

2. *An overview of the program.* The overview explains generally what the program will determine, such as optimal solution, optimal order quantity, and optimal assignment pattern. This section also describes the model variations (subproblems) within the program, and any data preparation that is necessary before data can be entered in the program. Model selection is from menu as discussed in the previous section of this chapter. Most of the programs offer a choice of model variations or subprograms (only LP, transportation, and assignment do not).

3. *A discussion of the data entry required by the program* (for each model/ variation included in this program). This may require a discussion of model selection, or entry form selection. For those programs with subprograms (more than one model/variation), the detailed discussion of data entry for the specific subproblem chosen may be presented under the specific model heading, for instance, EOQ DATA ENTRY.
   Data entry is made from prompted input and/or in a tabular format, as discussed earlier. All programs allow entry from a disk file. Each chapter will describe specifically what input is required by the program for problem solution, and how it should be entered. All programs with model selection require data entry from prompted input. The prompts are self-explanatory and most of the information needed to make an entry is provided on screen. Three models, LP, transportation, and assignment, have a data entry method menu to allow you to choose the manner in which data will be entered.

4. *A discussion of program output.* Output is the solution, the results that are determined by the program. These results frequently appear in easy to understand tabular form. The optimal solution is always so identified.

5. *A summary or summaries of program notes for quick reference.* Each chapter has at least one summary of program restrictions, rules, requirements, special hints, etc. These are intended to be used to find the answer to a specific question.

6. *Example problems.* A variety of example problems are presented to demonstrate how the program works and how to make optimal use of the various special features of the programs.

## 1.6   General Notations and Cautions

### Dos and Don'ts When Making Entries

■  Do enter a zero (0) and not the letter O in numeric entries.

■  Do drop the trailing zeros after the decimal place. Enter 7.9, not 7.90 and 63, not 63.00. It won't make any difference to the computer and it will save you keystrokes.

■  Do not enter dollar signs ($). Enter 14.95, not $14.95.

■  Do not enter commas (,). Enter 6000, not 6,000.

■  Do not enter the percent sign (%). When you are asked to enter a percent, enter the number only, 24, not 24% or 0.24.

■  Do not attempt to enter values with more than six significant digits. Enter large numbers in scientific notation, 6.5E6, not 6500000.

■  Do not enter variable names longer than five characters in length.

### Size Limitations of the Models

The size of the problems which each of the models can solve is limited. The specific limitations, such as the number of rows and the number of variables, are discussed in each chapter. Tabular output on large problems, like linear programming or transportation, may not fit within the 80 character width of the screen (or many printers). If this is the case, the tableau will be segmented and output in sections.

### Significant Digits

One should also remember that in most cases the IBM works only with values up to seven (7) digits, and only the first six digits will be accurate. Thus, if you enter a value of 983,216,074, the computer may convert that value to 9.83216E+8 internally.

When you are using the tabular input format, the programs will accept up to seven digits (characters) including a decimal point; 1234.56 would be acceptable. Large numbers may be entered in scientific notation form; thus, the number 10000000 could not be entered in this form, since it requires 8 digits, but it could be entered as 1E7 or 1E+7 (1 times 10 to the 7th power). In certain cases where numerical output values are very large or very small, the computer will automatically display the number in scientific notation. Thus, 1.23E9 would be 1,230,000,000 and 7.4E−6 would be 0.0000074.

## Rounding

In some cases output will be rounded to whole numbers, two decimal places, or three decimal places. For example, in linear programming tableaus, numbers are rounded to three decimal places and, if the number is too large to fit in the space provided, the decimals may be dropped entirely. The rounding procedure used is specified in each chapter.

Because values may be rounded, the values produced by these models will not always match the answers given in textbooks. They will be close, however. If your textbook rounds values to two or four decimal places before multiplying and the model rounds to three places, the resulting answers will obviously vary somewhat, especially if the rounded value is used in a later calculation. However, there should not be a serious discrepancy.

## Computer Irregularities

In addition to normal rounding problems, values are stored in microcomputers using binary notation. This notation may produce some strange results, although this occurs infrequently. For example, the value 0.9 will sometimes be stored (and later displayed) as .9000001 or .8999999 (or 9.000001E−1). Most of the output values have been formatted or rounded to avoid this problem.

## Scaling Your Input

Occasionally, you may want to scale your input so that the number of significant digits is consistent throughout the problem. For example, in a linear programming problem with the following constraints

$$A + 2B \quad\quad <= 12$$
$$8000000A + 12000000B <= 30000000$$

you may want to divide all values in the second constraint by 1 million, giving constraints of

$$A + \quad 2B <= 12$$
$$8A + 12B <= 30$$

This scaling will in no way change the correct answer in units of A and B, but may affect the computer's ability to determine the correct answer by avoiding the loss of significant digits in the calculations.

## 1.7 Special Keys

The keyboard has some keys which serve special purposes. These are described in the following list. When two keys are listed together with a hyphen, those keys should be pressed simultaneously.

- **Caps Lock**   This key is a soft switch which toggles you from lower case to upper case and back each time the key is pressed. It applies only to alphabetic keys.

- **Num Lock**   This is also a soft switch which turns the numeric keypad on and off. When the key is on, the numbers are activated. When the key is off, the arrow keys are in use.

- **⇆[TAB]**   The [TAB] key can be used with tabular entries and emulates the right arrow key to enable you to complete tabular entries from either side of the keyboard.

- **Ctrl-Num Lock**   These keys suspend the computer's operations temporarily. When output is about to scroll off the screen and you want more time to look at it, pressing these keys simultaneously will freeze the screen until you press the space bar or some other alphanumeric key (the computer's signal to begin again).

- **Ctrl-Scroll Lock**   These are the program termination keys. Pressing these keys stops the program execution and gives you the DOS prompt. Whenever you decide you don't want to wait for a program to terminate normally, you can press these keys, but you will then have to run the Main Menu program again to get back into the program, that is, type START.

- **Shift-PrtSc**   The print screen key allows you to send the image currently on the screen to the printer. It works at any time during program execution and is independent of the program command to send output to the printer. (The shift keys are the upward pointing arrow keys.)

- **Function Keys and Other Special Keys**   These programs make use of the function keys ([F3]−[F9]), the [Home], [End], [PgUp], [PgDn], and arrow keys, in tabular input format only. In these cases, the active keys are listed in a footer at the bottom of the screen. Normally, when entering data in a table or tableau, the [F3] key allows you to alter the type of problem, for example, from maximization to minimization; [F5] allows you to delete a row; [F6] adds a row; [F7] deletes a column; [F8] adds a column; and [F9] accepts the entries as being complete and correct. The arrow keys allow you to move in the direction indicated within the tableau, the [Home] key moves the cursor to the first column in the current row, the [End] key moves the cursor to the last column in the row. The [PgUp] key moves the cursor to the top row of the tableau, the

[PgDn] moves the cursor to the bottom row of the tableau. Note that the ⟨RET⟩ key and [TAB] key emulate the right arrow key. Using these makes it easier to use the numeric keypad on the IBM.

## 1.8    User Cautions

### Rational Entries

Some words of caution. Although many of these models have some checks built into them to prevent erroneous entries, they are not error-free. There is no way to anticipate all errors which might occur, for example, pressing the ⟨RET⟩ key before making an entry. Therefore, the models assume that the user is somewhat familiar with the basic model before he or she starts. The models also assume that the user has read the chapter and knows what form the data will take and any limitations such as maximum number of entries. For example, in the linear programming chapter, the text clearly states that negative right-hand sides cannot be entered. The model assumes, therefore, that the user is rational and knows better; it does not check for negative right-hand sides, and it produces erroneous results if they are entered. The models are also designed to work with most typical homework problems. Data input not normally acceptable, however, such as a cost of −12.95, 459 days per year, and expected completion time of 34,548,914 days, will all be accepted but will produce unreliable results. For the most part, the model assumes the data entered, once corrected and accepted by the user, are acceptable. If the program should terminate in an error, refer to section 1.9 of this chapter and start over.

## 1.9    Common Problems/Errors

While it is impossible to anticipate all of the problems you might encounter when running these programs on your computer, our experience has exposed some of the more common problems. They are discussed in the following sections.

### Stopping a Program While It Is Running

You can always terminate a program that is running by pressing the Ctrl-Scroll Lock keys—you may have to press them a few times. This will terminate the program and leave you with the DOS prompt. You should never open the door of the disk drive or turn the computer off while the red light on the disk drive is lit. Doing so could damage the information stored on the disk.

### Compatibility Problems

There are often slight differences between computers which may cause problems when running programs intended for the IBM PC family. Frequently, problems occur because a computer may not be totally IBM compatible. One example is the Zenith Z100 computer. The D&D programs have been run successfully on many of the compatibles, such as Compaq, AT&T, IT&T, Zenith, and Hewlett Packard, with no difficulty whatsoever. Problems have occurred, however, when one machine's version of DOS was installed on the D&D models disks during the installation procedure, and those disks were then used to attempt to boot the programs from a different manufacturer's machine. Problems have also occurred when using AT's or other machines with five-and-one-quarter inch disk drives using formats other than the standard 360 Kilobyte format (for example, 1.2 Megabyte drives). This problem usually results when the non-360K drive is used to write to a disk (storing a problem or print file). If you have problems with a non-IBM computer, check to make sure you have booted the system with the correct version of DOS. If you are still having problems, check the computer's user manual.

### Printer Errors

If you have specified that you wish printed output, but your printer is not turned on, you will get an error message. If you have a printer which is turned on, but not online, that is, the online or ready light is off, the program will hang until you press the button to bring the printer back online. You will also get an error message with most printers if there is no paper in the printer. This error does not terminate the program, however. Once you correct the mistake and "Press any key to continue," the printer should begin to print the output. If you have other printer errors, see the Installation section which refers to configuring your D&D models disk for the appropriate type of printer. If nothing seems to work, press the shift and PrtSc keys simultaneously. If nothing happens, there is a problem with your cable or printer.

### Disk Drive Errors

When you attempt to save a problem to a disk drive, you may see one of several error messages. The normal messages, with the solution to the problem, are given below:

DRIVE DOOR IS OPEN or DISK IS NOT IN DRIVE
CORRECT AND PRESS ANY KEY TO CONTINUE

Check to make sure you have a disk in the drive specified and the drive door is closed, then press the space bar.

YOUR DISK IS WRITE-PROTECTED.
REMOVE TAB OR REPLACE AND PRESS ANY KEY TO CONTINUE

As instructed, either remove the write-protect tab or replace the disk with a formatted, but not write-protected disk.

THE SPECIFIED PATH (DISK DRIVE OR SUBDIRECTORY) WAS NOT FOUND
REENTER VALID PATH

You specified a disk drive or subdirectory path which the computer cannot find. Check and try again by typing in the correct drive/path designation and file name.

YOUR DISK IS FULL
REPLACE AND PRESS SPACE BAR TO CONTINUE or PRESS RETURN KEY
TO CANCEL

There is no room on the disk you specified. Replace with another format-ted disk or press the ⟨RET⟩ key. When this happens, you may want to use the DIR/P command (at the DOS prompt) to check the files on your disk and the ERASE (ERASE filename) command to remove any files you no longer need. Caution: do *not* erase any of your D&D models files.

FILE ALREADY EXISTS. DO YOU WANT TO OVERWRITE IT ? (YES/NO)

There is already a file with the name you specified. Answering YES will replace it with your current problem. Answering NO will result in a prompt to "ENTER A DIFFERENT FILENAME BELOW" and a repetition of the original filename request prompt.

NO *model type* FILES FOUND IN THIS DIRECTORY

You attempted to find a problem file for a particular type of model, but the computer could find no files for that type of model on the disk specified. If you specify a file name that cannot be found but other files for that type of model are on the disk, you will see "CURRENT FILES ARE:" followed by a list of the available files (with suffixes). You will then be given another op-portunity to enter a file name.

### Cannot Find . . . Errors

These errors usually result when the program cannot find the run-time module or library file that it needs. These files are all on the D&D models disk #1. If you get this message, make sure disk #1 is in one of the disk drives and specify which one if prompted to do so.

### Program Termination Errors

The following errors are all program termination errors, and they will stop the program and return you to DOS. If you are running a program and this happens, you will find yourself looking at an error message and the instruction to press any key to return to the DOS system. To begin again, you must return to the Main Menu. You can do so by typing

    START

and pressing ⟨RET⟩. The most common program termination messages are listed with explanations in the following sections.

### Division by Zero Errors

Occasionally, an unusual set of entries will produce a situation where the computer attempts to divide by zero. In that case, you will see a message similar to

    division by zero   overflow error

and some of your output will contain the machine's equivalent of infinity. Usually this result is produced by erroneous input. Check your values carefully and try again. (Since this error will terminate the program, trying again will require reentering the Main Menu by typing START at the DOS prompt.) If the same result occurs, try another problem; you may have an atypical problem/situation.

### Memory Problem Errors

Most memory problem errors will result in either the program not running at all or in the program terminating after beginning to run. These errors result from having insufficient memory (RAM) installed in the computer. Common error messages are:

Out of Memory

Out of String Space

A similar problem is the overflow problem. It means that the values entered, when used in the necessary calculations, produce a result which is too large to be represented in the computer's floating point notation.

## 1.10  Summary of Chapters

The following is a brief description of each chapter/model.

### Linear Programming

This model uses the simplex linear programming algorithm to solve LP problems with up to a total of 30 variables and 30 constraints. It allows user-supplied variable names and constraints to be labeled. The model also performs sensitivity analysis.

### Integer Linear Programming

This chapter solves integer, mixed integer, and 0,1 integer linear programming problems using a branch and bound algorithm. ILP and MILP problems are limited to 25 variables and 25 constraints. 0,1 problems are limited to 12 variables and 12 constraints.

### Goal Programming

This model solves goal programming problems using the modified simplex procedure. Up to three priorities of goals are allowed, and goals may be weighted within any priority. Problems are limited to 25 variables (real variables and goal deviation variables) and 30 constraints.

### Transportation Model

This model solves distribution problems attempting to minimize the cost of shipping homogeneous units from several sources to several destinations. Problems are limited to 40 sources and 40 destinations. The model automatically adds dummy rows or columns to unbalanced problems, identifies infeasible problems, and calculates the total cost of the optimal allocation. The model can also be used for maximization problems.

### Assignment Model

This model solves assignment problems attempting to minimize the cost of one-to-one allocations. The model automatically adjusts for unbalanced problems, allows the user to designate unacceptable assignments, and calculates the total cost of the optimal allocation. It will solve problems with up to 40 allocations. The model can also be used for maximization problems. The error-correction routine allows it to be used repeatedly to solve traveling salesmen problems.

### Network Models

This model solves three common network problems: shortest-route, maximal flow, and minimal spanning tree. The shortest-route segment determines the shortest route between two points. The maximal flow segment determines the maximum flow of material through a network. The minimal spanning tree program connects all nodes in the network while covering the shortest possible distance. The programs are each limited to 30 nodes and 30 branches.

### PERT/CPM

This model determines the critical path in a project network consisting of 52 or fewer activities. The model has one variation which allows inputs using node numbers and another which identifies activities by letters and their predecessors. Both variations can be used to solve problems with either deterministic or probabilistic times. Activities on the critical path are identified, as are multiple critical paths, and the standard deviation and variance on solitary critical paths in probabilistic networks.

### Forecasting

This model is really a composite of three popular forecasting techniques: moving averages, exponential smoothing, and regression analysis. The moving averages can be simple or weighted. Exponential smoothing calculates both simple smoothed forecasts and trend-adjusted forecasts. It also allows the user to vary the values of the smoothing constants and has a built-in search option which determines the value of the smoothing constants which give the lowest forecast errors. Regression analysis determines a least squares regression line, the regression coefficient, the standard error of the estimate, and allows the user to forecast using the regression equation. All variations can accept up to 100 data points.

### Deterministic Inventory

This model contains four submodels: economic order quantity (EOQ); production lot size; EOQ with backorders; and quantity discount calculations. In addition to the order quantity, the submodels also calculate related items such as reorder points, cycle times, and orders per year.

### Probabilistic Inventory

This model contains three submodels: discrete demand (reorder point determination with discrete demand); continuous demand (reorder point or service level with continuous demand); and single period—marginal (single period marginal analysis).

### Decision Theory

This model allows the user to solve a decision matrix using the maximax, maximin, minimax regret, equal likelihood, and expected value criterion. It also determines posterior probabilities using Bayesian analysis and lists the optimal set of decisions. The expected value of perfect information and the expected value of sample information are also determined in the latter variations. Decision matrices can have up to 30 alternatives and 30 states of nature.

### Simulation

This model contains three different submodels. The first allows the user to enter a discrete distribution and then uses the Monte Carlo technique to simulate random events based upon the distribution. The second simulates an inventory reorder problem where the user makes reorder decisions over time, facing variable use rates with either fixed or variable lead times. The third submodel simulates a queuing situation with random interarrival rates and service times.

### Queuing Theory

The model calculates the traditional waiting line statistics—number in line, time in line, number in the system, time in the system—for a variety of queuing situations including single or multiple servers and infinite or finite queue lengths. It also determines the facility utilization rate and performs simple economic calculations, comparing the cost of waiting.

### Markov Analysis

This program will determine transitional probabilities over time, the probability or quantities in a resulting vector, and steady state probabilities and quantities. It also provides the fundamental matrix in the case of absorbing states. Problems are limited to 30 states.

# Chapter 1 Supplement

# Running the Models from a
# Nonbooting Disk

## IBM PC or Compatible

To run the models from the original diskettes without making disk #1 self-booting, start your computer with a DOS diskette in drive A (or from a hard disk—drive C). Enter the date and time when and if prompted to do so. When you have the DOS prompt ( A⟩ ), replace the DOS disk with your models disk #1, type **START**, and press ⟨RET⟩. (If you booted your computer from a hard disk, the DOS prompt will be C⟩. Type **A:** and press ⟨RET⟩, place models disk #1 in drive A, and type **START**.)

# Chapter 2

# Tutorial

In this chapter, we will take you, step by step, through the solution of example problems. It is intended to give hands-on experience, and not to be an all-inclusive discussion of the program being demonstrated. For a complete description of any given program, including all restrictions, limits, and special features, refer to the corresponding chapter discussion. We assume that you have properly installed the program as discussed in Chapter one, and that you have the computer on, and the D&D programs in place.

Note that once you have identified the problem, prepared the data for entry, and selected the program to be run, you will be following the instructions given by the program. Each program leads you through the solution procedure, prompting for input as it is needed.

To use the tutorial effectively, read each numbered section thoroughly *before making any entries*. Instructions are divided into the basic program parts (getting started, data entry, error correction, output, and ending). Each instruction in a given section is numbered, and is organized in this sequence:

An introductory statement that describes what you are going to do; for example, identify type of problem, prepare the data, or enter data, etc.

A specific instruction or command, in *italics* for emphasis; the keys you will strike, the words you will type, and any entry you are to make will be shown in **bold**.

Notes on, comments about, or explanation of this particular entry.

## 2.1 Problem 1: A Linear Programming Problem—Free Form Data Entry

Savoy Sausages produces a special bulk sausage for a Pancake Restaurant franchise. The sausage, produced in 2,500 pound batches, is a mixture of pork at a cost of $3.00 per pound, beef at $5.00 per pound, and cereal at $1.75 per pound. According to the franchise specifications, each batch must contain at least 600 pounds of pork, and at least 1,200 pounds of beef. The mix cannot contain more than 900 pounds of cereal. The company wants to find the optimal mix of ingredients that will minimize the total cost of the mixture.

### Getting Started

1. Identify the type of problem, prepare data and formulate.

   This is a linear programming problem. Using the following decision variables

   P = Number of pounds of pork in mixture

   B = Number of pounds of beef in mixture

   C = Number of pounds of cereal in mixture

   *Formulate the problem*

   MIN   3P + 5B + 1.75C

   Subject to:
   $$
   \begin{aligned}
   P & & &>= 600 \\
   & B & &>= 1200 \\
   & & C &<= 900 \\
   P + B &+ C & &= 2500
   \end{aligned}
   $$

   Note that it is possible to use variable names of your choosing, but they must begin with a letter of the alphabet. It is not necessary to include nonnegativity constraints. They are assumed by the program.

2. Select the program from the Main Menu (displayed in Figure 2.1).

   *Highlight* Linear Programming. *Press* ⟨**RET**⟩ (to complete this entry).

   This is the default menu selection, that is, it is already highlighted. Therefore, it is not necessary to use the up and down arrow keys to move the highlight. Note that the highlighted selection also shows up in the bottom rectangular box, which shows the program selected.

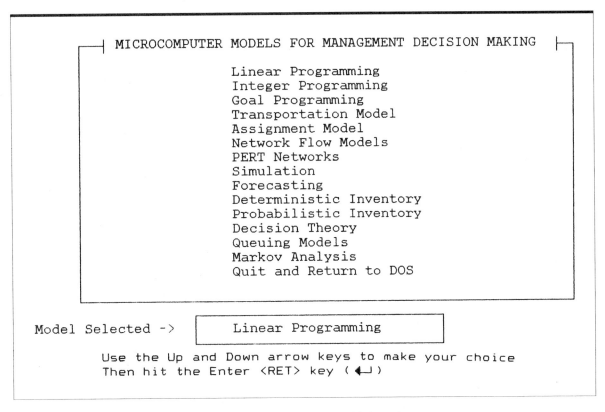

**Figure 2.1**    Main Menu with Linear Programming Model Selected

### Data Entry

From this point on, you are guided by the program—you do what the screen tells you to do. Screens are program specific. What you see depends on the program you are running. When the LP program selection entry is completed, the screen will change to display the data entry method menu.

1. Select the data entry method of choice from the DATA ENTRY METHOD menu, which is shown in Figure 2.2 (p. 32).

   *Select* Free Form Entry. *Press* ⟨**RET**⟩ (to complete the entry).

   The cursor, or highlight, is already by default on this choice, so it is not necessary to use the up or down arrow keys to move through the menu. Note, we chose this entry for this particular problem because of the size of the problem and the nature of the constraints (three of the four constraints have only one variable).

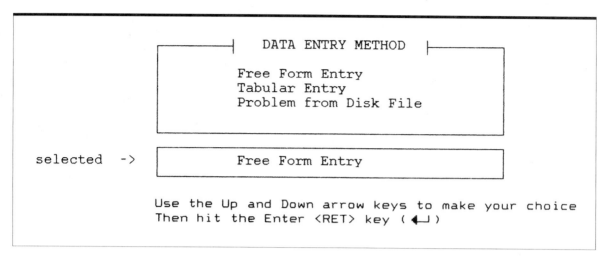

**Figure 2.2**    Data Entry Method Menu

After this selection is completed, the screen again changes. You will now be prompted to describe and enter the problem. Free form entry allows you to enter the problem much as you write it when it is formulated.

2. Respond to the prompts. The prompts will appear one at a time, as each entry is completed. The prompts you will see are shown in capital letters. The entries you should make in response are described following the prompts.

TYPE OF PROBLEM: MAX/ **MIN**

Identify the problem objective as maximization (MAX) or minimization (MIN).

*Select* MIN. *Press* ⟨**RET**⟩.

Selection is made by highlighting your choice and pressing ⟨RET⟩. Note that the default value, or the choice highlighted when the prompt first appears, is MIN. The left arrow key will move this cursor to MAX; the right arrow key will move it back to MIN.

ENTER OBJECTIVE FUNCTION
MIN

Note that the objective selected, MAX or MIN, appears automatically, followed by the blinking line (cursor).
*Type*   **3P+5B+1.75C** ⟨**RET**⟩

It does not matter whether variables are in upper or lower case. Nor does it matter if you put a space between the variable and the + sign.

If you make a mistake while typing, and recognize it before the ⟨RET⟩ key is pressed, use the backspace/erase key to erase it and retype. If you notice an error after the ⟨RET⟩ key is pressed, you will have to wait for the input summary to be able to make modifications.

ENTER THE CONSTRAINTS, ONE PER LINE, HERE. AFTER YOU HAVE ENTERED THE LAST CONSTRAINT, ENTER THE WORD    GO.

1 _

*Type the problem constraints, one constraint to a line, as shown below.*

1 **P>600 ⟨RET⟩**
2 **B>1200 ⟨RET⟩**
3 **C<900 ⟨RET⟩**
4 **P+B+C = 2500 ⟨RET⟩**
5 **GO ⟨RET⟩**

The program automatically numbers the constraints. Note, it is not necessary to type the equal (=) sign as part of the inequality expressions. Be sure to press ⟨RET⟩ after each constraint and to type GO ⟨RET⟩ to complete the constraint entries.

You have just entered the problem. You are now presented with the input summary, showing you what you have entered and offering you the opportunity to modify any of the data or correct any errors.

### Error Correction/Input Summary

1.  Check input. Make corrections/modifications. Figure 2.3 (p. 34) shows the input summary for this problem.

    *Respond NO, by pressing* **⟨RET⟩** *to the question "DO YOU WANT TO MODIFY THE DATA ?".* The default response is NO. We have made no entry errors, so we respond no. However, be sure to check your summary to make sure it is all right.

    If you did make an error:

    use the left arrow key to highlight YES, and press ⟨RET⟩.

    respond to the questions—each line is numbered for easy identification
    identify the line to be changed (line number and ⟨RET⟩)
    reenter the line

    check the summary as presented again and respond to the question "DO YOU WANT TO MODIFY THE DATA ?"

**Figure 2.3**
Input Summary

```
HERE IS WHAT YOU ENTERED:

0    MIN  3P+5B+1.75C
     SUBJECT TO:
1       1P>= 600
2       1B>= 1200
3       1C<= 900
4       1P+1B+1C= 2500

DO YOU WANT TO MODIFY THE DATA ? (YES/NO)
```

**Label Constraints**

The LP program allows you to label the constraints to make it easier to identify shadow prices and ranges. After the input summary has been accepted:

1.  Decide whether or not you wish to label the constraints.

> DO YOU WANT TO LABEL THE CONSTRAINTS ? (YES/NO)

*Respond* YES. *Press the* **left arrow key** *one time to move the cursor (highlight) to* YES. *Press* ⟨**RET**⟩.

Just for the practice, we will label these, although for such a small problem, we do not usually do so. Note that the default is "NO."

To label constraints, respond to the prompt:

> ENTER THE LABEL FOR EACH CONSTRAINT BELOW:

> CONSTRAINT   LABEL
>      1         ?

*Type the following labels*: note that you make the entry after the ?. The constraint number is given by the program.

> 1  ? **PORK** ⟨**RET**⟩
> 2  ? **BEEF** ⟨**RET**⟩
> 3  ? **CEREAL** ⟨**RET**⟩
> 4  ? **MIXTURE** ⟨**RET**⟩

Data entry/input is complete. The program now yields the following output.

### Output

1.  Figure 2.4 shows the first output screen for this problem, a summary of the slack, surplus, and artificial variables added to the tableau.

**Figure 2.4**
Slack, Surplus, and Artificial Variables. Press any key to continue. *Press the* **space bar**.

```
SLACK, SURPLUS AND ARTIFICIAL VARIABLES
ADDED TO MODEL (TABLEAU):

VARIABLE          TYPE            CONSTRAINT
- - - - - - - -   - - - - - - - -   - - - - - - - - - -
   A1          ARTIFICIAL          1    PORK
   S1          SURPLUS             1    PORK
   A2          ARTIFICIAL          2    BEEF
   S2          SURPLUS             2    BEEF
   S3          SLACK               3    CEREAL
   A3          ARTIFICIAL          4    MIXTURE


          Press any key to continue
```

2.  Decide whether you want to see tableaus displayed, and if so whether you want all the tableaus or just the final one. Figure 2.5 shows this menu.
    *Select* FINAL TABLEAU. *Press the* **down arrow key** *once. Press* ⟨**RET**⟩.
    NO TABLEAUS is the default choice. Use the down arrow key to move to the selection of choice, FINAL TABLEAU.

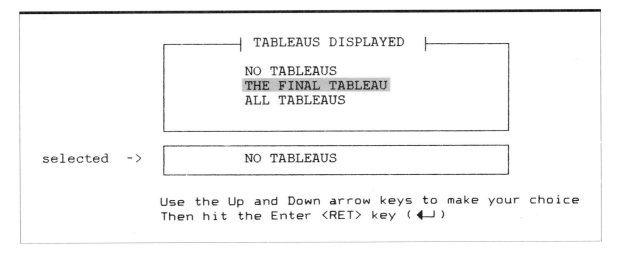

```
                    ┤ TABLEAUS DISPLAYED ├

                        NO TABLEAUS
                        THE FINAL TABLEAU
                        ALL TABLEAUS



selected  ->             NO TABLEAUS


        Use the Up and Down arrow keys to make your choice
        Then hit the Enter <RET> key ( ⬅⎌ )
```

**Figure 2.5**          Tableau Menu

3. *Tableau Output.* The tableau should be familiar to you, so we will not discuss it. Note, however, that instead of the M for the coefficient of an artificial variable, the computer uses the value 99999999. Note also that a screen width cannot necessarily display the entire tableau. In this case the tableau is split, as in our example. Pressing any key as directed reveals the rest of the tableau. Figure 2.6 shows this tableau as it appears on the screen.

When you are through examining the tableau, press any key to continue. You will see the final output, the optimal solution summary.

```
TABLEAU NUMBER   4

     C(j)            3        5        1.75     99999998 0        99999998 0
             Basis   P        B        C        A1       S1       A2       S2

    3          P     1        0        0        1        -1       0        0
    5          B     0        1        0        0        0        1        -1
    0          S3    0        0        0        1        -1       1        -1
    1.75       C     0        0        1        -1       1        -1       1

               Z     3        5        1.75     1.25     -1.25    3.25     -3.25
               C-Z   0        0        0        99999998 1.25     99999998 3.25

                   Press any key to continue

                  0        99999998
     Basis        S3       A3         RHS

       P          0        0          600
       B          0        0          1200
       S3         1        -1         200
       C          0        1          700

       Z          0        1.75       9025
       C-Z        0        99999998

                   Press any key to continue
```

**Figure 2.6**    Final Tableau

4. *Optimal Solution.* Figure 2.7 shows this output. Note that the optimal solution includes variable quantities and objective function value (Z value). It also includes a summary of shadow prices.

When you have examined the solution, you can decide whether or not you want to do sensitivity analysis.

5. *Sensitivity Analysis. Select* YES to the question asking ''DO YOU WANT TO DO SENSITIVITY ANALYSIS ?'' Figure 2.8 displays sensitivity analysis for the problem. After you have examined the results, *press any key to continue* (we suggest you *press the* **space bar**).

```
AFTER 3  ITERATIONS,
THIS SOLUTION IS OPTIMAL:

VARIABLE          QUANTITY
--------          --------
   P                 600
   B                1200
   C                 700
   S3                200


OPTIMAL Z =   9025

VARIABLE          SHADOW PRICE
--------          ------------
   P                  0
   B                  0
   C                  0
   S1                -1.25
   S2                -3.25
   S3                 0


DO YOU WANT TO DO SENSITIVITY ANALYSIS ?  (YES/NO)
```

**Figure 2.7**        Optimal Summary

```
SENSITIVITY ANALYSIS OF OBJECTIVE FUNCTION COEFFICIENTS

VARIABLE      LOWER          ORIGINAL       UPPER
  NAME        LIMIT          VALUE          LIMIT
--------      -----          --------       -----
   P          1.75           3              NO LIMIT
   B          1.75           5              NO LIMIT
   C          NO LIMIT       1.75           3

              Press any key to continue


SENSITIVITY ANALYSIS OF RIGHT HAND SIDE RANGES

              LOWER          ORIGINAL       UPPER
CONSTRAINT    LIMIT          VALUE          LIMIT
----------    -----          --------       -----
    1         400            600            1300        PORK
    2         1000           1200           1900        BEEF
    3         700            900            NO LIMIT    CEREAL
    4         1800           2500           2700        MIXTURE

              Press any key to continue
```

**Figure 2.8**        Sensitivity Analysis

### Ending

1.  The Ending Menu is shown in Figure 2.9. Decide what you want to do at this time.

    *Select* Save to a Disk File. *Press the* **down arrow key** *two times. Press* ⟨**RET**⟩.

    In case you want to use this problem later, give it a file name, and save it to a disk. Here are the instructions:

    > Enter the filename beginning with the disk drive designation.
    > d:xxxxxxxx   or   d:\ssssss\xxxxxxxx   Do not enter a file suffix.
    > (where d = disk drive and ssssss is an existing subdirectory)

    *Type* **B:SAVOY**. *Press* ⟨**RET**⟩.

    Note, the disk drive designation is for drive B. If you do not have two disk drives or are using a hard disk, check Chapter one for instructions. File names can be entered in all capital or lower-case letters.

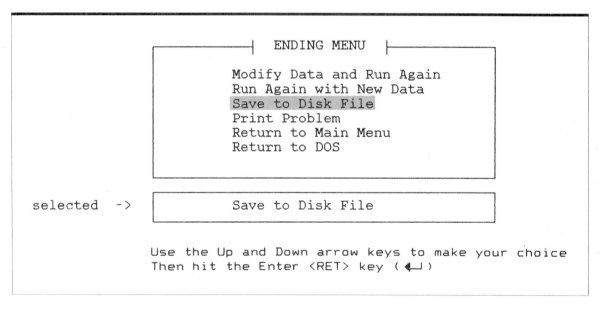

**Figure 2.9**        Ending Menu

2.  Return to Main Menu. After you have saved to the disk file, the Ending Menu reappears. This time we want to return to the Main Menu to run another program.

    *Select* Return to Main Menu. *Press the* **down arrow key** *4 times. Press* ⟨**RET**⟩.

Note that you had several choices. You could have chosen, for example, to "Return to DOS". At the DOS prompt you are no longer using the D&D programs.

## 2.2 Problem 2: A Transportation Problem

Plowshares, Inc. ships heavy duty snow plow blades from factories in Buffalo, Syracuse, Corning, and Albany to five upstate New York cities: Rochester, Potsdam, Utica, Elmira, and Old Forge. Given the following supply, demand and cost figures, find the optimal allocation to minimize total shipping costs.

| Factory | Supply | City | Demand |
|---|---|---|---|
| Buffalo | 100 | Rochester | 75 |
| Syracuse | 150 | Potsdam | 100 |
| Corning | 100 | Utica | 100 |
| Albany | 100 | Elmira | 75 |
| | | Old Forge | 100 |

**Shipping Costs:**

| From | Rochester | Potsdam | To Utica | Elmira | Old Forge |
|---|---|---|---|---|---|
| Buffalo | 14 | 11 | 23 | 16 | 22 |
| Syracuse | 12 | 19 | 20 | 18 | 23 |
| Corning | 16 | 14 | 19 | 15 | 25 |
| Albany | 14 | 16 | 21 | 17 | 26 |

### Getting Started

1. Identify the type of problem, prepare data and formulate.

   This is a *transportation* problem.

   *Formulate the problem, that is, set up the transportation tableau.*

   Use the first letter of each name as the variable for that city:

| From \ To | R | P | U | E | O | Supply |
|---|---|---|---|---|---|---|
| B | 14 | 11 | 23 | 16 | 22 | 100 |
| S | 12 | 19 | 20 | 18 | 23 | 150 |
| C | 16 | 14 | 19 | 15 | 25 | 100 |
| A | 14 | 16 | 21 | 17 | 26 | 100 |
| Demand | 75 | 100 | 100 | 75 | 100 | |

Note that it is possible to use any variable name, up to five characters in length. As you will see the program uses the default variables D1, S1, etc.

2. Select the program from the Main Menu.

*Select Transportation.* Use the **down arrow key** to move to transportation. *Press* ⟨**RET**⟩ (to complete the entry). Note that the selection is highlighted and repeated in the selected −> box. Figure 2.1 (p. 31) shows the Main Menu.

### Data Entry

From this point on, you are guided by the program—you do what the screen tells you to do. Screens are now program specific. What you see, depends on the program you are running. When the TRANSPORTATION program selection entry is completed, the screen will change to display the data entry method menu.

1. Select the data entry method of choice from the DATA ENTRY METHOD menu, which is shown in Figure 2.10.

*Select* ENTRY FROM KEYBOARD. *Press* ⟨**RET**⟩ (to complete the entry).

The cursor, or highlight, is already by default on this choice, so it is not necessary to use the up or down arrow keys to move through the menu.

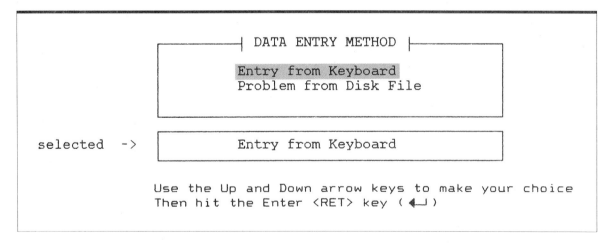

**Figure 2.10**     Data Entry Method Menu

2. Respond to the prompts. The prompts require you to describe the problem (max or min, number of rows and columns). Succeeding prompts appear after a response to a prompt has been entered. The prompts you will see are in all capital letters. Your responses for this problem are given here:

TYPE OF PROBLEM: (MAX/ MIN )

*Select* MIN. *Press* ⟨**RET**⟩.

Minimization is the default choice, or the selection offered by the program. Selection is made by highlighting your choice and pressing ⟨RET⟩. The left arrow key will move this cursor to MAX; the right arrow key will move it back to MIN.

HOW MANY ROWS (SOURCES) IN THE TABLEAU ?

*Type* **4**

The program is limited to 40 rows (not counting dummies, which are added automatically by the program). However, anything over 10 causes the top rows to scroll out of sight as the bottom of the screen is reached.

HOW MANY COLUMNS (DESTINATIONS) IN THE TABLEAU ?

*Type* **5**

The program limit is 40. Note that not all 40 can appear on one line, because of screen width. The screen will scroll horizontally to allow additional entries.

Now that the problem has been described, the program can set up the tableau for you to fill in.

3.  Fill in the tableau values, per unit costs, demands, and supplies. Change variable names if desired. Figure 2.11 shows the tableau as it appears ready for the first entry. Entries are made by typing them. The cursor movement keys allow you to move around in the table to where you want to type the entry.

**Figure 2.11**
Transportation
Tableau Ready
for Entries

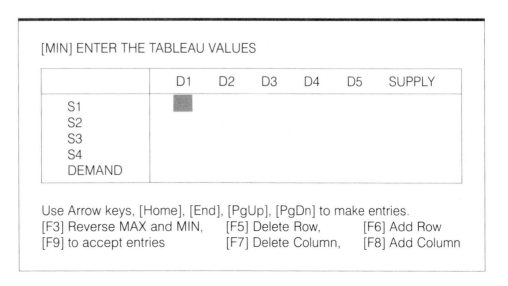

[MIN] ENTER THE TABLEAU VALUES

|  | D1 | D2 | D3 | D4 | D5 | SUPPLY |
|---|---|---|---|---|---|---|
| S1 |  |  |  |  |  |  |
| S2 |  |  |  |  |  |  |
| S3 |  |  |  |  |  |  |
| S4 |  |  |  |  |  |  |
| DEMAND |  |  |  |  |  |  |

Use Arrow keys, [Home], [End], [PgUp], [PgDn] to make entries.
[F3] Reverse MAX and MIN,      [F5] Delete Row,        [F6] Add Row
[F9] to accept entries              [F7] Delete Column,    [F8] Add Column

Note that the instructions for using the cursor movement keys and function [F] keys to move through the tableau to make entries are given below. The cursor (highlighted rectangle) is in cell S1-D1. The problem is identified as minimization [MIN] above the table.

To move around the table:

Arrow keys move cursor right, left, up, down.

[HOME] key moves cursor to left-hand edge of a line.

[END] key moves cursor to right edge of a line.

[PgUp] moves cursor to first row of the cell values section of the tableau.

[PgDn] moves cursor to last row of the cell values section.

The [TAB] key and the ⟨RET⟩ key emulate the right arrow key.

To use the function keys to make/edit entries:

[F3] reverses MAX/MIN.

[F5] deletes a row (used to eliminate a source).

[F6] adds a row (used to add a source).

[F7] deletes a column (used to eliminate a destination).

[F8] adds a column (used to add a destination).

[F9] accepts the entries. This key must be pressed to continue the program and achieve a solution.

*Type the tableau entries as follows:*

1.  Name the variables. Change the default demand variables from D1, D2, etc. to our problem variables, R, P, U, E, and O.

    *Press the* **up arrow key** *to move the cursor to the D1. Type* **R**. *Press the* **right arrow key** *or the* ⟨**RET**⟩ *key to move to the D2. Type* **P**, *etc.*

    Change the default supply variables from S1, S2, etc. to B, S, C, and A for our problem.

    *Use the* **arrow keys** *to move to S1, type* **B**. *Move to S2, type* **S**, *etc.*

2.  Enter the shipping costs, supplies, and demands.

    *Use* **cursor movement keys** *to move to each cell. Type the entry.* For example:

    Move the cursor to the upper left-hand cell (B-R), *type* **14**. *Press the* **right arrow key** *or the* ⟨**RET**⟩ *key to move one cell to the right, to cell B-P. Type* **11**. Continue until all entries have been made.

**Editing/Making Corrections**

1.  If you catch a typing mistake just as you are making it, that is, before leaving that cell, use the backspace/erase key and retype it.

2. If you notice a mistake in a cell that you are no longer in, move to that cell and type the correct value over the incorrect value.

Let's demonstrate:

Put your cursor on cell A-R. Assume that you entered the supply from Buffalo incorrectly. Press [END]. The cursor should move to the supply value for this row. Press the up arrow key three times. You should be in the cell with the supply from Buffalo. Retype the 100.

Modifications (error corrections, changes, etc.) have to be made before the entries are accepted. *Check the data carefully after you have entered it.*

### Accepting the Entries

When all entries have been made and checked for accuracy, they have to be accepted in order for the program to solve the problem.

1. Accept the entries if they are all correct.

*Press the* **[F9] key**. The [F9] function key tells the program to continue.

Figure 2.12 shows the completed tableau for this problem.

```
[MIN] ENTER THE TABLEAU VALUES:


              R      P      U      E      O     SUPPLY

      B      14     11     23     16     22     100
      S      12     19     20     18     23     150
      C      16     14     19     15     25     100
      A      14     16     21     17     26     100
   DEMAND    75    100    100     75    100




Use Arrow keys, [Home], [End], [PgUp], [PgDn] to make entries.
[F3] Reverse MAX and MIN,      [F5] Delete Row,       [F6] Add Row
[F9] to accept entries         [F7] Delete Column,    [F8] Add Column
```

**Figure 2.12**    Completed Transportation Tableau

### Output

Output for the transportation program is very simple and straightforward. It is the tableau showing the optimal allocation and the solution value. Figure 2.13 shows it for this problem. After you have looked it over, follow the screen instructions to "Press any key to continue." We will use the Ending Menu to change this problem to demonstrate some of the transportation program features.

```
OPTIMAL ALLOCATION:


          | R       P       U       E       O       SUPPLY

    B     | 0       100     0       0       0       100
    S     | 50      0       0       0       100     150
    C     | 0       0       100     0       0       100
    A     | 25      0       0       75      0       100

 DEMAND   | 75      100     100     75      100

SOLUTION VALUE =   7525

          Press any key to continue
```

**Figure 2.13**    Optimal Solution Transportation Problem

### Ending

1. Use the Ending Menu to Modify Data and Run Again. The Ending Menu was shown in Figure 2.9.

   *Select* Modify Data and Run Again. *Press* ⟨**RET**⟩. Note that this is the default choice offered by the program.

### Returning to the Problem to Modify Data

The Problem Revisited

Plowshares, Inc. has to temporarily close the Albany factory. The Buffalo factory can increase production and supply an additional 60 blades. Corning can supply 25 more. Syracuse cannot increase production at all. What do these changes do to the shipping allocations and the total cost? Plowshares still desires to minimize total shipping costs.

## Modifying Data

Note that when you selected "Modify Data and Run Again," the program provides you with the tableau that you had previously completed under a "HERE IS WHAT YOU ENTERED" heading. Figure 2.14 shows this.

```
[MIN] HERE IS WHAT YOU ENTERED:


               R       P       U       E       O      SUPPLY

       B       14      11      23      16      22      100
       S       12      19      20      18      23      150
       C       16      14      19      15      25      100
       A       14      16      21      17      26      100
    DEMAND     75      100     100     75      100




Use Arrow keys, [Home], [End], [PgUp], [PgDn] to make entries.
[F3] Reverse MAX and MIN,      [F5] Delete Row,        [F6] Add Row
[F9] to accept entries         [F7] Delete Column,     [F8] Add Column
```

**Figure 2.14**    Summary of Tableau Entries

1. Move through the table and make the required changes. We will make them as follows:

   Eliminate the Albany source.

   *Place the cursor anywhere in that row (one row above the demand row).*
   *Press the* **[F5] key** to delete the row.

   Note that when you make this command ([F5]) the program asks you if you are sure that you want to delete the row. The default answer is NO. *Select* YES. The tableau on screen now has that row deleted.

Change the supply from Buffalo.

*Use the* **arrow keys***; move to the supply figure from Buffalo. Type* **160**. Note that you are typing over the 100.

Change the supply from Corning.

*Use the* **down arrow key***; move down two rows to the Corning supply. Type* **125**.

2. Check these entries, correct any typos, and accept the entries.

*Press the* **[F9] key**.

Note that the problem is no longer balanced. This doesn't matter to the program. Dummy rows and/or columns are added automatically. Figure 2.15 shows the tableau with the dummy row.

```
UNBALANCED SUPPLY AND DEMAND.   DEMAND EXCEEDS SUPPLY.

ADDING A DUMMY ROW WITH   15   UNITS AND ZERO VALUE IN EACH CELL.

NEW TABLEAU:


           R        P        U        E        O       SUPPLY
        ---------------------------------------------------------
    B   | 14       11       23       16       22       160
    S   | 12       19       20       18       23       150
    C   | 16       14       19       15       25       125
  DUMMY | 0        0        0        0        0        15
        ---------------------------------------------------------
  DEMAND| 75       100      100      75       100


            Press any key to continue
```

**Figure 2.15**     Transportation Tableau with Dummy Row Added

*Press any key to continue.*

### Output

The revised output is shown in Figure 2.16.

After you have looked at the output, *Press any key to continue.* When the Ending Menu appears, *select* Return to Main Menu, if you want to continue working on the tutorial. Otherwise, make the selection of your choice. Return to DOS allows you to quit.

```
OPTIMAL ALLOCATION:

         | R      P      U      E      O      SUPPLY
---------+------------------------------------------
    B    | 0      100    0      0      60     160
    S    | 75     0      50     0      25     150
    C    | 0      0      50     75     0      125
  DUMMY  | 0      0      0      0      15     15
---------+------------------------------------------
 DEMAND  | 75     100    100    75     100

SOLUTION VALUE =   6970

          Press any key to continue
```

**Figure 2.16**     Optimal Allocation, Revised Transportation Problem

## 2.3  Problem 3: Deterministic Inventory—EOQ

Great Sounds! sells a car stereo, completely installed, for $225. The stereo components cost Great Sounds! $95. They install 10,000 of these units a year. The cost of placing an order is $30, and inventory holding costs are charged at 25 percent of average inventory value. What is the economic order quantity? Given a lead time of 7 days, and a work year of 360 days, find the reorder point and the cycle time.

### Getting Started

1.  Identify the type of problem, and prepare data.

    This is a deterministic inventory problem. We are seeking to determine the economic order quantity; it is an EOQ problem. *Prepare the data for the problem.*

    Data preparation in this case is actually the identification of the pertinent data needed to solve the problem. Thus we can identify:

    | | |
    |---|---|
    | Annual demand | 10,000 |
    | Ordering cost | $30.00 |

Carrying cost        25% of $95
Lead time            7 days
Working days/year    360

2. Select the program from the Main Menu (Main Menu is displayed in Figure 2.1 on page 31).

   *Highlight* Deterministic Inventory. *Press the* **down arrow key** *to move to this selection. Press* ⟨**RET**⟩.

   Note the highlighted selection also shows up in the bottom rectangular box, which shows the program selected.

### Data Entry

1. Select the subprogram to be run from the subprogram menu. Figure 2.17 shows this menu.

   *Select* EOQ (the default choice). *Press* ⟨**RET**⟩.

   Since EOQ is the default choice, it is necessary only to press ⟨RET⟩ to complete the entry. Be sure to check the selected box and the highlight to be certain you have made the correct choice before pressing the ⟨RET⟩ key.

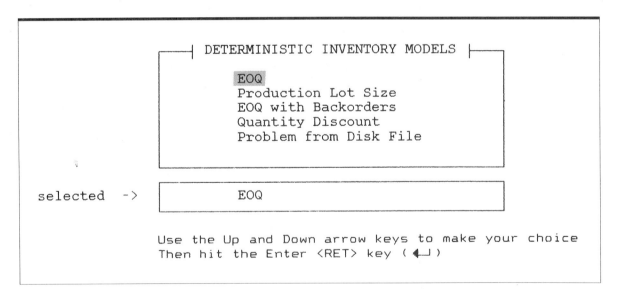

**Figure 2.17**    Deterministic Inventory Models Menu

Data entry is in the form of prompted input. You will respond to a series of questions appearing on the screen. Your responses describe the problem and provide the data necessary to solve it.

If you make a mistake while typing and recognize it before the ⟨RET⟩ key is pressed, use the backspace/erase key to erase it and retype. If you notice an error after the ⟨RET⟩ key is pressed, you will have to wait for the input summary to be able to make modifications.

The prompts, shown in capital letters, and the required responses are very easy to understand and are very straightforward.

2. Respond to the prompts as follows:

WHAT IS THE ANNUAL DEMAND IN UNITS ?

*Type* **10000**. *Press* ⟨**RET**⟩. Note: do not type the comma.

WHAT IS THE COST OF PLACING AN ORDER ?

*Type* **30**. *Press* ⟨**RET**⟩. Note: do not use the $ or the 00 after the decimal.

IS CARRYING COST EXPRESSED AS:

$ (Dollar/unit) or % (Percent of inventory value) ? ( $ / % )

*Select %. Press* ⟨**RET**⟩. % is the default value.

WHAT IS THE PRICE PER UNIT OF THE ITEM ?

*Type* **95**. *Press* ⟨**RET**⟩. Note: do not use the $ or trailing 00s.

CARRYING COST IS WHAT PERCENT OF THE INVENTORY VALUE ?

*Type* **25**. *Press* ⟨**RET**⟩. Note: this is the percentage without the percent (%) sign. Do not enter the decimal equivalent of 0.25.

These last two questions are asked because we responded that carrying costs are expressed as a percent of inventory value. If we said it is expressed as a dollar value per unit, we would have been asked to enter the carrying cost in dollars and cents.

WHAT IS THE LEAD TIME IN DAYS (IF NONE, HIT ⟨RET⟩) ?

*Type* **7**. *Press* ⟨**RET**⟩.

You are entering the number of days it takes to receive an order after it has been placed. You need this to determine when to reorder. If you do not want to determine reorder point merely press ⟨RET⟩.

HOW MANY WORKING DAYS PER YEAR
          (HIT ⟨RET⟩ FOR 365) ?

*Type* **360**. *Press* ⟨**RET**⟩.
Note: the default value is 365 days. If the company/firm works 365 days, or if you are not looking for a reorder point, just press ⟨RET⟩.

### Error Correction/Input Summary

1.  Check input. Make corrections/modifications. Figure 2.18 shows the input summary for this problem.

```
HERE IS WHAT YOU ENTERED:

(1) ANNUAL DEMAND                    10000
(2) COST OF PLACING AN ORDER      $  30
(3) CARRYING COST                    25 % OF $ 95   OR $ 23.75
(4) NUMBER OF DAYS PER YEAR          360
(5) LEAD TIME IN DAYS                7

DO YOU WANT TO MODIFY THE DATA ? (YES/NO)
```

**Figure 2.18**     Input Summary EOQ

We are going to demonstrate an error correction. Our problem said that carrying cost was 25 percent of inventory value. We now discover that this was incorrect. The actual figure is 20 percent. We need to make this correction in our input. Note, in the input summary that number (3) is carrying cost.

2.  Respond YES to the question "DO YOU WANT TO MODIFY THE DATA ?" (YES/NO).
    *Use the* **left arrow key** *to move to YES. Press* ⟨**RET**⟩.

3.  Respond to the prompts to make the change as follows:
    WHICH LINE DO YOU WISH TO CHANGE ?

    *Type* **3**. *Press* ⟨**RET**⟩.

    We have already noted that this is the line that refers to carrying cost.

    ENTER THE CORRECT VALUE BELOW:

    PRICE OF ITEM ?

    *Type* **95**. *Press* ⟨**RET**⟩.

    CARRYING COST (PERCENT) ?

    *Type* **20**. *Press* ⟨**RET**⟩. This is the new or modified value.

4.  Respond NO to the question "DO YOU WANT TO MODIFY THE DATA ?" (YES/ NO ).

    *Select* NO (the default value). *Press* ⟨**RET**⟩.

    Once we have made one modification, we are shown the new input summary and have to answer the question again. Thus, only one modification/correction can be made at a time. It is necessary to respond NO to get a solution.

### Output

Figure 2.19 shows the output.

**Figure 2.19**
Output EOQ

```
THE OPTIMAL EOQ VALUE =  177.7   UNITS

ANNUAL COSTS (EXCLUDING ITEM COSTS):

        CARRYING COST =    $1,688.19
        ORDERING COST =    $1,688.19
        TOTAL COSTS   =    $3,376.38

THE REORDER POINT IS  194.44   UNITS

THE NUMBER OF ORDERS PER YEAR IS  56.27


THE CYCLE TIME IS  6.4   DAYS

                Press any key to continue.
```

Pressing any key to continue, takes you to the Ending Menu, shown previously in Figure 2.9 (p. 38). When it appears, select Return to DOS. You have completed the tutorial.

We hope these practice exercises have given you sufficient experience with the data entry formats to make you more comfortable, or at least, less uncomfortable with the use of these models.

# Chapter 3

# Linear Programming

Linear programming is a mathematical technique designed to help managers make the best use of an organization's resources. It is used for the allocation of restricted or constrained resources in an attempt to achieve a single objective. It is widely used by organizations wishing to maximize or minimize some quantity (such as profit or costs) in the presence of constrained resources that limit the pursuit of this objective.

A linear programming problem must contain: 1. an objective function; 2. constraints or restrictions, that is, resources that are in limited supply and need to be allocated; 3. interaction between variables such that there are alternative courses of action; and 4. a linear or direct relationship among the variables. Moreover, the objective and limitations must be able to be expressed in mathematical form as equations or inequalities. Linear programming will identify the optimal feasible solution to the problem.

LP can be and has been used by organizations for a broad range of applications. One of the most common uses is the determination of product mix, where a company must allocate limited resources in the manufacture of selected products in order to either minimize cost or maximize profit. It has also been used effectively in such widely diverse applications as media selection or marketing strategy, portfolio selection, assignment or labor problems, transportation problems, ingredient and blending problems, and goal planning.

## 3.1 The LP Program

This program uses the simplex method, a general purpose linear programming technique used to solve large scale problems that involve multiple variables and constraints. The program will solve LP problems having a single objective function and up to 30 variables and 30 constraints.

The objective of the LP program is to identify the optimal feasible solution to the problem. The program solves for variable values and objective function values, identifying slack, surplus, and/or artificial variables added to the constraints. It also identifies shadow prices. In addition, the program will perform sensitivity analysis on the objective function coefficients and the right-hand sides. It can be used to perform postoptimality analysis and to solve both maximization and minimization problems.

To prepare a problem for computer input, it is necessary to first formulate the LP model. The objective function and the constraints of the problem have to be identified and stated in mathematical form. However, it is not necessary to state the problem in standard or tableau form. The program automatically converts the inequalities of the problem to equalities, adding or subtracting slack, surplus, and artificial variables as necessary to set up the initial tableau. The program also automatically assumes the nonnegativity constraints.

## 3.2 Data Entry

The problem data are entered in one of three ways: free form, tabular (a spreadsheet like input), or from a disk file. Selection is made from the data entry method menu by using the up and down arrow keys to move to the selection of choice and pressing ⟨RET⟩ to complete the entry.

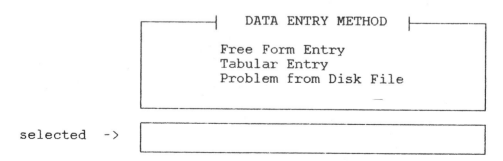

```
                    |  DATA ENTRY METHOD  |
                    Free Form Entry
                    Tabular Entry
                    Problem from Disk File


selected  ->   [                                        ]


          Use the Up and Down arrow keys to make your choice
          Then hit the Enter <RET> key ( ◄┘ )
```

Note that while it is possible to enter data from a disk file, this disk file must have been created previously, using one of the two entry methods as discussed in Chapter one. Therefore, entry from disk file will not be presented in this chapter.

Both the free form and the tabular mode begin by requiring you to identify the problem as a maximization or a minimization problem:

TYPE OF PROBLEM: MAX/ MIN

The arrow keys highlight the correct choice and the ⟨RET⟩ key enters it.

## Free Form Entry

The free form entry is an instructional tool for smaller problems (or for problems having several 0 (zero) coefficients). It eases the transition from manual solution to computer solution. Thus, the free form entry resembles the LP model that has been formulated from the problem, for example,

```
MAX 5X1 + 3X2
SUBJECT TO:
        2X1 + 4X2 <= 20
        4X1 + 2X2 <= 22
               X2 >= 3
```

Once the type of problem has been identified, data is entered in response to prompts (prompted input). As prompted:

1. Enter (type) the objective function at the cursor (MAX or MIN appear automatically). Press ⟨RET⟩ to complete the entry.
2. Enter the constraints, one constraint to a line, each followed by ⟨RET⟩.
3. Enter GO (as the final entry, after the last constraint has been entered). The program automatically numbers each line.

If the objective function or any constraint is longer than one screen line (80 characters), it will automatically wrap to the next line when it reaches the right edge of the screen. A typical entry would look like Figure 3.1 (p. 56).

## Tabular Entries

The tabular entry form is especially useful for entering and editing data in larger problems (up to 30 variables and 30 constraints). In response to prompts asking for the number of variables and the number of constraints the program sets up the table for data entry. Enter the data spreadsheet fashion. In other words, use the cursor movement keys (the arrow keys,

**Figure 3.1**
Free Form Entry
for LP

TYPE OF PROBLEM: **MAX** /MIN

ENTER OBJECTIVE FUNCTION
MAX  5X1  +  3X2

ENTER THE CONSTRAINTS, ONE PER LINE, HERE. AFTER YOU HAVE
ENTERED THE LAST CONSTRAINT, ENTER THE WORD GO
1      2X1  +  4X2 <= 20
2      4X1  +  2X2 <= 22
3      X2  >= 3
4      GO

[Home], [End], [PgUp], and [PgDn]) to move through the table; type the
entry in the correct location. Press the [F9] key to accept the entries and
begin the solution procedure. The tabular entry form is a two step process:

1.  Respond to the prompts to describe the problem. The program
    prompts for type of problem, number of variables, and number of
    constraints. Figure 3.2 shows an example of the initial entries (the
    example uses a two variable, three constraint maximization problem).

**Figure 3.2**
Initial Entries
Tabular Form LP

TYPE OF PROBLEM: MAX/ **MIN**

NUMBER OF VARIABLES ? 2

NUMBER OF CONSTRAINTS ? 3

Recall that the ⟨RET⟩ key has to be pressed to complete each entry.

2.  Fill in the table. The program provides a fill-in-the-blank table based
    on the number of variables and constraints described. Row one is for
    objective function coefficients; row two shows the variables (with
    default names X1, X2, etc., which can be changed); and the remaining
    rows, three, four, etc., are for constraints. Top-of-the-screen
    messages prompt for required input and indicate the type of problem
    [MAX] or [MIN]. These prompts reflect the cursor location; for
    example, when the cursor is in the first row, the prompt reads [MAX]
    or [MIN] INPUT OBJECTIVE FUNCTION COEFFICIENTS. Figure 3.3
    shows this table.

**Figure 3.3**
Tabular Entry Form

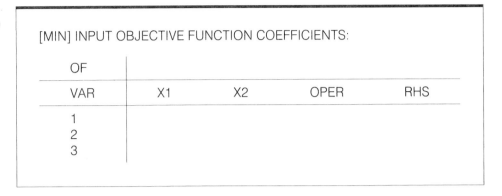

[MIN] INPUT OBJECTIVE FUNCTION COEFFICIENTS:

| OF | | | | |
|---|---|---|---|---|
| VAR | X1 | X2 | OPER | RHS |
| 1 | | | | |
| 2 | | | | |
| 3 | | | | |

Use the cursor movement keys to move around in the table. Type the entry. To change an entry, type over what is currently there. Note the top message line changes to reflect the row where the cursor is. The [F3] key will reverse the MAX/MIN selection. When all entries have been made, checked for accuracy, and edited, if necessary, press the [F9] key to accept the entries. Figure 3.4 shows a completed table. Entry specifics are as follows:

1.  Enter the objective function *coefficients*. A zero (0) coefficient does not have to be entered; a coefficient of one (1) must be entered. Do not enter the variable names; you are entering coefficients only. It is not possible to enter coefficients for variables that are not there. Variables can be added or deleted by using [F7] to delete a column and [F8] to add a column.

2.  Name the variables. The table comes up showing the default variable names (X1,X2, etc.). These can be changed. Move the cursor to the variable, and type over the default name. Variables can be added or deleted as described in step one using the [F7] and [F8] keys.

**Figure 3.4**
Sample Tabular
Entry Form

| OF | 5 | 3 | | |
|---|---|---|---|---|
| VAR | P1 | P2 | OPER | RHS |
| 1 | 2 | 4 | < | 20 |
| 2 | 4 | 2 | < | 22 |
| 3 | | 1 | > | 3 |

3.  Enter each constraint coefficient, operator, and right-hand side value.
    Note, all values are limited to 7 characters. Scientific notation can be
    used for larger values. Do not enter variables. Constraints can be
    added or deleted. The [F5] key deletes a row and the [F6] adds a row.
    Only 10 constraint rows show on screen at a time. The rows scroll up
    as you reach the bottom of the display area.

## 3.3 Editing/Error Correction

Error correction was detailed in Chapter one. However, because this is the
initial model chapter, and because LP is the most widely used model, we
are going to repeat much of the error correction/editing discussion. Our
purpose is to reinforce what you have learned.

Error correction is dependent on the type of data entry method selected. However, with either method, if the mistake is made while the entry is being typed, use the backspace key to erase the mistake and retype.

### Free Form Entry

If you do not discover the mistake until after you have entered it, you can
correct it using the error correcting routine, but only after you have completed all entries for the problem. In general, the routine displays the entries with each line numbered, asks if you wish to make any modifications,
and provides you an opportunity to modify the data one line at a time.
Prompts then lead you step by step through the procedure:

1.  Identify the line which contains the error (0 is the objective function;
    1, 2, . . . are the constraints)

2.  Reenter the line correctly. To add a constraint, use the next
    consecutive line number. To delete a line, press ⟨RET⟩ when
    prompted to reenter the line correctly.

Note that you can change only one line at a time. Once this line is entered,
the error correction routine repeats, allowing you to make another modification. Once the problem is entered to your satisfaction, the error correction routine is terminated by responding NO to the question "DO YOU
WANT TO MODIFY THE DATA ?"

### Tabular Entry

Errors can be corrected only before you press the [F9] key to accept the
entries. Use the cursor movement keys and designated function keys
([F3],[F5],[F6],[F7],[F8]) can be used to move throughout the table to make
corrections and changes or modifications—to add and delete variables

and constraints and change the problem type. It is a good idea to carefully verify the data in a given table, before pressing the [F9] key.

### Disk File

When you retrieve a file from disk, it automatically comes up in tabular entry form. At this time, it is possible for you to use the cursor movement keys to move through one table at a time to make modifications. If the data are acceptable, the [F9] key has to be pressed before the program will continue.

Note that it is also possible to make changes in problems in order to modify data, correct errors, and do postoptimality analyses after a problem has been completed and a solution has been determined. To do so use the Modify Data option in the Ending Menu, shown here and discussed in Chapter one.

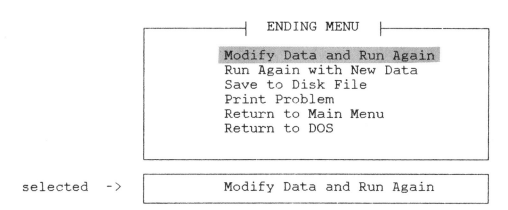

```
                   ┤  ENDING MENU  ├
        ┌─────────────────────────────────────────┐
        │                                           │
        │        Modify Data and Run Again          │
        │        Run Again with New Data            │
        │        Save to Disk File                  │
        │        Print Problem                      │
        │        Return to Main Menu                │
        │        Return to DOS                      │
        │                                           │
        │                                           │
        └─────────────────────────────────────────┘

selected  ->  ┌─────────────────────────────────────────┐
              │        Modify Data and Run Again          │
              └─────────────────────────────────────────┘
```

## 3.4   Labeling Constraints

Both entry forms permit the labeling of constraints, which makes identifying shadow prices and ranges easier. After the data have been entered and modified, you are allowed, through prompted input, to label the constraints. Labeling the constraints is a simple prompted input procedure:

1.  Respond NO to the prompt "DO YOU WANT TO LABEL THE CONSTRAINTS?" to leave the constraints unlabeled.

2.  Respond YES to label the constraints. The program then displays the constraint numbers (the constraints are numbered 1, 2, . . . by the program).

3. Enter the name, up to 12 characters, press ⟨RET⟩. Do not use commas. Repeat the entering procedure.

4. If you make a typing mistake, use the backspace key to erase it and retype it correctly before pressing ⟨RET⟩. You will not be given a chance to change these entries.

## 3.5  Output and Solution

The output for the LP program is independent of the entry form used. Output includes:

1. A summary of slack, surplus and artificial variables added to the model (tableau) by the program as needed.

2. The tableaus (if desired). You are given the opportunity, by menu selection, to have no tableaus displayed, only the final tableau displayed, or to have all tableaus displayed. Note any time there are more than six variables, the tableau will wrap. A typical final tableau for a problem with six variables will look like Figure 3.5.

**Figure 3.5**
Sample Final
Tableau

TABLEAU NUMBER 4

| C(j) | | 3 | 5 | 2 | 0 | 0 | −999999 | |
|---|---|---|---|---|---|---|---|---|
| | Basis | P1 | P2 | P3 | S1 | S2 | A1 | RHS |
| 5 | P2 | 0 | 1 | 0 | .38 | −.25 | .25 | 2.75 |
| 2 | P3 | 0 | 0 | 1 | −.5 | 1 | −3 | 3 |
| 3 | P1 | 1 | 0 | 0 | 0 | 0 | 1 | 3 |
| | Z | 3 | 5 | 2 | .875 | .75 | −1.75 | 28.75 |
| | C–Z | 0 | 0 | 0 | −.875 | −.75 | −999999 | |

### Tableau Notes

■ Because of the way the computer stores numbers in binary notation (described in Chapter one), and because large numbers in the tableaus are frequently truncated, you may get some unusual results. For example, in a problem minimizing .05A, .07B, and .09C (MIN .05A + .07B + .09C), some computers have shown the following tableau:

| C | .05 | .07 | 9.0000 |
|---|---|---|---|
| | A | B | C |

- That coefficient of 9.0000 displayed for variable C is really the value 9.00000E−02 which has been truncated. It is the equivalent of .09, although it doesn't appear that way in the tableau. This occurs infrequently, but you should be aware of the possibility.

- In a tableau having artificial variables, a coefficient of −999999 or 999999 appears instead of the letter −M (or +M) with which you may be more familiar.

- If the value of the objective function is large, it will be displayed in scientific notation.

- If the problem is unbounded or infeasible the message "THIS PROBLEM IS UNBOUNDED OR INFEASIBLE" will appear. Infeasible problems may produce the alternative message:

    THERE IS NO FEASIBLE SOLUTION TO THIS PROBLEM
    . . . OR SIMPLY BEYOND MY LIMITED CAPABILITIES
    BESIDES, I'M GETTING A HEADACHE!

- If the problem has more than 13 constraints, the output may begin to scroll off the screen. You can freeze the screen by pressing the CTRL and NUM LOCK keys (see Chapter one). To continue press any key.

3. The optimal solution. The solution indicates the number of iterations required and gives the optimal value for each variable, objective function value, and shadow prices (and/or dual values).

    Note, in the solution, that the column labeled SHADOW PRICE contains the C−Z values for the real variables as well. Some authors refer to these values as "REDUCED COST" or "DUAL VALUES". Although the term **shadow price** may be a misnomer for these values, we have chosen to use it rather than list the variety of different terms in use today.

4. Sensitivity analysis, which gives the range of values for the objective function coefficients and right-hand side values. Sensitivity analysis is optional. After the optimal solution has been displayed, you are asked if you want to do sensitivity analysis.

## 3.6  Examples

### Example 1: Linear Programming Maximization Problem—Free Form Entry

Mary Jane's bakery finds it can sell all of the specialty party cakes it bakes. Each layered cake requires two cups of flour and each large sheet cake requires four cups of flour. Each layered cake requires four eggs and each sheet cake uses two eggs. The baker finds she has only twenty cups of flour and twenty-two eggs available for these cakes. In addition, Mary Jane's has an order for three of the large sheet cakes. If Mary Jane's makes $5 on each layered cake and $3 on each large sheet cake, how many cakes of each type should it bake to be sold the next day?

Figure 3.6 shows the entries you must make for this problem. Note that you first must formulate the model, which you then use to make the entries for the objective function and the constraints. The error correction routine shows no mistakes have been made in input. Figure 3.7 shows the labels for the constraints. The output/solution is shown in Figures 3.8–3.10. Only the final tableau is shown. Sensitivity analysis is not performed for the problem.

```
TYPE OF PROBLEM:  MAX/MIN

ENTER OBJECTIVE FUNCTION
MAX 5X1+3X2

ENTER THE CONSTRAINTS, ONE PER LINE, HERE.  AFTER YOU HAVE
ENTERED THE LAST CONSTRAINT, ENTER THE WORD  GO.

  1    2X1+4X2<20
  2    4X1+2X2<22
  3    X2>3
  4    GO




HERE IS WHAT YOU ENTERED:

  0   MAX  5X1+3X2
      SUBJECT TO:
  1      2X1+4X2<= 20
  2      4X1+2X2<= 22
  3      1X2>= 3

DO YOU WANT TO MODIFY THE DATA ? (YES/NO)
```

**Figure 3.6**      Example 1: LP Input

We see, with little effort on our part, that Mary Jane's should bake four of the layered cakes and three sheet cakes. If she does, she will make a profit of $29.

**Figure 3.7**
Example 1: LP
Constraint Labels

```
DO YOU WANT TO LABEL THE CONSTRAINTS ? (YES/NO)
ENTER THE LABEL FOR EACH CONSTRAINT BELOW:

CONSTRAINT    LABEL
----------    -----
        1     ? FLOUR
        2     ? EGGS
        3     ? ORDERED
```

**Figure 3.8**
Example 1: LP
Output—Variables
Added to Model

```
SLACK, SURPLUS AND ARTIFICIAL VARIABLES
ADDED TO MODEL (TABLEAU):

VARIABLE        TYPE            CONSTRAINT
--------        --------        ----------
   S1           SLACK              1    FLOUR
   S2           SLACK              2    EGGS
   A1           ARTIFICIAL         3    ORDERED
   S3           SURPLUS            3    ORDERED


        Press any key to continue
```

```
TABLEAU NUMBER   3
```

| C(j) | | 5 | 3 | 0 | 0 | -99999998 | 0 | |
|---|---|---|---|---|---|---|---|---|
| | Basis | X1 | X2 | S1 | S2 | A1 | S3 | RHS |
| 5 | X1 | 1 | 0 | .5 | 0 | -2 | 2 | 4 |
| 0 | S2 | 0 | 0 | -2 | 1 | 6 | -6 | 0 |
| 3 | X2 | 0 | 1 | 0 | 0 | 1 | -1 | 3 |
| | Z | 5 | 3 | 2.5 | 0 | -7 | 7 | 29 |
| | C-Z | 0 | 0 | -2.5 | 0 | -99999998 | -7 | |

```
        Press any key to continue
```

**Figure 3.9**    Example 1: LP Output—Final Tableau

```
AFTER 2  ITERATIONS,
THIS SOLUTION IS OPTIMAL:

VARIABLE          QUANTITY
--------          --------
   X1                4
   X2                3
   S2                0


OPTIMAL Z =   29

VARIABLE          SHADOW PRICE
--------          ------------
   X1                0
   X2                0
   S1               -2.5
   S2                0
   S3               -7


DO YOU WANT TO DO SENSITIVITY ANALYSIS ? (YES/NO)
```

**Figure 3.10**     Example 1: LP Output—Optimal Solution

### Example 2: Linear Programming Minimization Problem with Error Correction

Mary Jane's Bakery blends three different frosting mixes, brands A, B, and C, to make frosting for its cakes. The brands cost 5, 7, and 10 cents per ounce, respectively. Mary Jane's needs to blend at least 80 ounces of frosting for its current batch of cakes. In addition, the brands contain 10 percent, 20 percent, and 50 percent sugar per ounce. The bakery wants its total blend to contain at least 24 ounces of sugar. Because MJ's is currently overstocked with brand B, they wish to use at least 20 ounces of brand B. How many ounces of each brand of frosting mix should MJ's use if it wishes to minimize the cost of its blend?

Figure 3.11 shows the input for this problem. We are using free form entry, but the selection screen is not shown. Note that there is a constraint missing in the entry. Then check the input summary and the error correction routine to see that we entered the missing constraint. We are not labeling the constraints this time. Figures 3.12–3.14 (pp. 66–67) show the output and solution (final tableau only). Again we do not ask for sensitivity analysis.

```
TYPE OF PROBLEM:   MAX/MIN

ENTER OBJECTIVE FUNCTION
MIN .05A+.07B+.10C

ENTER THE CONSTRAINTS, ONE PER LINE, HERE.  AFTER YOU HAVE
ENTERED THE LAST CONSTRAINT, ENTER THE WORD   GO.

  1    A+B+C>80
  2    .1A+.2B+.5C>24
  3    GO


HERE IS WHAT YOU ENTERED:

  0    MIN   .05A+.07B+.1C
       SUBJECT TO:
  1       1A+1B+1C>= 80
  2       .1A+.2B+.5C>= 24

DO YOU WANT TO MODIFY THE DATA ? (YES/NO)
WHICH LINE DO YOU WISH TO CHANGE? 3

ENTER NEW LINE(S). TO STOP, TYPE GO
  3    B>20
  4    GO


HERE IS WHAT YOU ENTERED:

  0    MIN   .05A+.07B+.1C
       SUBJECT TO:
  1       1A+1B+1C>= 80
  2       .1A+.2B+.5C>= 24
  3       1B>= 20

DO YOU WANT TO MODIFY THE DATA ? (YES/NO)
```

**Figure 3.11**    Example 2: LP Input

As you can see, after 4 iterations, you have an optimal solution of 25 ounces of brand A, 20 ounces of brand B, and 35 ounces of brand C, at a cost of $6.15.

66    *Chapter 3*

```
DO YOU WANT TO LABEL THE CONSTRAINTS ? (YES/NO)

SLACK, SURPLUS AND ARTIFICIAL VARIABLES
ADDED TO MODEL (TABLEAU):

VARIABLE          TYPE              CONSTRAINT
--------          --------          ----------
   A1             ARTIFICIAL            1
   S1             SURPLUS               1
   A2             ARTIFICIAL            2
   S2             SURPLUS               2
   A3             ARTIFICIAL            3
   S3             SURPLUS               3


          Press any key to continue
```

**Figure 3.12**        Example 2: LP—Variables Added to Model

```
TABLEAU NUMBER   5
```

| $C(j)$ | | .05 | .07 | .1 | 99999998 | 0 | 99999998 | 0 |
|---|---|---|---|---|---|---|---|---|
| | Basis | A | B | C | A1 | S1 | A2 | S2 |
| .05 | A | 1 | 0 | 0 | 1.25 | -1.25 | -2.5 | 2.5 |
| .1 | C | 0 | 0 | 1 | -.25 | .25 | 2.5 | -2.5 |
| .07 | B | 0 | 1 | 0 | 0 | 0 | 0 | 0 |
| | Z | .05 | .07 | .1 | .038 | -.037 | .125 | -.125 |
| | C-Z | 0 | 0 | 0 | 99999998 | .037 | 99999998 | .125 |

```
          Press any key to continue
```

| | 99999998 | 0 | |
|---|---|---|---|
| Basis | A3 | S3 | RHS |
| A | -.75 | .75 | 25 |
| C | -.25 | .25 | 35 |
| B | 1 | -1 | 20 |
| Z | .007 | -.007 | 6.15 |
| C-Z | 99999998 | .007 | |

```
          Press any key to continue
```

**Figure 3.13**        Example 2: LP Output—Final Tableau

```
AFTER 4  ITERATIONS,
THIS SOLUTION IS OPTIMAL:

VARIABLE        QUANTITY
--------        --------
    A              25
    B              20
    C              35

OPTIMAL Z =  6.15

VARIABLE        SHADOW PRICE
--------        ------------
    A               0
    B               0
    C               0
    S1            -.037
    S2            -.125
    S3            -.007

DO YOU WANT TO DO SENSITIVITY ANALYSIS ? (YES/NO)
```

**Figure 3.14**     Example 2: LP Output/Solution

### Example 3: Tabular Entry and Sensitivity Analysis

Consider the following LP model:

$$\text{Max}\quad 2X_1 + 4X_2 + X_3 + 5X_4$$
$$\text{ST}$$
$$3X_1 + 2X_2 + X_3 + 4X_4 <= 90$$
$$3X_2 \qquad + 2X_4 <= 42$$
$$X_3 \qquad >= 10$$

1.  Enter using tabular entry and solve.
2.  Determine the optimal range for all $C_j$ values.
3.  Determine the feasible range for all right-hand sides.

Figure 3.15 (p. 68) shows the initial entries for this problem. Figure 3.16 shows the table with input. Output/solution is shown in Figures 3.17–3.20 (pp. 69–71). Notice that we asked to see only the final tableau. The important feature of this example is the inclusion of the sensitivity analysis.

```
                  ┌──────────┤ DATA ENTRY METHOD ├──────────┐
                  │                                          │
                  │          Free Form Entry                 │
                  │          Tabular Entry                   │
                  │          Problem from Disk File          │
                  │                                          │
                  └──────────────────────────────────────────┘

      selected  ->    ┌────────────────────────────────┐
                       │          Tabular Entry         │
                       └────────────────────────────────┘

                  Use the Up and Down arrow keys to select the model
                  Then hit the Enter <RET> key (  ◄┘  )


  TYPE OF PROBLEM:  MAX/MIN


  NUMBER OF VARIABLES ? 4


  NUMBER OF CONSTRAINTS ? 3
```

**Figure 3.15**        Example 3: LP Initial Entries

```
  [MAX] ENTER THE CONSTRAINT COEFFICIENTS, OPERATORS (<,=,>) AND RHS VALUES:

  OF │ 2       4       1       5
  ───┼─────────────────────────────────────────────────────────
  VAR│ X1      X2      X3      X4      OPER    RHS
  ───┼─────────────────────────────────────────────────────────
   1 │ 3       2       1       4       <       90
   2 │         3               2       <       42
   3 │                 1               >       10
  ───┴─────────────────────────────────────────────────────────



  Use Arrow keys, [Home], [End], [PgUp], [PgDn] to make entries.
  [F3] Reverse MAX and MIN,     [F5] Delete Row,       [F6] Add Row
  [F9] to accept entries        [F7] Delete Column,    [F8] Add Column
```

**Figure 3.16**        Example 3: LP Table Entries

```
      DO YOU WANT TO LABEL THE CONSTRAINTS ? (YES/NO)

      SLACK, SURPLUS AND ARTIFICIAL VARIABLES
      ADDED TO MODEL (TABLEAU):

      VARIABLE          TYPE              CONSTRAINT
      --------          --------          ----------
          S1            SLACK                 1
          S2            SLACK                 2
          A1            ARTIFICIAL            3
          S3            SURPLUS               3


                      Press any key to continue
```

**Figure 3.17**     Example 3: LP—Variables Added to Model

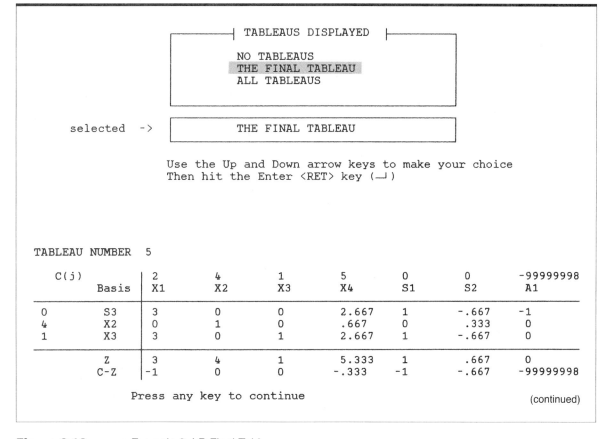

```
                    ┤ TABLEAUS DISPLAYED ├

                      NO TABLEAUS
                      THE FINAL TABLEAU
                      ALL TABLEAUS


      selected  ->          THE FINAL TABLEAU


             Use the Up and Down arrow keys to make your choice
             Then hit the Enter <RET> key (⌐ )




TABLEAU NUMBER  5

   C(j)            2       4       1       5       0       0     -99999998
          Basis    X1      X2      X3      X4      S1      S2      A1
          ──────────────────────────────────────────────────────────────
   0       S3      3       0       0       2.667   1      -.667   -1
   4       X2      0       1       0       .667    0       .333    0
   1       X3      3       0       1       2.667   1      -.667    0
          ──────────────────────────────────────────────────────────────
           Z       3       4       1       5.333   1       .667    0
          C-Z     -1       0       0      -.333   -1      -.667   -99999998

             Press any key to continue                         (continued)
```

**Figure 3.18**     Example 3: LP Final Tableau

```
          0
  Basis   S3        RHS

    S3    1         52
    X2    0         14
    X3    0         62

    Z     0         118
   C-Z    0

              Press any key to continue
```

**Figure 3.18**        (continued)

```
    AFTER 4  ITERATIONS,
    THIS SOLUTION IS OPTIMAL:

    VARIABLE        QUANTITY
    --------        --------
       X2              14
       X3              62
       S3              52

    OPTIMAL Z =  118

    VARIABLE        SHADOW PRICE
    --------        ------------
       X1              -1
       X2               0
       X3               0
       X4              -.333
       S1              -1
       S2              -.667
       S3               0

    DO YOU WANT TO DO SENSITIVITY ANALYSIS ? (YES/NO)
```

**Figure 3.19**        Example 3: LP Output/Solution

The optimal feasible solution to this problem is X2 = 14 and X3 = 62 with an optimal Z value of 118. The sensitivity analysis of the objective function coefficients shows us that variable X2 is optimal when its coefficient is between 3.5 and infinity. For variable X3, the coefficient range is between

```
SENSITIVITY ANALYSIS OF OBJECTIVE FUNCTION COEFFICIENTS

VARIABLE        LOWER           ORIGINAL        UPPER
   NAME         LIMIT           VALUE           LIMIT
--------        -----           --------        -----
    X1          NO LIMIT        2               3
    X2          3.5             4               NO LIMIT
    X3          .875            1               2
    X4          NO LIMIT        5               5.33

            Press any key to continue




SENSITIVITY ANALYSIS OF RIGHT HAND SIDE RANGES

                LOWER           ORIGINAL        UPPER
CONSTRAINT      LIMIT           VALUE           LIMIT
----------      -----           --------        -----
    1           38              90              NO LIMIT
    2           0               42              120
    3           NO LIMIT        10              62

            Press any key to continue
```

**Figure 3.20**    Example 3: LP Sensitivity Analysis

.875 and 2. The range of infeasibility—the objective function coefficient range over which the variables will not enter the basis—is negative infinity (no lower limit) to 3 for variable X1 and negative infinity (no lower limit) to 5.33 for variable X4. The sensitivity analysis of right-hand sides reveals the following feasible ranges, i.e., ranges of right-hand side values over which the shadow prices for those constraints remain constant: constraint 1 (S1) is feasible between 38 and infinity; constraint 2 (S2) is feasible between 0 and 120; and constraint 3 (S3) has no lower limit and can be as large as 62.

## 3.7

**Summary Notes**
for the LP Program

1. *Size*: both the free form and tabular entry form have a 30 variables and 30 constraints limit (however, we recommend using free form for smaller problems); coefficients and RHS values are limited to 7 digit numbers (larger numbers can be stated in scientific notation form).

2. *Variables*: (a) all variables must appear in the objective function (even

those with a 0 coefficient); (b) if a variable name is repeated in the objective function, i.e., if it appears more than once, an error message will indicate that it is a duplicate and ask you to change the entry; (c) variable names are limited to 5 characters; (d) almost any variable name may be used as long as the variable begins with a letter (A–Z). Recall that the letters A and S are used by the program for slack and artificial variables; (e) in the tabular form coefficients of one (1) must be entered; (f) variable names using subscripts use this form: X2, Y3, etc.

3. *Constraints*: (a) constraints can be entered in any order; (b) variables with 0 coefficients do not have to be entered; (c) if a constraint contains a variable not found in the objective function, an error message indicates this and allows you to enter it in the objective function with a 0 coefficient or correct the typo; (d) constraints may not have negative right-hand sides; if they do, you will have to convert them (multiplying by −1) before entering them (remember to change the direction of the inequality); (e) when entering inequalities using < or >, it is not necessary to add the equal sign (=), that is, <= or >=; the program assumes these to save you keystrokes.

4. When entering coefficients in the table using the tabular entry form, be sure not to type the variable with the coefficient.

5. *Moving around the table (tabular entry)*: Arrow keys move right, left, up, down; [TAB] and ⟨RET⟩ emulate the right arrow key; [HOME] moves cursor to left-hand edge of line; [END] moves cursor to right edge of line; [PgUp] moves cursor to first row of the *constraint* section of table; [PgDn] moves cursor to the last row of the *constraint* section.

6. *Function keys in tabular entries*: [F3] reverses MAX/MIN; [F5] deletes a row (used to eliminate a constraint); [F6] adds a row (used to add a constraint); [F7] deletes a column (used to eliminate a variable); [F8] adds a column (used to add a variable); [F9] accepts the entries. This key must be pressed to continue the program and get a solution.

7. Because of the way the computer stores numbers in binary notation (described in Chapter one), and because large numbers in the tableaus are frequently truncated, you may get some unusual results.

8. A coefficient of −999999 or 999999 appears in tableaus which have artificial variables (not the more familiar letter M).

9. Screen messages indicate unbounded or infeasible problems.

10. Very large objective function values are displayed in scientific notation.

11. The output for a problem with more than 13 constraints may begin to scroll off the screen (freeze the screen by pressing the CTRL and NUM LOCK keys).

12. In the solution, the column labeled SHADOW PRICE contains the C–Z values for the real variables as well.

# 3.8

**Problems**

1. Solve the following LP problem:

Max $3X1 + 5X2 + X3$
    Subject to:
        $2X1 + 3X2 + 2X3 <= 20$
        $2X1 \qquad + \quad X3 <= 16$
        $X1 + 4X2 \qquad <= 20$
        $X1,X2,X3 >= 0$

2. Solve the following:

Max $3X1 + 4X2 + 3X3$
    Subject to:
        $2X1 \qquad + X3 \quad <= 120$
        $4X1 + 2X2 \qquad >= \quad 60$
        $3X2 + 2X3 <= 140$
        $X1 \qquad\qquad = \quad 10$
        $X1,X2,X3 >= 0$

3. Solve the following LP problem:

Min $2X1 + 3X2 + 2X3$
    Subject to:
        $2X1 + \quad X2 + 2X3 >= 60$
        $3X1 + 2X2 + \quad X3 >= 84$
        $X1 + 3X2 + 2X3 >= 72$
        $X1,X2,X3 >= 0$

4. Given the following LP problem:

Max $7X1 + 12X2 + 4X3$
    Subject to:                     Constraint
        $3X1 + 6X2 + \quad X3 <= 300$       A
        $4X1 + 5X2 + 2X3 <= 280$       B
        $6X1 + 8X2 + 2X3 <= 340$       C
        $X1,X2,X3 >= 0$

    a.  What is the value of the optimal solution?
    b.  If 10 units could be added to one of the constraints (A, B or C), which constraint would you increase? Why?
    c.  What is the maximum amount you would pay for each unit of the increase in part b?
    d.  Will the values of X1, X2, and X3 change if $C_2$ is changed to 15?
    e.  Referring to the increase in units discussed in parts b and d, what would be the maximum increase?

**5.** Given the following LP problem:

Max 5X1 + 10X2 + 3X3
 Subject to:
    X1 + 3X2 + 4X3 <= 450
    X1 + 2X2 + 2X3 <= 360
         X2 + 2X3 <= 200
   X1,X2,X3 >=0

   **a.** Solve the problem for the optimal solution.
   **b.** Determine the range of optimality or insignificance for the objective function coefficients.
   **c.** Determine the right-hand side range.

**6.** Big Buy Distributors have 1000 Cutsie Poo dolls in stock. Since these dolls are in great demand, Big Buy can sell them all. Big Buy supplies three different types of stores: chain stores, specialty stores, and discount stores. Each type of store yields a different profit per unit and requires different shipping times. Those figures are shown below:

| Store | Profit/unit | Shipping time/unit |
|---|---|---|
| Chain | 8 | 0 min* |
| Specialty | 16 | 18 min |
| Discount | 5.50 | 12 min |

*The chain store sends its own trucks to pick up this item.

Because these dolls are in such great demand, Big Buy wishes to supply a minimum of 200 to each type of store to maintain good will. In addition, the shipping department has a total of 130 hours available. How many dolls should Big Buy sell to each type of store if it wishes to maximize profits?

**7.** The Bilkmore Investment Company has $700,000 to invest. They are considering the following investments:

| Investment | Yield | Risk Factor/$1000 |
|---|---|---|
| Treasury bonds | 8% | 1 |
| Industrial bonds | 10% | 4 |
| Real estate | 15% | 8 |
| New stock issues | 20% | 17 |

Bilkmore's president has stated at least 60% of the funds must be invested in bonds; no more than 30% can be invested in new stock; and the total risk factor cannot exceed 3500. What investments should Bilkmore make if it wishes to maximize its yield? What will be the annual amount of that yield?

**8.** The Bright Feather Bird Seed Company is blending a special 16 ounce box of parakeet seed mix using two different seeds, types A and B. Information on the two types of seeds is shown below:

| Type | Cost/oz | Protein | Fat | Fiber |
|---|---|---|---|---|
| A | $ .04 | 8% | 4% | 6% |
| B | .07 | 15% | 3% | 8% |

Bright Feather wants this blend to contain at least 2 ounces of crude protein and ½ ounce of fat. They also want it to contain no more than 1.5 ounce of crude fiber. How should they blend these seeds to achieve the most economical mixture?

9. The Slick Move Company manufactures two products, figure skates and hockey skates. It makes $12 on each pair of figure skates and $9 on each pair of hockey skates. Each type of skate must pass through the shoe department and the blade department. Figure skates require 1 hour in the shoe department and 1½ hours in the blade department. Hockey skates require 2 hours and ¾ hours in the respective departments. There are currently 48 hours/day available in the shoe department and 56 hours/day in the blade department.
   a. Assuming SMC can sell all the skates it can produce, what product mix will optimize profits?
   b. SMC can increase production by scheduling overtime in one of the departments. Which department should get the overtime?
   c. Any skates produced on overtime net $2 less because of the higher costs. If 16 hours of overtime are scheduled for this department, how many skates of each type should be produced?

10. The Acme Production Company makes an electrical component for a control mechanism. The component can be made using design A, which calls for 2 diodes, 5 resistors, and 4 transistors, or design B, which calls for 4 diodes, 7 resistors, and 1 transistor. Both methods provide equal performance. Diodes cost $.10 each, resistors $.06, and transistors $.17. The company currently has a contract to supply 180 components. Thirty of these components must be of design A, while the remaining 150 may be of either design. If the company has only 500 diodes available, how many components of each design should it produce if it wishes to minimize its costs?

# 4

# Integer
# Linear Programming

Integer linear programming is an extension or variation of linear programming. However, LP solutions are not necessarily integer (the divisibility assumption). Such fractional solutions are not always practicable or sensible in the real world. Some problems require that some or all of the variables have integer values, i.e., that the solution to the problem is an integer. Merely rounding off is not necessarily the answer. Such solutions may be either not feasible or not optimal. Integer linear programming finds the optimum integer solution without violating any of the constraints.

ILP problems, like LP problems, must contain an objective function and constraints or restrictions. However, with ILP there are additional constraints defining the integer requirements for the variables. A problem can require that all variables be integer, that some but not all variables be integer, or that the integer variables assume only the values 0 or 1.

Because of its avoidance of fractional values, ILP is usually preferred for problems in capital budgeting and distribution system design. Moreover, binary ILP (0 or 1) is widely used wherever flexibility in developing logical, that is, either/or, constraints is required.

## 4.1  The ILP Program

The program uses a branch and bound technique (branching only on the node with the higher upper bound for maximization problems or the lower bound for minimization problems) to identify the optimal feasible integer solution for either maximization or minimization problems. It solves pure integer, mixed integer and 0,1 problems having a single objective function and up to 15 variables and 15 constraints. The program solves for variable values and objective function values. Unlike the LP program in the previous chapter, it does not identify either the slack, surplus, and/or artificial variables added to the constraints or the shadow prices. Nor does the program perform sensitivity analysis. However, it is still possible to perform postoptimality analysis, using the Ending Menu option to "Modify Data."

As with an LP problem, it is important to first formulate the ILP model—identify the objective function and the constraints of the problem, and state them in mathematical form. However, it is not necessary to state the problem in standard or tableau form. The program automatically converts the inequalities of the problem to equalities, adding or subtracting slack, surplus and artificial variables as necessary to set up the initial tableau. The program also automatically assumes the nonnegativity constraints.

## 4.2 Data Entry

Data entry begins with the selection of data entry method from the menu, shown below, which offers you two options.

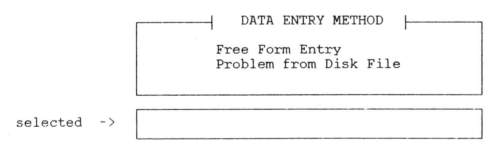

Recall, the free form entry method for LP was described in the previous chapter, and entry from disk file was discussed in Chapter one.

For ILP problems, you must also identify what type of problem is being solved—0,1, mixed integer, or pure integer. The identification is made from menu selection, shown in Figure 4.1.

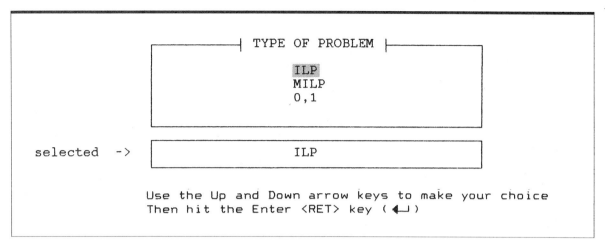

```
                    ┤ TYPE OF PROBLEM ├
                              ILP
                             MILP
                              0,1




selected  ->  │              ILP                │


        Use the Up and Down arrow keys to make your choice
        Then hit the Enter <RET> key ( ◄┘ )
```

**Figure 4.1**        Type of ILP Problem Menu

If you select ILP, the program automatically assumes all variables are integer values. If you select 0,1, the program assumes all variables have a value of 0 or 1. If you select MILP, you will have the opportunity later, after entering the constraints, to identify which variables must have integer values.

As with LP, you must also describe the problem as a maximization or a minimization problem

TYPE OF PROBLEM: MAX/ MIN

again using the arrow keys to highlight your choice and the ⟨RET⟩ key to enter it.

Then as prompted:

1.  Enter the objective function at the cursor (MAX or MIN appear automatically). Press ⟨RET⟩ to complete the entry. The program limits ILP and MILP problems to 25 variables; 0,1 problems to 12 variables.

2.  Enter the constraints, one constraint to a line, each followed by ⟨RET⟩. ILP and MILP problems are limited to 25 constraints. 0,1 problems are limited to 12 constraints.

3.  Enter GO (as the final entry, after the last constraints ⟨RET⟩ has been entered). The program automatically numbers each line.

Note that if the objective function or any constraint is longer than one screen line (80 characters), it will automatically wrap to the next line when it reaches the right edge of the screen. Do not hit the ⟨RET⟩ key until you have compléted the entry.

If the problem has been identified as MILP, the program next lists the variables and asks if it has an integer value. The prompt will look like this:

IS VARIABLE AN INTEGER ?

| VARIABLE | INTEGER |
|----------|---------|
| X1 | YES/NO |
| X2 | YES/NO |
| . | . |

Use the right and left arrow keys to answer YES or NO, and press ⟨RET⟩ to complete the entry.

Figure 4.2 shows a sample entry for a problem already identified as MILP.

**Figure 4.2**
Sample Entry
for ILP

TYPE OF PROBLEM: MAX /MIN

ENTER OBJECTIVE FUNCTION
MAX   X1 + X2 + X3

ENTER THE CONSTRAINTS, ONE PER LINE, HERE. AFTER YOU HAVE
ENTERED THE LAST CONSTRAINT, ENTER THE WORD GO
1      2X1 + 4X2 + X3 < 220
2      .25X1 + 5X2 + 3X3 < 280
3      1.3X2 > 10
4      GO

IS VARIABLE AN INTEGER ?

| VARIABLE | INTEGER? |
|----------|----------|
| X1 | YES / NO |
| X2 | YES / NO |
| X3 | YES / NO |

Error correction, discussed in Chapter one, is of the input summary type:

HERE IS WHAT YOU ENTERED
DO YOU WANT TO MODIFY THE DATA ? ( YES /NO)
WHICH LINE DO YOU WANT TO CHANGE ?

Note that with MILP there are two summaries. The additional one shows the identification of the integer variables. To change the YES or NO identifying a given variable as integer, it is necessary only to identify the variable number (provided by the program). The change is automatic (it can be only one or the other).

Recall that it is necessary for you to respond NO to "DO YOU WANT TO MODIFY THE DATA" in order for the solution to proceed.

## 4.3  **Output and Solution**

Output for the ILP program includes results at each branch and the optimal solution. Each screen (each branch) will show:

1. The branching variable and value, for example, BRANCHING: X2 <=17.

2. The node number, for example, AT NODE 2. NODE 1 will also be identified as the LP RELAXATION.

3. The value for each variable.

4. The upper bound and the lower bound.

5. Whether the solution at the node is a feasible integer solution (the word "FEASIBLE" will appear). This is not to be confused with the message "THERE IS NO FEASIBLE SOLUTION," which refers to a feasible LP solution.

At each branch, you may continue viewing the branches or proceed immediately to the final solution. On screen instructions offer you this option.

Press Space Bar to continue, [F9] key to show optimal solution only.

The final or optimal solution gives the optimal value for each variable and the optimal Z value (objective function value).

Figure 4.3 shows a sample output, showing 2 branches and the final solution.

**Figure 4.3**
ILP Sample Output

SOLUTION AT NODE 1 (LP RELAXATION)

| VARIABLE | QUANTITY |
|----------|----------|
| X1 | 56.72 |
| X2 | 7.69 |
| X3 | 75.79 |

UB = 140.202     LB = 138.692

Press Space Bar to continue, [F9] key to show optimal solution only.

(continued)

**Figure 4.3**
(continued)

BRANCHING: X3 <= 75

SOLUTION AT NODE 2

| VARIABLE | QUANTITY |
|----------|----------|
| X1 | 57.12 |
| X2 | 7.69 |
| X3 | 75 |

UB = 139.812    LB = 139.692

Press Space Bar to continue, [F9] key to show optimal solution only.

BRANCHING: X3 >= 76

SOLUTION AT NODE 3

| VARIABLE | QUANTITY |
|----------|----------|
| X1 | 54.15 |
| X2 | 7.69 |
| X3 | 76 |

UB = 137.842    LB = 137.692

Press Space Bar to continue, [F9] key to show optimal solution only.

THIS IS THE OPTIMAL MILP SOLUTION:

| VARIABLE | QUANTITY |
|----------|----------|
| X1 | 57 |
| X2 | 7.75 |
| X3 | 75 |

OPTIMAL Z VALUE = 139.75

Press any key to continue.

## 4.4 Examples

### Example 1: Pure (Total) ILP

Problem: Max 2X1 + 3X2
Subject to:
3X1 + X2 <= 150
4X1 + 9X2 <= 330
X1, X2 >= 0 and integer

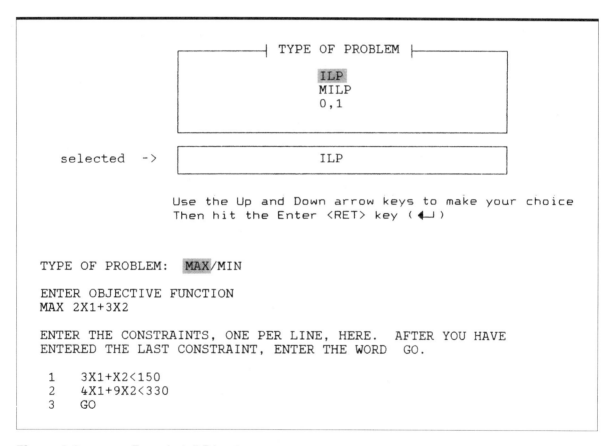

```
                         ┤ TYPE OF PROBLEM ├

                                ILP
                                MILP
                                0,1


    selected  ->             ILP


           Use the Up and Down arrow keys to make your choice
           Then hit the Enter <RET> key ( ◄┘ )



TYPE OF PROBLEM:   MAX/MIN

ENTER OBJECTIVE FUNCTION
MAX 2X1+3X2

ENTER THE CONSTRAINTS, ONE PER LINE, HERE.   AFTER YOU HAVE
ENTERED THE LAST CONSTRAINT, ENTER THE WORD   GO.

   1    3X1+X2<150
   2    4X1+9X2<330
   3    GO
```

**Figure 4.4**      Example 1: ILP Input

Figure 4.4 shows the input (including the initial input identifying the problem as all integer) for this problem. We choose to look at each branch in the solution. Figure 4.5 shows the solution. Note the solution at each node.

84     *Chapter 4*

```
         SOLUTION AT NODE  1 (LP RELAXATION)

         VARIABLE     QUANTITY
         --------     --------
            X1          44.35
            X2          16.96
         UB =  139.565     LB =  136


Press Space Bar to continue, [F9] key to show optimal solution only.


         BRANCHING:  X2   <= 16
         SOLUTION AT NODE  2

         VARIABLE     QUANTITY
         --------     --------
            X1          44.67
            X2          16
         UB =  137.333     LB =  136


Press Space Bar to continue, [F9] key to show optimal solution only.


         BRANCHING:  X2   >= 17
         SOLUTION AT NODE  3

         VARIABLE     QUANTITY
         --------     --------
            X1          44.25
            X2          17
         UB =  139.5       LB =  136


Press Space Bar to continue, [F9] key to show optimal solution only.


         BRANCHING:  X1   <= 44
         SOLUTION AT NODE  4

         VARIABLE     QUANTITY
         --------     --------
            X1          44
            X2          17.11
         UB =  139.333     LB =  139


Press Space Bar to continue, [F9] key to show optimal solution only.
```

**Figure 4.5**      Example 1: ILP Output

```
        BRANCHING:   X1    >= 45
        SOLUTION AT NODE   5

        THERE IS NO FEASIBLE SOLUTION


Press Space Bar to continue, [F9] key to show optimal solution only.


        BRANCHING:   X2    <= 17
        SOLUTION AT NODE   6

        VARIABLE      QUANTITY
        --------      --------
          X1            44
          X2            17
        UB =  139          LB =  139              FEASIBLE


Press Space Bar to continue, [F9] key to show optimal solution only.


        BRANCHING:   X2    >= 18
        SOLUTION AT NODE   7

        VARIABLE      QUANTITY
        --------      --------
          X1            42
          X2            18
        UB =  138          LB =  135              FEASIBLE


Press Space Bar to continue, [F9] key to show optimal solution only.


        THIS IS THE OPTIMAL  ILP  SOLUTION:

        VARIABLE         QUANTITY
        --------         --------
          X1               44
          X2               17

        OPTIMAL Z VALUE =                 139

            Press any key to continue.
```

**Figure 4.5**        (continued)

### Example 2: MILP

Max   3X1 + 5X2
Subject to:
     2X1 + 4X2 <= 5
     4X1 + 2X2 <= 6
      X1,X2 >= 0
      X1 integer

Figures 4.6 and 4.7 show the input and solution to this problem. Input includes the identification of the problem as a mixed integer problem and the designation of the integer valued variables. We include the input summary to show the two summaries (one for designating integer valued variables). We are showing only the final (optimal) solution.

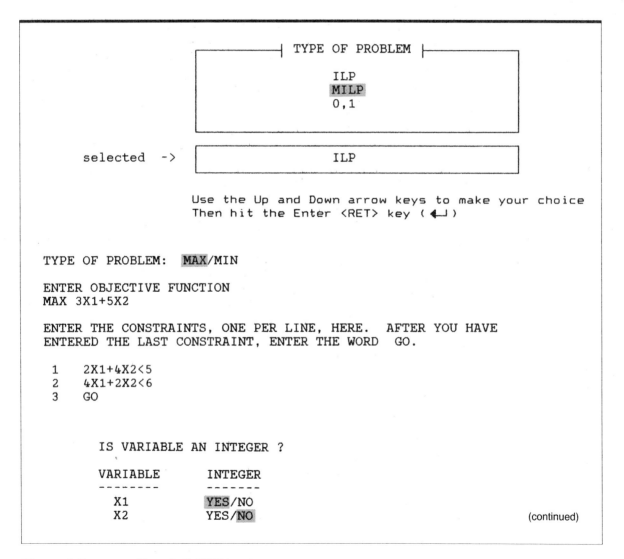

**Figure 4.6**    Example 2: MILP Input

```
HERE IS WHAT YOU ENTERED:     ( MILP )

 0    MAX  3X1+5X2
      SUBJECT TO:
 1      2X1+4X2<= 5
 2      4X1+2X2<= 6

DO YOU WANT TO MODIFY THE DATA ? (YES/NO)


HERE IS WHAT YOU ENTERED (MILP - INTEGER VARIABLES):

VARIABLE      VARIABLE       INTEGER
 NUMBER        NAME        VARIABLE?
--------      --------      ---------
    1            X1            YES
    2            X2            NO

DO YOU WISH TO MODIFY THIS DATA ? (YES/NO)
```

**Figure 4.6**          (continued)

```
    SOLUTION AT NODE  1 (LP RELAXATION)

    VARIABLE     QUANTITY
    --------     --------
        X1          1.17
        X2          .67
    UB =  6.833        LB =  6.333


Press Space Bar to continue, [F9] key to show optimal solution only.


    THIS IS THE OPTIMAL  MILP  SOLUTION:

    VARIABLE          QUANTITY
    --------          --------
       X1                1
       X2                .75

    OPTIMAL Z VALUE =                 6.75

        Press any key to continue.
```

**Figure 4.7**     Example 2: MILP Solution

### Example 3: 0,1

Solve the following knapsack problem:

Max 36X1 + 64X2 + 26X3 + 120X4 + 108X5
Subject to:
    12X1 + 16X2 + 13X3 + 15X4 + 18X5 <= 45
    X1,X2,X3,X4,X5 = 0 or 1

Figure 4.8 (p. 88) shows the input for this problem. Figure 4.9 (pp. 88–91) shows the output (all branches).

```
TYPE OF PROBLEM:   MAX/MIN

ENTER OBJECTIVE FUNCTION
MAX  36X1+64X2+26X3+120X4+108X5

ENTER THE CONSTRAINTS, ONE PER LINE, HERE.   AFTER YOU HAVE
ENTERED THE LAST CONSTRAINT, ENTER THE WORD   GO.

   1     12X1+16X2+13X3+15X4+18X5<45
   2     GO
```

**Figure 4.8**    Example 3: 0,1 Problem Input

```
        SOLUTION AT NODE   1 (LP RELAXATION)

        VARIABLE       QUANTITY
        --------       --------
           X2            .75
           X4           1
           X5           1
     UB =   276            LB =   228


  Press Space Bar to continue, [F9] key to show optimal solution only.

                                                        (continued)
```

**Figure 4.9**    Example 3: 0,1 Problem Output/Solution

```
         BRANCHING:   X2    <= 0
         SOLUTION AT NODE   2

         VARIABLE      QUANTITY
         --------      --------
            X1            1
            X2            0
            X4            1
            X5            1
     UB =  264          LB =  264                        FEASIBLE


Press Space Bar to continue, [F9] key to show optimal solution only.



         BRANCHING:   X2    >= 1
         SOLUTION AT NODE   3

         VARIABLE      QUANTITY
         --------      --------
            X2            1
            X4            1
            X5           .78
     UB =  268          LB =  184


Press Space Bar to continue, [F9] key to show optimal solution only.



         BRANCHING:   X5    <= 0
         SOLUTION AT NODE   4

         VARIABLE      QUANTITY
         --------      --------
            X1            1
            X2            1
            X3           .15
            X4            1
            X5            0
     UB =  224          LB =  220


Press Space Bar to continue, [F9] key to show optimal solution only.



         BRANCHING:   X5    >= 1
         SOLUTION AT NODE   5

         VARIABLE      QUANTITY
         --------      --------
            X2            1
            X4           .73
            X5            1
     UB =  260          LB =  172


Press Space Bar to continue, [F9] key to show optimal solution only.

                                                            (continued)
```

**Figure 4.9**    (continued)

```
      BRANCHING:   X4    <= 0
      SOLUTION AT NODE   6

      VARIABLE      QUANTITY
      --------      --------
         X1           .92
         X2          1
         X4          0
         X5          1
   UB =   205             LB =   172
```

Press Space Bar to continue, [F9] key to show optimal solution only.

```
      BRANCHING:   X4    >= 1
      SOLUTION AT NODE   7

      THERE IS NO FEASIBLE SOLUTION
```

Press Space Bar to continue, [F9] key to show optimal solution only.

```
      BRANCHING:   X1    <= 0
      SOLUTION AT NODE   8

      VARIABLE      QUANTITY
      --------      --------
         X1          0
         X2          1
         X3           .85
         X4          0
         X5          1
   UB =   194             LB =   172
```

Press Space Bar to continue, [F9] key to show optimal solution only.

```
      BRANCHING:   X1    >= 1
      SOLUTION AT NODE   9

      THERE IS NO FEASIBLE SOLUTION
```

Press Space Bar to continue, [F9] key to show optimal solution only.

```
      BRANCHING:   X3    <= 0
      SOLUTION AT NODE   10
```

(continued)

**Figure 4.9**        (continued)

```
        VARIABLE       QUANTITY
        --------       --------
           X1             0
           X2             1
           X3             0
           X4             0
           X5             1
   UB =   172            LB =   172                    FEASIBLE


Press Space Bar to continue, [F9] key to show optimal solution only.


        BRANCHING:   X3    >= 1
        SOLUTION AT NODE   11

        THERE IS NO FEASIBLE SOLUTION


Press Space Bar to continue, [F9] key to show optimal solution only.


        THIS IS THE OPTIMAL  0,1  SOLUTION:

        VARIABLE          QUANTITY
        --------          --------
           X1                1
           X2                0
           X3                0
           X4                1
           X5                1

   OPTIMAL Z VALUE =                    264

            Press any key to continue.
```

**Figure 4.9**        (continued)

## 4.5

**Summary**
**Notes**
for the ILP
Program

1. The ILP and MILP programs have a size limit of 25 variables and 25 constraints. The 0,1 program has a limit of 12 variables and 12 constraints.

2. Coefficients and RHS values are limited to 7 digit numbers (larger numbers can be stated in scientific notation form).

3. All variables must appear in the objective function (even those with a 0 coefficient); if a variable name appears more than once in the objective function, an error message will indicate that it is a duplicate

and ask you to change the entry; variable names are limited to 5 characters, but almost any variable name may be used as long as the variable begins with a letter (A–Z), remembering that A and S are used by the program for artificial and slack variables; variable names using subscripts use this form: X2, Y3, etc.

4. Constraints can be entered in any order; variables with 0 coefficients do not have to be entered; if a constraint contains a variable not found in the objective function, an error message indicates this and allows you to enter it in the objective function with a 0 coefficient or to correct the typo; constraints may not have negative right-hand sides; if they do, you will have to convert them (multiplying by −1) before entering them (remember to change the direction of the inequality); when entering inequalities using < or >, it is not necessary to add the equal sign (=), that is, enter < or > rather than <= or >=; the program assumes the equal sign to save you keystrokes.

## 4.6

### Problems

1. Max $9X1 + 5X2$
   Subject to:
   $X1 + 2X2 < 41$
   $3X1 + X2 < 50$
   $X2 > 5$
   $X1,X2 > 0$ and integer

2. Max $10X1 + 7X2 + 9X3$
   Subject to:
   $7X1 + 5X2 + 6X3 < 60$
   $4X1 + 5X3 < 45$
   $5X1 + 3X2 < 48$
   $X1,X2,X3 > 0$ and integer

3. Max $A + B + C$
   Subject to:
   $2A + 4B + C < 100$
   $5B + 3C < 140$
   $A,B,C > 0$ and $A,B$ integer

4. Max $3A + 4B + 3C$
   Subject to:
   $A + B + C < 10$
   $B - 1.5C > 0$
   $A + 2B < 7$
   $A,B,C > 0$ and integer

5. Min $5A + 4B$
   Subject to:
   $2A + 5B > 120$
   $3A + B > 100$
   $B > 10$
   $A,B > 0$ and integer

6. Min $20X + 16Y$
   Subject to:
   $4X + 5Y > 93$
   $9X + 10Y > 152$
   $Y > 5$
   $X,Y > 0$ and integer

7. Modify Problem 6 and resolve such that only Y is integer.

8. Max $18X1 + 20X2 + 14X3$
   Subject to:
   $12X1 + 14X2 + 10X3 < 125$
   $10X1 + 8X2 < 92$
   $10X2 + 6X3 < 98$
   $X1,X2,X3 > 0$, $X1,X2$ integer

9. The Westmore Company is considering the purchase of five different machines, all with approximately equal cost. Westmore has decided it can afford only three of the five machines. They have also found that if they purchase machine B, they must also purchase machine A (although the reverse is not true). In addition, machines C and D will do the same job, so the company has no need for both; however, the production manager has stated that at least one of the machines must be purchased. The net present worth of each of the machines is shown below. What decision should Westmore make?

| Machine | NPW ($000) |
|---------|-----------|
| A | 5 |
| B | 7 |
| C | 4 |
| D | 6 |
| E | 10 |

10. Song of the Sea, a resort in Southwest Florida, would like to make recreational water craft available for guest rental. Under consideration for purchase are catamarans, wind surfers, and water buggies. Song of the Sea has earmarked $12,000 as an initial investment and has 52 feet of beach frontage for storage (the craft can be stored only one deep on this space). Management would like to purchase the combination of water craft that will yield the greatest profit. Research indicates that they should purchase at least 5 wind surfers; at least one, but no more than 3 catamarans, and at least 2 water buggies. Given the following figures on cost and size, what purchases should Song of the Sea make?

| | RENT | COST | SIZE (width) |
|---------|------|------|--------------|
| Catamaran | $20/hr | $2,000 | 7 ft |
| Wind Surf | 10/hr | 500 | 3 |
| Buggy | 15/hr | 1,000 | 4 |

11. Tai Martini wants to invest $500,000 in two stock offerings, real estate, and industrial bonds. He wishes to structure his investment in such a way as to maximize the total annual yield (in dollars). The cost and yield figures for Tai's four options are listed below:

| Investment Alternative | Cost | Annual Yield |
|-----------------------|------|--------------|
| Stock A | $35.00/share | 18% |
| Stock B | $42.50/share | 22% |
| Real Estate | — | 15% |
| Industrial Bonds | $1000/bond | 12% |

In order to reduce the overall risk of his investment, Tai has established the following criteria for his investment: (a) no more than 50 percent of the investment can be in stock; and (b) at least 20 percent of the investment must be in industrial bonds. Stocks can be bought only in whole shares and bonds in $1000 amounts, while the investment in real estate can be in any denomination. To maximize his dollar yield, how many shares of each stock should Tai buy? How much should he invest in real estate?

# Chapter 4 Supplement

# Solving ILP Using Branch and Bound with the LP Program

It is possible to solve ILP problems using the branch and bound technique in conjunction with the LP program presented in Chapter three. Recall that branch and bound is an efficient, quick-enumeration technique based on the principle of partitioning the area of feasible solutions into smaller parts until the best solution is found.

The LP (simplex) program from Chapter two determines an initial solution to the problem (with the integer restrictions relaxed). This is the starting point for the ILP solution. The relaxed simplex solution and the round down solution provide the upper and lower bounds of the optimal solution.

Once the initial optimal feasible solution (the LP relaxation) has been determined, the "Modify Data" option in the Ending Menu allows you to add or replace constraints as you partition and evaluate feasible solutions until the optimal integer solution is determined. In other words, you must branch from this initial solution and repeat the process until an optimal solution is reached.

This process requires you to make a series of decisions regarding the variables to add, replace, and branch on. We strongly suggest that you draw a diagram with branches and nodes to help you keep track of where you are.

To most clearly explain how to use this program to solve an ILP problem using branch and bound, we will lead you through a problem and then summarize the steps required. We will use the ILP Example 1, so that you can compare results.

## 4S.1  The Branch and Bound Technique

In solving this problem:

    Max  2X1 + 3X2
    Subject to:
          3X1 +  X2 <= 150
          4X1 + 9X2 <= 330
               X1, X2 >= 0 and integer

our initial step is to solve for LP relaxation using the LP model introduced in Chapter two. Figure 4S.1 shows the output/solution for this problem. Notice that we have not shown you the initial input or the shadow prices in the output.

**Figure 4S.1**
LP Relaxation
Solution

```
AFTER 2  ITERATIONS,
THIS SOLUTION IS OPTIMAL:

VARIABLE         QUANTITY
--------         --------
   X1              44.348
   X2              16.957

OPTIMAL Z =   139.565
```

Once we have this solution, we can use these values to determine the upper and lower bounds (UB and LB) and to evaluate the solution for optimality. Because we are working on a maximization problem the Z value of our relaxed solution, 139.58, is the UB. The LB, 136, is determined by rounding down the solution variables and solving the objective function using these values. (If this were a minimization problem, the optimal solution would be the lower bound and we would round up to find the upper bound.) We now know that the value of the optimal solution to our problem will lie between these two values. This solution, with the upper and lower bounds, constitute the first node, which is shown in Figure 4S.2 (p. 96). Since this solution is not a feasible integer solution, we have to branch from this node.

Branching creates two new solution subsets. In order to continue the solution using the LP model, we must first select the "Modify Data" option on the Ending Menu and then respond YES to the prompt, "DO YOU WANT TO MODIFY THE DATA ? (YES/NO)." This allows us to add (or

**Figure 4S.2**
Node 1

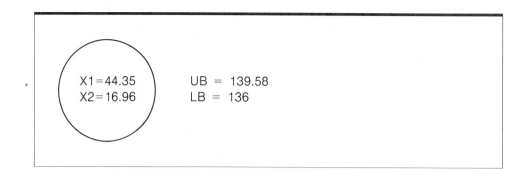

X1 = 44.35        UB = 139.58
X2 = 16.96        LB = 136

replace) a constraint (one at a time). Selecting the constraint with the larger fractional part to branch on, X2 (16.96), gives us one branch for X2<16 and one branch for X2>17. Note that when we add a constraint, we must respond with the next sequential line number (3) to the prompt question "WHICH LINE DO YOU WISH TO CHANGE". Later, when we replace this constraint (X2<16) with the constraint X2>17, we will respond with the line number of the constraint being changed. After adding the constraint, we type GO as directed and get the new solution: X1=44.67 and X2=16, with Z=137.34. Repeating the solution procedure and replacing the constraint X2<16 with X2>17 gives us the alternate values of X1=44.25 and X2=17, with the Z of 139.5. From these we determine the new UB and LB. However, note that since neither solution is integer, the lower bound remains the LB from the first rounding down. It is essential to remember to go through the solution procedure twice, once for each new constraint. Figure 4S.3 shows the entries and solution with the constraint X2<16 added. Figure 4S.4 (p. 98) shows the entries and solution when we replace X2<16 with X2>17. Figure 4S.5 (p. 99) shows nodes 2 and 3 added to the first node.

Evaluating the solutions at the descendant nodes 2 and 3 reveals that we do not have an optimal integer solution (neither node has an integer solution). It is necessary to continue branching. In general, the solution at a node is optimal when it is integer and the UB at that node is greater than or equal to the UB at any other ending node. We branch from the node that has the higher upper bound (in keeping with most current texts)—node 3 with a UB of 139.5. Again we select the variable with the greatest fractional part, develop two new constraints, and use the "Modify Data" option of the Ending Menu to get new LP solutions. At node 3, X2 is integer (X2=17). We therefore branch on X1, developing the two alternate constraints, X1<44 and X1>45. Because we are branching from node 3, the constraint we added to get that solution, X2>17, is left in the model. Figures 4S.6 and 4S.7 (pp. 99–101) show the entries and solutions for each of these constraints. Figure 4S.8 (p. 101) shows the addition of nodes 4 and 5.

```
                          ┤ ENDING MENU ├
                    Modify Data and Run Again
                    Run Again with New Data
                    Save to Disk File
                    Print Problem
                    Return to Main Menu
                    Return to DOS


    selected  ->        Modify Data and Run Again


                Use the Up and Down arrow keys to make your choice
                Then hit the Enter <RET> key ( ◄┘ )


HERE IS WHAT YOU ENTERED:

 0    MAX   2X1+3X2
      SUBJECT TO:
 1       3X1+1X2<= 150
 2       4X1+9X2<= 330

DO YOU WANT TO MODIFY THE DATA ? (YES/NO)
WHICH LINE DO YOU WISH TO CHANGE? 3

ENTER NEW LINE(S). TO STOP, TYPE GO
 3    X2<16
 4    GO


HERE IS WHAT YOU ENTERED:

 0    MAX   2X1+3X2
      SUBJECT TO:
 1       3X1+1X2<= 150
 2       4X1+9X2<= 330
 3       1X2<= 16

DO YOU WANT TO MODIFY THE DATA ? (YES/NO)


AFTER 2  ITERATIONS,
THIS SOLUTION IS OPTIMAL:

VARIABLE        QUANTITY
--------        --------
   X1             44.667
   X2             16
   S2             7.333

OPTIMAL Z =   137.333
```

**Figure 4S.3**    Entries and Solution with Constraint X2<16

```
┤ ENDING MENU ├

        Modify Data and Run Again
        Run Again with New Data
        Save to Disk File
        Print Problem
        Return to Main Menu
        Return to DOS


selected  ->        Modify Data and Run Again


        Use the Up and Down arrow keys to make your choice
        Then hit the Enter <RET> key ( ◄┘ )
```

HERE IS WHAT YOU ENTERED:

```
0    MAX   2X1+3X2
     SUBJECT TO:
1       3X1+1X2<= 150
2       4X1+9X2<= 330
3       1X2<= 16
```

DO YOU WANT TO MODIFY THE DATA ? (YES/NO)
WHICH LINE DO YOU WISH TO CHANGE? 3

(IF YOU WISH TO DELETE THIS LINE, HIT RETURN)

```
REENTER LINE    3
 3    X2>17
```

HERE IS WHAT YOU ENTERED:

```
0    MAX   2X1+3X2
     SUBJECT TO:
1       3X1+1X2<= 150
2       4X1+9X2<= 330
3       1X2>= 17
```

DO YOU WANT TO MODIFY THE DATA ? (YES/NO)


AFTER 3  ITERATIONS,
THIS SOLUTION IS OPTIMAL:

```
VARIABLE          QUANTITY
--------          --------
   X1                44.25
   X2                17
   S1                .25
```

OPTIMAL Z =  139.5

**Figure 4S.4**        Entries and Solution with Constraint X2>17

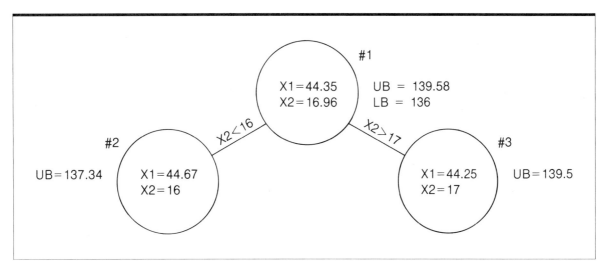

**Figure 4S.5**    Nodes 2 and 3 First Solution Subset

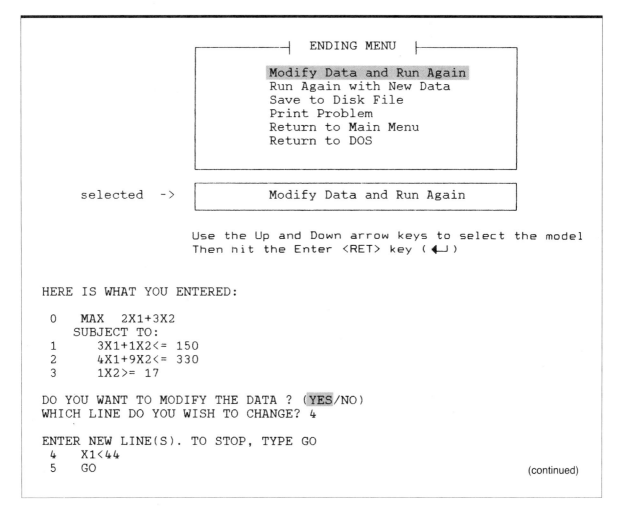

```
                    ┤ ENDING MENU ├

                Modify Data and Run Again
                Run Again with New Data
                Save to Disk File
                Print Problem
                Return to Main Menu
                Return to DOS


    selected  ->        Modify Data and Run Again


                Use the Up and Down arrow keys to select the model
                Then hit the Enter <RET> key ( ◄┘ )

HERE IS WHAT YOU ENTERED:

0    MAX   2X1+3X2
     SUBJECT TO:
1       3X1+1X2<= 150
2       4X1+9X2<= 330
3       1X2>= 17

DO YOU WANT TO MODIFY THE DATA ? (YES/NO)
WHICH LINE DO YOU WISH TO CHANGE? 4

ENTER NEW LINE(S). TO STOP, TYPE GO
  4    X1<44
  5    GO                                          (continued)
```

**Figure 4S.6**    Entries and Solution with Constraint X1<44

```
HERE IS WHAT YOU ENTERED:

0    MAX   2X1+3X2
     SUBJECT TO:
1       3X1+1X2<= 150
2       4X1+9X2<= 330
3       1X2>= 17
4       1X1<= 44

DO YOU WANT TO MODIFY THE DATA ? (YES/NO)


AFTER 3  ITERATIONS,
THIS SOLUTION IS OPTIMAL:

VARIABLE        QUANTITY
--------        --------

   X1              44
   X2              17.111
   S1              .889
   S3              .111

OPTIMAL Z =   139.333
```

**Figure 4S.6**      (continued)

**Figure 4S.7**
Entries and
Solution with
Constraint X1>45

```
HERE IS WHAT YOU ENTERED:

0    MAX   2X1+3X2
     SUBJECT TO:
1       3X1+1X2<= 150
2       4X1+9X2<= 330
3       1X2>= 17
4       1X1<= 44

DO YOU WANT TO MODIFY THE DATA ? (YES/NO)
WHICH LINE DO YOU WISH TO CHANGE? 4

(IF YOU WISH TO DELETE THIS LINE, HIT RETURN)

REENTER LINE    4
   4    X1>45
```
      (continued)

**Figure 4S.7**
(continued)

```
HERE IS WHAT YOU ENTERED:

0    MAX   2X1+3X2
     SUBJECT TO:
1      3X1+1X2<= 150
2      4X1+9X2<= 330
3      1X2>= 17
4      1X1>= 45

DO YOU WANT TO MODIFY THE DATA ? (YES/NO)


          CALCULATING TABLEAU   4

THERE IS NO FEASIBLE SOLUTION TO THIS PROBLEM
...OR SIMPLY BEYOND MY LIMITED CAPABILITIES
BESIDES, I'M GETTING A HEADACHE!


            Press any key to continue
```

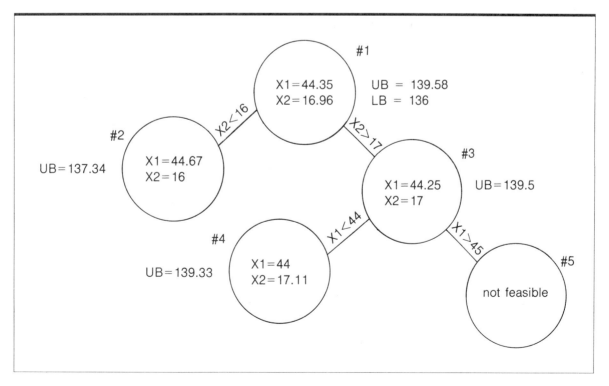

**Figure 4S.8**      Nodes 4 and 5–Second Solution Subset

We again evaluate the solutions at the nodes. This time we are evaluating nodes 4 and 5. Since there is no optimal integer solution, we have to again branch from one of the nodes, develop two new constraints, and solve. Node 5 does not have a feasible solution. Therefore, we branch from node 4, developing the two alternate constraints, X2<=17 and X2>=18, and retaining the constraint previously above, X1<44. Since we changed the fourth constraint to X1>45 at node 5, we have to change it back before we branch from node 4. Figures 4S.9, 4S.10 and 4S.11 show these entries, solutions, and nodes 6 and 7.

Evaluating the solutions at each of these nodes, we discover that there are two feasible integer solutions. Since we have an integer solution, it is necessary to calculate new LBs also. When we do so, we see that in both nodes UB=LB, sometimes cited as the stopping point, the point at which an optimal solution has been found. In this case, with two such solutions, we clearly see that node 6 offers the optimal solution with the higher UB (thus the higher LP value or optimal Z value).

**Figure 4S.9**
Entries and Solution with Constraint X2<17

```
HERE IS WHAT YOU ENTERED:

0    MAX   2X1+3X2
     SUBJECT TO:
1       3X1+1X2<= 150
2       4X1+9X2<= 330
3       1X2>= 17
4       1X1>= 45

DO YOU WANT TO MODIFY THE DATA ? (YES/NO)
WHICH LINE DO YOU WISH TO CHANGE? 4

(IF YOU WISH TO DELETE THIS LINE, HIT RETURN)

REENTER LINE    4
  4    X1<44
```

```
HERE IS WHAT YOU ENTERED:

0    MAX   2X1+3X2
     SUBJECT TO:
1       3X1+1X2<= 150
2       4X1+9X2<= 330
3       1X2>= 17
4       1X1<= 44

DO YOU WANT TO MODIFY THE DATA ? (YES/NO)
WHICH LINE DO YOU WISH TO CHANGE? 5

ENTER NEW LINE(S). TO STOP, TYPE GO
 5   X2<17
 6   GO


HERE IS WHAT YOU ENTERED:

0    MAX   2X1+3X2
     SUBJECT TO:
1       3X1+1X2<= 150
2       4X1+9X2<= 330
3       1X2>= 17
4       1X1<= 44
5       1X2<= 17

DO YOU WANT TO MODIFY THE DATA ? (YES/NO)


AFTER 3  ITERATIONS,
THIS SOLUTION IS OPTIMAL:

VARIABLE          QUANTITY
--------          --------
   X1                44
   X2                17
   S1                1
   S2                1
   S3                0

OPTIMAL Z =   139
```

```
HERE IS WHAT YOU ENTERED:

0    MAX   2X1+3X2
     SUBJECT TO:
1       3X1+1X2<= 150
2       4X1+9X2<= 330
3       1X2>= 17
4       1X1<= 44
5       1X2<= 17

DO YOU WANT TO MODIFY THE DATA ? (YES/NO)
WHICH LINE DO YOU WISH TO CHANGE? 5

(IF YOU WISH TO DELETE THIS LINE, HIT RETURN)

REENTER LINE    5
  5    X2>18


HERE IS WHAT YOU ENTERED:

0    MAX   2X1+3X2
     SUBJECT TO:
1       3X1+1X2<= 150
2       4X1+9X2<= 330
3       1X2>= 17
4       1X1<= 44
5       1X2>= 18

DO YOU WANT TO MODIFY THE DATA ? (YES/NO)


AFTER 4  ITERATIONS,
THIS SOLUTION IS OPTIMAL:

VARIABLE        QUANTITY
--------        --------
   X1              42
   X2              18
   S1               6
   S3               1
   S4               2

OPTIMAL Z =  138

              Press any key to continue
```

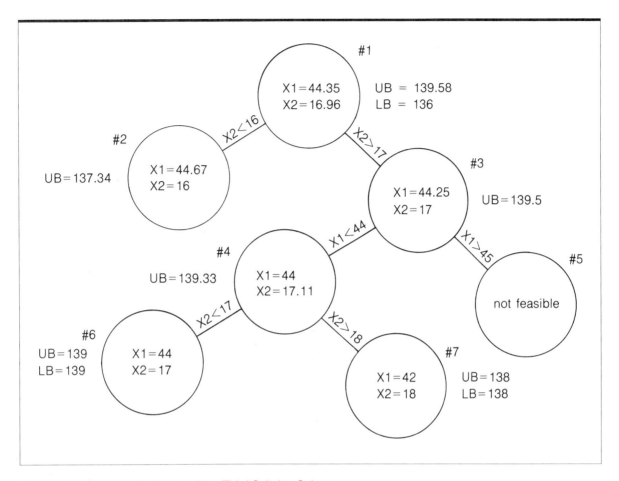

**Figure 4S.11**     Nodes 6 and 7—Third Solution Subset

## 4S.2  **Summary of Branch and Bound Steps**

In summary, the steps required to solve an ILP problem using the LP model with the branch and bound technique are listed below:

Step 1: Solve the LP relaxation using the LP model.

Step 2: Determine the UB and LB. Evaluate the UB for optimality.

Step 3: Branch, creating two descendant nodes. Select the constraint with the larger fractional part to branch on. Use the "Modify Data" option of the Ending Menu twice, to add or replace each of the alternate constraints developed from the solution at the node from which you are branching (that is, the one with the higher UB), and get two new solutions to evaluate.

Step 4: Continue to evaluate, branch, and solve the LP problem with newly developed constraints, that is, repeat steps 2 and 3 until the optimal integer solution is reached.

## 4S.3 MILP and 0,1 Problems

The basic steps (with a few differences) outlined and described above can be used to solve mixed integer linear programming problems (MILP) and binary (0,1) problems. You should also remember that if you are solving a minimization problem, the Z value will be the lower bound and the upper bound will be obtained by rounding the noninteger values upwards. In the case of minimization problems, you are attempting to minimize the lower bound value, so you will branch from the node which has the lower LB.

To solve MILP problems: 1. At node 1, to determine the LB, round down (for maximization problems) only those variables with integer restrictions. 2. To determine which variable to branch from (the variable with the greatest fractional part), consider only those variables which must be integer. The optimal solution has been reached at a node when it is the maximum UB of all ending nodes and meets the specified integer requirements.

To solve 0,1 problems: 1. 0,1 restrictions for variables must be stated in the model as constraints ($X_j <= 1$). 2. When the variable with the greatest fractional part is selected to branch on, the two new constraints developed are $X=1$ and $X=0$. These two constraints form the branches at each succeeding node.

Chapter **5**

# Goal Programming

The goal programming model is a variation or extension of the LP model which allows decision makers to handle problems involving multiple objectives. Recall that the LP model, structured with a single objective function subject to specified system constraints, solves problems having a single optimization objective, usually to maximize profit or minimize cost. However, in reality, many decision makers face situations having multiple, and sometimes even conflicting, goals or objectives. Goal programming provides an alternate solution technique for handling multicriteria decision-making within the general LP framework. This approach seeks a satisfactory solution (satisfactory levels of goal attainment representing the best possible combination of goal achievements) to problems with more than one objective, allowing the decision maker to incorporate a preemptive, preferential system of goal levels and priorities into the decision-making process. With the GP model, while all goals are considered, it is understood that some goals may be achieved only at the expense of other, lower-ranked goals.

Since GP is a form of LP, it is formulated under the same limitations and assumptions as LP (linearity, divisibility, etc.). Moreover, a goal programming problem contains elements that are similar to the elements in the LP model: decision variables, system constraints that represent the absolute restrictions, and an objective function. However, GP problems differ from LP problems because the objective function always seeks to minimize the undesirable deviations from the specified goals. Thus, GP offers the advantage of not having to meet goals exactly, i.e., it allows deviations from targets or goals, thus introducing flexibility into the decision-making process. With LP, it is not always possible to achieve a feasible solution when a constraint cannot be met exactly. GP, on the other hand, produces a feasible (optimal LP) solution showing what can be accomplished and identifying any failure to reach the stated goals in the form of the deviations from those goals.

Goal programming is therefore especially appropriate for business firms seeking to attain satisfactory levels in multiple objectives simultaneously, for instance, contribution to profit, labor relations, environmental protection, and social responsibility. It is also useful for government agencies and nonprofit organizations facing a variety of social objectives.

## 5.1   The GP Program

The modified simplex method used by this program is similar to the simplex method, but it uses multiple $Z_j$, and $C_j - Z_j$ rows to represent different priority levels. This program will solve GP problems with up to five different priority levels, 25 variables, and 30 constraints.

The objective of the program is to identify the optimal solution to the problem; the solution occurs when the deviations from the stated goals have been minimized. It should be recognized that in GP, the decision maker is looking for a satisfactory solution given target goals and constraints, rather than a truly optimal solution. Thus, we have a decision maker who is attempting to "satisfice" using a mathematical model designed to optimize by formulating the problem (in such a way as to allow for deviations, priorities, and weights) differently. The program allows deviational variables to be assigned both different priority levels and different weights. It then attempts to satisfy the goals by minimizing the deviations from those goals based upon the priority level assigned, i.e., deviations from first priority level goals are minimized first.

## 5.2   Data Entry

Data entry for the goal programming model is a slightly modified version of the LP entry routine, with the addition of several prompts necessary to fully describe the goal programming problem, such as real variables, deviational variables, priorities, and weights. Thus, it is necessary to first select the data entry method from the menu shown on page 109 (and discussed in Chapter one).

With either the free form or the tabular entry selection, data entry is in two parts. Part one, from prompted input, describes the problem. Note that it is no longer necessary to identify a problem as MAX/MIN since all goal programming problems are, by definition, attempting to minimize the undesirable deviations. Part two is a modified version of either the free

```
                    ┌─────────┤ DATA ENTRY METHOD ├─────────┐
                    │                                        │
                    │       Free Form Entry                  │
                    │       Tabular Entry                     │
                    │       Problem from Disk File            │
                    │                                        │
                    │                                        │
                    └────────────────────────────────────────┘

   selected  ->     ┌────────────────────────────────────────┐
                    │                                        │
                    └────────────────────────────────────────┘
```

Use the Up and Down arrow keys to select the model
Then hit the Enter <RET> key ( ↵ )

form or tabular entry already described in detail in Chapter three with LP problems.

## Part One

In response to the prompts:

1. Enter the number of decision variables in the problem. The program is limited to a total of 25 variables (decision plus deviational).

2. Enter the names of the variables. Variable names are limited to 5 characters and must begin with a letter. Be sure to keep decision and deviational variable names distinct. Variable names with subscripts use the form X1, A1, Z2 . . . (recall that the ⟨RET⟩ key completes each entry).

3. Enter the number of deviational variables in the problem.

4. Enter the names of the deviational variables. It is not possible to use the + or − with the deviational variables when using free form entry. We have used A for above and B for below, for example, D1A, D2A, D1B. *You must enter all negative deviational variables first, for example, DB1, DB2, DB3.* Because of the way the modified simplex procedure works in the program, this entry order is essential for certain problems but not for others. It is easier to enter all problems this way, rather than to remember under which problem circumstances the order is important for correct solution.

5. For each deviational variable listed, enter the corresponding weight and priority, completing each entry with ⟨RET⟩. Recall, with goal programming problems, it is possible to have problems with priorities and weights, with priorities but no weights (that is, all weights of 1), with neither priorities (all priority 1) nor weights (all 1), with no priorities (all priority 1) but with weights. The program allows 5 priority levels. Figure 5.1 (p. 110) shows a sample input for these entries.

**Figure 5.1**
Sample Input:
Initial GP Entries

HOW MANY DECISION VARIABLES ARE IN THE PROBLEM ? 2

ENTER NAMES OF DECISION VARIABLES BELOW:

| VAR | NAME |
| --- | --- |
| 1 | ? X1 |
| 2 | ? X2 |

HOW MANY DEVIATIONAL VARIABLES ARE IN THE PROBLEM ? 4

ENTER NAMES OF DEVIATIONAL VARIABLES BELOW:

| VAR | NAME |
| --- | --- |
| 1 | ? D1B |
| 2 | ? D2B |
| 3 | ? D1A |
| 4 | ? D2A |

FOR EACH DEVIATIONAL VARIABLE, ENTER THE WEIGHT AND THE
PRIORITY LEVEL (1–5):

| VARIABLE | WEIGHT | PRIORITY |
| --- | --- | --- |
| D1B | ? 2 | ? 1 |
| D2B | ? 1 | ? 1 |
| D1A | ? 0 | |
| D2A | ? 1 | ? 2 |

When making these entries, you must keep in mind that these entries
are determining the objective function. Thus, a weight of 0 eliminates the
variable from the objective coefficient. This means you *must enter a weight
of at least one (>=1)* for any deviational variable to be minimized. If the
problem is not weighted, then all the deviational variables that are to appear in the objective function have a weight of 1. If you enter a 0, you are
not even given the opportunity to enter a corresponding priority level. If
there are no priority levels, in other words, all goals have the same priority
level, enter a priority level of 1 for each deviational variable.

Once these initial entries have been made, the program will show you
an input summary and give you the opportunity to modify any of the entries. In effect, the error correction routine for goal programming has been
broken into two distinct parts, as has the entire entry process. This input
summary and error correction process have been discussed in Chapter one.
Modifications are made one at a time by identifying the line number where
the change is to occur and then, as directed, entering the modified data.

**Part Two**

In part two, both the system and goal constraints (30 total) are entered. Recall that entry method now depends upon the initial selection made from the data entry method menu.

For free form entry:

- Enter the constraints, one constraint per line, each followed by ⟨RET⟩. Unlike LP, there is no need to enter the objective function. The information needed for the objective function has already been entered in the earlier responses.

- Enter the word GO after all the constraints have been entered.

- Note that if any of the constraints are longer than one screen line, they will automatically wrap to the next line when they reach the edge of the screen.

- There is an input summary for data modification/error correction for these entries.

For tabular entry:

- In response to the prompt, enter the number of constraints (system plus goal) in the problem.

- Fill in the table, entering the constraint coefficients, operators, and RHS values. Use the cursor movement keys and designated function keys as directed on the screen to move throughout the table and to change the table. In entering the variable coefficients, recall that deviational variables always have a coefficient of 1 or −1. If a variable does not appear in a given constraint, it is not necessary to make an entry in that cell—a cell can be blank. Coefficients are again limited to 7 characters. Only 10 constraint rows can be displayed on screen at a time. The rows scroll up as you reach the bottom of the display area. Figure 5.2 shows a sample tabular entry.

- Note that it is not possible to add or to eliminate a variable in this table, but it is possible to add or to eliminate a constraint. It is not possible to make changes in the objective function. Those changes must be made in the part one error correction routine.

- The [F9] key accepts the entries. Any modification to input should be made before this key is pressed.

## 5.3  Output and Solution

As with LP, output is independent of the entry form used and includes:

**Figure 5.2**
Sample Tabular
Entry: GP
Constraints

NUMBER OF CONSTRAINTS ?   3

[MIN] ENTER THE CONSTRAINT COEFFICIENTS, OPERATORS ($<,=,>$)
AND RHS VALUES:

| OF | 0 | 0 | 2P1 | 0 | P1 | P2 | | |
|---|---|---|---|---|---|---|---|---|
| VAR | X1 | X2 | D1B | D2B | D1A | D2A | OPER | RHS |
| 1 | 1 | 1 | | | | | $>$ | 120 |
| 2 | 1 | | 1 | | $-1$ | | $=$ | 65 |
| 3 | | 1 | | 1 | | $-1$ | $=$ | 45 |

Use Arrow keys, [HOME], [END], [PgUp], [PgDn], to make entries.
[F9] to accept entries            [F5] Delete Row,            [F6] Add Row

1.  The tableaus (none, final, or all as selected from the tableaus
    displayed menu). Figure 5.3 shows a sample final tableau. Note that
    the modified simplex for goal programming has a Z and C–Z row for
    each priority level. We are not showing a Z row or C–Z rows. Instead
    we have chosen to display Z–C rows (the negative of C–Z).

TABLEAU NUMBER   4

| C(j) | Basis | 0 X1 | 0 X2 | 2P1 D1B | P1 D2B | 0 D1A | P2 D2A | 0 A1 |
|---|---|---|---|---|---|---|---|---|
| 0 | D1A | 0 | 0 | $-1$ | $-1$ | 1 | 1 | 1 |
| 0 | X1 | 1 | 0 | 0 | $-1$ | 0 | 1 | 1 |
| 0 | X2 | 0 | 1 | 0 | 1 | 0 | $-1$ | 0 |
| Z–C P2 | | 0 | 0 | 0 | 0 | 0 | $-1$ | 0 |
| Z–C P1 | | 0 | 0 | $-2$ | $-1$ | 0 | 0 | $-99999998$ |

Press any key to continue.

| Basis | 0 S1 | RHS |
|---|---|---|
| D1A | $-1$ | 10 |
| X1 | $-1$ | 75 |
| X2 | 0 | 45 |
| Z–C P2 | 0 | 0 |
| Z–C P1 | 0 | 0 |

Press any key to continue.

**Figure 5.3**        Sample GP Final Tableau

Again, we caution you to be aware that computer storage of numbers in binary notation can result in some unusual appearing numbers. Also, instead of M, the tableau displays the large number 99999998.

2. The optimal solution. The solution indicates the number of iterations required and gives the optimal value for each variable in the final solution. It also evaluates the objective function for each priority level as shown in the following display.

```
AFTER 3 ITERATIONS,
THIS SOLUTION IS OPTIMAL:
```

| VARIABLE | QUANTITY |
|----------|----------|
| X1 | 75 |
| X2 | 45 |
| D1A | 10 |

ANALYSIS OF THE OBJECTIVE FUNCTION

| PRIORITY | NON-ACHIEVEMENT |
|----------|-----------------|
| P1 | 0 |
| P2 | 0 |

## 5.4  Examples

### Example 1: A Multiple Objective Problem with Priorities

The Williamson Company manufactures three products: X, Y, and Z. The products contribute $1.00, $1.40 and $2.00 to profit respectively. The products must also pass through two departments, A and B. Product X requires 2 hours in department A and 5 hours in department B; product Y, 1.5 hours in A and 6 hours in B; and product Z, 1.75 hours in A and 7 hours in B. The company currently wishes to produce at least 850 units of product Y to meet a prior commitment. Williamson wishes to set up its production schedule for these three products for the coming quarter in such a way that:

1. Profit contribution is at least $5,000.

2. The number of hours worked in department A does not exceed 5,500.

3. The number of hours worked in department B does not exceed 16,000.

4. At least 850 units of product Y are produced.

```
HOW MANY DECISION VARIABLES ARE IN THE PROBLEM ? 3

ENTER NAMES OF DECISION VARIABLES BELOW:

VAR        NAME
---        ----
 1      ? X
 2      ? Y
 3      ? Z

HOW MANY DEVIATIONAL VARIABLES ARE IN THE PROBLEM ? 8

ENTER NAMES OF DEVIATIONAL VARIABLES BELOW:

VAR        NAME
---        ----
 1      ? D1B
 2      ? D2B
 3      ? D3B
 4      ? D4B
 5      ? D1A
 6      ? D2A
 7      ? D3A
 8      ? D4A



FOR EACH DEVIATIONAL VARIABLE, ENTER THE WEIGHT AND THE PRIORITY LEVEL (1-5):
VARIABLE          WEIGHT          PRIORITY
   D1B            ? 1               ? 1
   D2B            ? 0
   D3B            ? 0
   D4B            ? 1               ? 4
   D1A            ? 0
   D2A            ? 1               ? 2
   D3A            ? 1               ? 3
   D4A            ? 0



HERE IS WHAT YOU ENTERED (Part 1):

        NAME     WEIGHT     PRIORITY    OF VALUE
        ----     ------     --------    --------
 1      X
 2      Y
 3      Z
 4      D1B        1          1           1P1
 5      D2B        0          0
 6      D3B        0          0
 7      D4B        1          4           1P4
 8      D1A        0          0
 9      D2A        1          2           1P2
10      D3A        1          3           1P3
11      D4A        0          0
12      DECISION VARIABLES  =          3
13      DEVIATIONAL VARIABLES  =   8

DO YOU WANT TO MODIFY THIS DATA ? (YES/NO)                    (continued)
```

**Figure 5.4**       Example 1: GP Input

```
ENTER THE CONSTRAINTS, ONE PER LINE, HERE.  AFTER YOU HAVE
ENTERED THE LAST CONSTRAINT, ENTER THE WORD  GO.

 1    X+1.4Y+2Z+D1B-D1A=5000
 2    2X+1.5Y+1.75Z+D2B-D2A=5500
 3    5X+6Y+7Z+D3B-D3A=16000
 4    Y+D4B-D4A=850
 5    GO


HERE IS WHAT YOU ENTERED:

   MIN  P1D1B+P4D4B+P2D2A+P3D3A
    SUBJECT TO:
 1     1X+1.4Y+2Z+1D1B-1D1A= 5000
 2     2X+1.5Y+1.75Z+1D2B-1D2A= 5500
 3     5X+6Y+7Z+1D3B-1D3A= 16000
 4     1Y+1D4B-1D4A= 850

DO YOU WANT TO MODIFY THE DATA ? (YES/NO)
```

**Figure 5.4**        (continued)

The objectives for the production schedule listed above are in order of the company's priorities. Formulate and solve this problem. Figure 5.4 shows the input for this problem using free form entry. We have also shown the input summaries for both parts of the input. Figure 5.5 shows the output for the problem, including the final tableau.

```
TABLEAU NUMBER   3
```

| C(j) |  | 0 | 0 | 0 | P1 | 0 | 0 | P4 |
|------|------|------|------|------|------|------|------|------|
|  | Basis | X | Y | Z | D1B | D2B | D3B | D4B |
| P3 | D3A | -1.5 | -1.1 | 0 | 3.5 | 0 | -1 | 0 |
| 0 | D2B | 1.125 | .275 | 0 | -.875 | 1 | 0 | 0 |
| 0 | Z | .5 | .7 | 1 | .5 | 0 | 0 | 0 |
| P4 | D4B | 0 | 1 | 0 | 0 | 0 | 0 | 1 |
| Z-C | P4 | 0 | 1 | 0 | 0 | 0 | 0 | 0 |
| Z-C | P3 | -1.5 | -1.1 | 0 | 3.5 | 0 | -1 | 0 |
| Z-C | P2 | 0 | 0 | 0 | 0 | 0 | 0 | 0 |
| Z-C | P1 | 0 | 0 | 0 | -1 | 0 | 0 | 0 |

```
           Press any key to continue.
```

(continued)

**Figure 5.5**        Example 1: GP Output

| Basis | 0<br>D1A | P2<br>D2A | P3<br>D3A | 0<br>D4A | RHS |
|-------|------|------|------|------|------|
| D3A | -3.5 | 0 | 1 | 0 | 1500 |
| D2B | .875 | -1 | 0 | 0 | 1125 |
| Z | -.5 | 0 | 0 | 0 | 2500 |
| D4B | 0 | 0 | 0 | -1 | 850 |
| Z-C  P4 | 0 | 0 | 0 | -1 | 850 |
| Z-C  P3 | -3.5 | 0 | 0 | 0 | 1500 |
| Z-C  P2 | 0 | -1 | 0 | 0 | 0 |
| Z-C  P1 | 0 | 0 | 0 | 0 | 0 |

```
                Press any key to continue.




AFTER 2  ITERATIONS,
THIS SOLUTION IS OPTIMAL:

VARIABLE        QUANTITY
--------        --------
   Z             2500
   D2B           1125
   D4B            850
   D3A           1500

ANALYSIS OF THE OBJECTIVE FUNCTION:
   PRIORITY    NON-ACHIEVEMENT
   --------    ---------------
     P1            0
     P2            0
     P3          1500
     P4           850

        Press any key to continue.
```

**Figure 5.5**        (continued)

Priority level 3, showing a nonachievement of 1,500, indicates that the firm has exceeded that goal—no more than 16,000 hours to be worked in department B—by 1,500 hours. They have also underachieved the fourth goal—to produce at least 850 units of product Y—by 850 units, that is, they have not produced any of product Y. However, they did achieve the first two priority level goals (profit contribution and hours to be worked in department A).

It is important to recognize that in GP a solution may, in fact, be unacceptable to the decision maker. It is not uncommon for goals to be redefined and the problem resolved once the decision maker is confronted with the "optimal" results. This redefinition process may continue until the most acceptable result is found.

### Example 2: A Problem with Priorities and Weights

The Williamson Company from the previous example did not produce the 850 units of product Y to meet its requirement. It now wishes to do so at a branch plant. It can do so by using either skilled or unskilled labor. Each skilled worker can produce 3 units per hour, and each unskilled worker can produce 2 units per hour. There are 280 skilled hours and 190 unskilled hours available. Management must decide how many hours of each type of labor to assign to this job given the following goals listed in order of importance.

1. Produce exactly 850 units. Overproduction is considered as undesirable as a shortage.

2. Use 280 hours of skilled labor. Because of a labor contract, underutilization is given a weight of 3 and overtime is given a weight of 2.

3. Use 190 hours of unskilled labor. Underutilization is twice as bad as overtime.

Figure 5.6 shows the input for this problem (but no error correction routine). We are using tabular entry. However, there are too many columns (variable coefficients, operators, and RHS values) to fit on one screen. As we reach the right-hand edge when making entries, the screen scrolls across to allow the next entry. Note that the problem has three priority levels, and that priority levels 2 and 3 have weights assigned to the deviational variables. Figure 5.7 shows the optimal solution. No tableaus are shown.

```
HOW MANY DECISION VARIABLES ARE IN THE PROBLEM ? 2

ENTER NAMES OF DECISION VARIABLES BELOW:

VAR        NAME
---        ----
 1       ? X1
 2       ? X2

HOW MANY DEVIATIONAL VARIABLES ARE IN THE PROBLEM ? 6

ENTER NAMES OF DEVIATIONAL VARIABLES BELOW:

VAR        NAME
---        ----
 1       ? D1B
 2       ? D2B
 3       ? D3B
 4       ? D1A
 5       ? D2A
 6       ? D3A                                          (continued)
```

**Figure 5.6**      Example 2: GP Input

```
FOR EACH DEVIATIONAL VARIABLE, ENTER THE WEIGHT AND THE PRIORITY LEVEL (1-5):
VARIABLE         WEIGHT       PRIORITY
    D1B          ? 1          ? 1
    D2B          ? 3          ? 2
    D3B          ? 2          ? 3
    D1A          ? 1          ? 1
    D2A          ? 2          ? 2
    D3A          ? 1          ? 3


NUMBER OF CONSTRAINTS ? 3


[MIN] ENTER THE CONSTRAINT COEFFICIENTS, OPERATORS (<,=,>) AND RHS VALUES:
```

| OF | 0 | 0 | P1 | 3P2 | 2P3 | P1 | 2P2 | P3 | | |
|----|----|----|-----|-----|-----|-----|-----|-----|------|-----|
| VAR | X1 | X2 | D1B | D2B | D3B | D1A | D2A | D3A | OPER | RHS |
| 1 | 3 | 2 | 1 | | | -1 | | | = | 850 |
| 2 | 1 | | | 1 | | | -1 | | = | 280 |
| 3 | | 1 | | | 1 | | | -1 | = | 190 |

```
Use Arrow keys, [Home], [End], [PgUp], [PgDn] to make entries.
[F9] to accept entries          [F5] Delete Row,          [F6] Add Row
```

**Figure 5.6**    (continued)

**Figure 5.7**
Example 2:
GP Optimal
Solution Output

```
AFTER 3  ITERATIONS,
THIS SOLUTION IS OPTIMAL:

VARIABLE          QUANTITY
--------          --------
    X1               280
    X2               5
    D3B              185

ANALYSIS OF THE OBJECTIVE FUNCTION:
    PRIORITY    NON-ACHIEVEMENT
    --------    ---------------
      P1              0
      P2              0
      P3              370

        Press any key to continue.
```

The optimal solution shows that the first priority level goal has been achieved. With X1 = 280 and X2 = 5, there is neither overachievement nor underachievement of the desired goal of 850. The second priority level goal is also achieved with X1 = 280. The third priority level is under-achieved by 370, X2 = 5, an underachievement of 185 (D3B = 185). However, it was twice as important that underachievement not occur. The result is a nonachievement value of 370 (185 times a weight of 2).

### Example 3: No Priorities

Solve the following problem:

$$\text{MIN} \quad \text{P1D1B} + \text{P1D1A} + \text{P1D2B} + \text{P1D2A}$$

SUBJECT TO

$$X1 + \quad X2 <= 80$$
$$3X1 + 7.5X2 + D1B - D1A = 375$$
$$2X1 + \quad X2 + D2B - D2A = 200$$
$$X1,X2,D1B,D1A,D2B,D2A >= 0$$

Figure 5.8 shows the input (free form, no error correction summaries) for this problem. Since there is only one priority level (and it is unweighted), notice the entries for priority and weights. Figure 5.9 shows the output, including the final tableau.

```
HOW MANY DECISION VARIABLES ARE IN THE PROBLEM ? 2

ENTER NAMES OF DECISION VARIABLES BELOW:

VAR        NAME
---        ----
 1       ? X1
 2       ? X2

HOW MANY DEVIATIONAL VARIABLES ARE IN THE PROBLEM ? 4

ENTER NAMES OF DEVIATIONAL VARIABLES BELOW:

VAR        NAME
---        ----
 1       ? D1B
 2       ? D2B
 3       ? D1A
 4       ? D2A


FOR EACH DEVIATIONAL VARIABLE, ENTER THE WEIGHT AND THE PRIORITY LEVEL (1-5):
VARIABLE        WEIGHT        PRIORITY
   D1B          ? 1           ? 1
   D2B          ? 1           ? 1
   D1A          ? 1           ? 1
   D2A          ? 1           ? 1              (continued)
```

**Figure 5.8**    Example 3: GP Input

```
ENTER THE CONSTRAINTS, ONE PER LINE, HERE.  AFTER YOU HAVE
ENTERED THE LAST CONSTRAINT, ENTER THE WORD  GO.

   1    X1+X2<80
   2    3X1+7.5X2+D1B-D1A=375
   3    2X1+X2+D2B-D2A=200
   4    GO
```

**Figure 5.8**      (continued)

**Figure 5.9**
Example 3: GP
Output with
Final Tableau

```
AFTER 2  ITERATIONS,
THIS SOLUTION IS OPTIMAL:

VARIABLE         QUANTITY
--------         --------
    X1              50
    X2              30
    D2B             70


ANALYSIS OF THE OBJECTIVE FUNCTION:
  PRIORITY   NON-ACHIEVEMENT
  --------   ---------------
    P1             70

          Press any key to continue.
```

In the case of equal priority, the model simply sums the deviational variables. Here, the third goal was underachieved by 70 units.

## 5.5

**Summary Notes**
for the Goal Programming Program

1. Goal programming problems are limited to 25 variables (decision variables plus deviational variables) and 30 constraints (system plus goal). Coefficients and RHS values are limited to 7-digit numbers (with larger numbers stated in scientific notation).

2. Almost any variable name may be used as long as the variable begins with a letter (A–Z, recall that the letter D is frequently used for deviational variables), but variable names are limited to 5 characters. Variable names using subscripts use this form: X2, Y3, etc. With free

form entry, it is not possible to use + and − with the deviational variables. We use A for above and B for below, for example, D1A, D1B, etc.

3. When entering the names of the deviational variables, all of the negative deviational variables must be entered first.

4. It is possible to have problems with priorities and weights, with priorities but no weights (all weight 1), with neither priorities (all priority 1) nor weights, with no priorities but with weights. The program allows 5 priority levels.

5. Entering a weight of 0 eliminates the variable from the objective function. Therefore, you *must enter a weight of at least one (>=1)* for any deviational variable to be minimized. If the problem is not weighted, then all the deviational variables that are to appear in the objective function have a weight of 1. If there are no priority levels, in other words, all goals have the same priority level, enter a priority level of 1 for each deviational variable.

6. It is not necessary to enter the objective function for either entry method. This is handled automatically (minimizing the undesirable deviations). Moreover, once you have moved on to part two of the data entry, it is not possible to make changes to the objective function. However, when the problem is completed, it is possible to use the "Modify Data" option of the Ending Menu to make changes.

7. When entering the constraints, 0 coefficients do not have to be entered—blank spaces may be left in the tabular entry—and the variables can be omitted in the free form entry. Constraints may not have negative right-hand sides. When entering inequalities using < or >, it is not necessary to add the equal sign (=), that is, <= or >=. The program assumes these to save you keystrokes.

8. To move around the table (tabular entry) use the arrow keys to move right, left, up, and down; [TAB] and ⟨RET⟩ emulate the right arrow key; use [HOME] to move to left-hand edge of line; use [END] to move to right-hand edge of line; use [PgUp] to move to the first row of the constraint section of the table; use [PgDn] to move to the last row of the constraint section.

9. To change the constraint part of the problem, use the designated function keys in tabular entries: [F5] deletes a row (used to eliminate a constraint); [F6] adds a row (used to add a constraint).

10. It is not possible to make changes in the objective function or to add or delete a variable as it was in LP.

11. Use the [F9] to accept the entries. This key must be pressed to continue the program and get a solution.

## 5.6

**Problems**

1. Min $D1^- + D1^+ + D2^- + D2^+ + D3^- + D3^+ + D4^- + D4^+$
   st:
   $$7X1 + 12X2 + 4X3 + D1^- - D1^+ = 600$$
   $$3X1 + 6X2 + X3 + D2^- - D2^+ = 280$$
   $$4X1 + 5X2 + 2X3 + D3^- - D3^+ = 280$$
   $$6X1 + 8X2 + 2X3 + D4^- - D4^+ = 280$$

2. Solve the following problem:
   $$\text{Min } P1D2^- + P2D1^+ + P3D3^-$$
   st:
   $$X1 + X2 + D1^- - D1^+ = 20$$
   $$2X1 + 3X2 + D2^- - D2^+ = 16$$
   $$X2 + D3^- - D3^+ = 14$$

   If the objective function to the above problem were

   $$\text{Min } P1D2^- + P2D1^+ + P3D3^-$$

   how would the answer change?

3. The Bilkmore Investment Company has $700,000 to invest. They are considering the following investments:

   | Investment | Yield | Risk Factor/$1000 |
   |---|---|---|
   | Treasury bonds | 8% | 1 |
   | Industrial bonds | 10% | 4 |
   | Real estate | 15% | 8 |
   | New stock issues | 20% | 17 |

   Bilkmore's president has specified the following goals in order of importance:
   a. The total yield should be at least $80,000.
   b. At least 70 percent of the funds must be invested in bonds.
   c. No more than 25 percent of the investment should be in new stock.
   d. The total risk factor should not exceed 3,000 (note, risk factor is per $1,000 invested).
   What investments should Bilkmore make if it wishes to achieve these goals? Are all the goals achieved, and if not, which ones are not achieved?

4. What happens in problem 3 if the following changes are made in the priorities:
   b. The total risk factor should not exceed 3,000.
   c. At least 70 percent of the funds must be invested in bonds.
   d. No more than 25 percent of the investment should be in new stock.

5. The Bright Feather Bird Seed Company is blending a special 16 ounce box of parakeet seed mix using two different seeds, types A and B. Information on the two types of seeds is shown below:

   | Type | Cost/oz | Protein | Fat | Fiber |
   |---|---|---|---|---|
   | A | $ .04 | 8% | 4% | 6% |
   | B | .07 | 15% | 3% | 8% |

Bright Feather wants this blend to contain at least 2 ounces of crude protein and 0.5 ounce of fat. They also want it to contain no more than 1.5 ounces of crude fiber. They want to spend no more than 90¢ per 16 ounce box. All the goals have the same priority level, but Bright Feather management feels keeping the cost below 90¢ per box is 3 times as important as the other goals.

How should they blend the seeds to achieve these goals?

6. How does the answer to problem 5 change if Bright Feather decides that all the goals have equal priority and weight?

7. Senator Briggston is planning the advertising campaign for his upcoming senatorial race. The senator's media advisor has provided the following information:

| Medium | Cost/ad | Younger Audience/ad | Older Audience/ad |
|--------|---------|---------------------|-------------------|
| TV | $1,500 | 5,000 | 3,500 |
| Radio | 150 | 3,000 | 1,000 |
| Newspaper | 400 | 2,500 | 6,000 |

The senator has established the following goals and priorities:
a. His total advertising budget should not exceed $25,000.
b. He wishes to reach at least 140,000 older voters and at least 125,000 younger voters. He feels it is twice as important to reach older voters than younger voters.
c. He does not wish to place more than 10 TV ads, 20 radio ads, or 15 newspaper ads.
Determine the number of ads the senator should place in each medium and the extent to which each of his goals is met.

8. How much does the solution to problem 7 change if the senator has only $17,500 to spend?

9. A manufacturing firm produces three products: A, B, and C. Products A and B each require 8 hours to produce; product C requires 8.5 hours. The plant has 4,800 hours of production capacity available per week. Product A contributes $27 per unit to profit, product B, $25 per unit, and product C, $30 per unit. The sales department estimates sales of 200, 240, and 220 units of products A, B, and C respectively.

The firm wishes to determine the optimum production schedule for the coming week given the following multiple goals, listed in order of their importance.
a. Achieve the stated sales goals. Use the profit contribution as weights.
b. Avoid the underutilization of normal production capacity.
c. Avoid overtime as much as possible.

10. Big Boy Manufacturing received an order for 600 units of its X3 widget. Two machines that can produce this widget are currently available. Machine A has 44 hours of available production time and machine B has 60 hours of available time. Machine A costs $15 per hour to operate and produces 6 units per hour. Machine B costs $17 per hour and produces 4.5 units per hour. Management goals in order of importance are:
a. Fill the order for 600 units.

    **b.** Keep maximum overtime hours to 8 hours total.
    **c.** Avoid underutilization of either machine.
    **d.** Spend no more than $1,600 on production, excluding overtime and other costs.

**11.** Change problem 10 as follows:
    **d.** Spend no more than $1,600 on production. Overtime hours are charged as follows: machine costs remain the same, but there is an additional charge of $12 per hour for machine A and $15 per hour for machine B.

Chapter **6**

# Transportation

Transportation problems deal with the physical distribution or allocation (transportation) of homogeneous goods from several sources (points of supply) to several destinations (points of demand). Each source of supply has a given or fixed capacity, and therefore, a limited quantity of available goods. Each destination has a given demand, specified order quantity, or limited capacity. There are a variety of alternate shipping routes available and a variety of costs for using these routes. The manager's objective is (usually) to minimize the cost of distribution, i.e., find the lowest total shipping cost while meeting all destination demands. Obviously, the manager's problem is to determine how many units to ship from each source to each destination in order to meet this objective.

## 6.1 The Transportation Program

Although transportation problems can be solved using linear programming, more efficient special purpose algorithms have been developed, such as stepping stone and MODI. As with LP, these methods require finding an initial feasible solution and then proceeding iteratively, making step-by-step improvements until the optimal solution is found. These algorithms are designed to optimize some objective, which in transportation is usually to minimize transportation costs (but can be to maximize some objective such as profit).

This transportation program uses a specialized algorithm which requires only that you identify the objective as maximization or minimization, define the tableau size (the number of rows and columns in the matrix), and then enter the supply available at each source, demand required at each destination, and per unit cost (or profit) for each route. The program allows you to determine the minimum cost route with either balanced or unbalanced supply and demand. It solves problems involving an unacceptable transportation route and it solves for both minimization and maximization objectives.

Before entering the data for this program, it is a good idea to set up the transportation tableau. It provides a convenient way to visualize the problem and summarize the data, and it makes it easier to correctly enter the data.

## 6.2 Data Entry

The data entry method menu offers two entry methods: entry from the keyboard, which is a tabular entry, or entry from disk file. As discussed in Chapter one, all programs allow data to be entered from a disk file, provided the problem has previously been saved to a file.

Data entry is a simple two-step procedure. First the problem objective is identified (MAX/MIN), and the tableau is described (number of rows and columns). Then the data (costs, supplies, demands) are entered in a fill-in-the-blank tableau provided by the program.

1. As prompted, describe the type and size of the problem (up to 40 rows by 40 columns, *not including dummies*). Entering a number in excess of 40 results in an error message. You are then given a chance to reenter the program. Recall that each entry has to be completed with the ⟨RET⟩ key. Figure 6.1 gives an example of these initial prompts.

**Figure 6.1**
Initial
Transportation
Entries

TYPE OF PROBLEM: MAX/ MIN

HOW MANY ROWS (SOURCES) IN THE TABLEAU? 4

HOW MANY COLUMNS (DESTINATIONS) IN THE TABLEAU? 5

2. Fill in the tableau. The program provides a transportation tableau, with the default variables S1, S2, etc., for sources, and D1, D2, etc., for destinations. The blank cells in the body of the tableau are the shipping routes. Use the cursor movement keys (arrow keys, [HOME], [END], [PgUp], [PgDn]) to move through the tableau. The [TAB] and ⟨RET⟩ keys emulate the right arrow key. Enter the supplies

in the column designated, demands in the row designated, and cell values, such as per unit shipping costs, in the body of the table. Any entry (including variable names) can be changed by typing over it. The number of rows (sources) and columns (destinations) can be changed with the [F5], [F6], [F7], and [F8] keys. For a more detailed explanation of these keys, see the summary notes for this chapter (Section 6.5) or Chapter one.

Entries must be accepted by pressing the [F9] key. This key should be pressed only after all the entries have been input and verified. Figure 6.2 shows this table with a sample input.

**Figure 6.2**
Transportation
Tableau Entry

[MIN] ENTER THE TABLEAU VALUES

|  | D1 | D2 | D3 | D4 | D5 | SUPPLY |
|---|---|---|---|---|---|---|
| S1 | 6 | 8 | 7 | 9 | 10 | 75 |
| S2 | 12 | 11 | 13 | 12 | 9 | 60 |
| S3 | 7.5 | 8.25 | 8.75 | 7.9 | 8.15 | 70 |
| S4 | 9.75 | 7.85 | 8.5 | 6.75 | 11.1 | 85 |
| DEMAND | 50 | 65 | 80 | 50 | 45 | |

Use Arrow keys, [Home], [End], [PgUp], [PgDn] to make entries.
[F3] Reverse MAX and MIN,     [F5] Delete Row,     [F6] Add Row
[F9] to accept entries,          [F7] Delete Column,  [F8] Add Column

The screen can display only 7 columns and/or 10 rows at a time. When you reach the right edge of the screen, the screen scrolls to reveal the next column. When the 10 rows are completed, near the bottom of the display area, the screen scrolls to allow the next row to be entered. Cell values are restricted to 7-digit numbers (scientific notation can be used). In most problems you can avoid size difficulties by simply scaling the values downward before entering them, in other words, drop the 000 when values are given in thousands, remembering to be consistent and to add the values back in to the optimal solution value. Numbers do not have to be integer.

## 6.3  Output and Solution

The output for the transportation program is very simple and straightforward. It shows:

1. The tableau with the optimal shipping pattern. This tableau shows how many units should be shipped from each source to each destination in order to optimize the given objective. Note that the display of large tableaus (more than 7 destinations) will be displayed in segments. Output for tableaus with more than 15 sources will scroll off the screen. To freeze the screen, press [CTRL] and [NUM LOCK]. To continue the display, press any key.

   Note that messages in the output identify unbalanced problems and notify the user that dummies are added by the program, for example,

   UNBALANCED SUPPLY AND DEMAND. SUPPLY EXCEEDS DEMAND.

   ADDING A DUMMY COLUMN WITH . . . UNITS AND ZERO COST IN EACH CELL.

   NEW TABLEAU:

2. The solution value, that is, the total cost (or profit) that results from these allocations.

3. When there are alternate optima. Recall that transportation problems can have alternate optimal solutions. The output will indicate that alternate optima exist, but it will not give an alternate allocation or shipping pattern. However, recall that the solution value will be the same regardless of the pattern.

   Figure 6.3 shows a sample output.

**Figure 6.3**
Transportation
Output/Solution

OPTIMAL ALLOCATION

|     | D1 | D2 | D3 | D4 | D5 | SUPPLY |
|-----|----|----|----|----|----|--------|
| S1  | 0  | 0  | 75 | 0  | 0  | 75 |
| S2  | 0  | 15 | 0  | 0  | 45 | 60 |
| S3  | 50 | 15 | 5  | 0  | 0  | 70 |
| S4  | 0  | 35 | 0  | 50 | 0  | 85 |
| DEMAND | 50 | 65 | 80 | 50 | 45 | |

SOLUTION VALUE =      2249.75

Press any key to continue

### Infeasible Problems

In rare instances, a cell identified as unacceptable may be required for an optimal solution. For example, in the following tableau, cell 1,2 has been given a cost of M (9E+10).

|        | 1  | 2  | SUPPLY |
|--------|----|----|--------|
| 1      | 4  | M  | 50     |
| 2      | 2  | 4  | 50     |
| DEMAND | 40 | 60 |        |

As you can see, however, 10 units must be shipped to this cell to meet the supply and demand requirements. Since this outcome has already been identified as unacceptable, we have defined an infeasible problem. The program will alert you to this fact with the message "THIS IS AN INFEASIBLE PROBLEM" preceding the output of the allocations. This output will include the necessary allocation to the unacceptable route. Total costs will be omitted. This is shown in Figure 6.4.

**Figure 6.4**
Transportation Output—Infeasible Problem

THIS IS AN INFEASIBLE PROBLEM

OPTIMAL ALLOCATION:

|        | 1  | 2  | SUPPLY |
|--------|----|----|--------|
| 1      | 40 | 10 | 50     |
| 2      | 0  | 50 | 50     |
| DEMAND | 40 | 60 |        |

## 6.4  Examples

### Example 1: Transportation—Balanced Problem

Dennco manufactures widgets in 3 locations, Buffalo, Boston and Denver. These are shipped to plants in Orlando, Reading, New York and San Diego. The supply available from each source, the demand at each destination and the per-unit shipping cost are shown in the next table. What shipping route do you recommend, and what is the total cost?

| From Origin | Orlando | To Destination Reading | N.Y. | San Diego | Supply |
|---|---|---|---|---|---|
| Buffalo | 18 | 13 | 13 | 26 | 350 |
| Boston | 16 | 13 | 11 | 24 | 150 |
| Denver | 21 | 24 | 19 | 13 | 200 |
| Demand | 100 | 250 | 200 | 150 | |

Figure 6.5 shows the input for this problem. Figure 6.6 shows the solution. When you are through with the problem, press any key, as directed, to continue. This will bring the Ending Menu on screen. We are going to modify this data and use it for the next problem example. Figure 6.7 shows the Ending Menu, with the selection highlighted.

```
                      ┤ DATA ENTRY METHOD ├
              ┌─────────────────────────────────────┐
              │       Entry from Keyboard           │
              │       Problem from Disk File        │
              │                                     │
              └─────────────────────────────────────┘

              ┌─────────────────────────────────────┐
 selected  -> │         Entry from Keyboard         │
              └─────────────────────────────────────┘

              Use the Up and Down arrow keys to select the model
              Then hit the Enter <RET> key ( ◄┘ )


TYPE OF PROBLEM:  (MAX/MIN)


HOW MANY ROWS (SOURCES) IN THE TABLEAU ? 3

HOW MANY COLUMNS (DESTINATIONS) IN THE TABLEAU ? 4


[MIN] ENTER THE TABLEAU VALUES:
```

|      | D1  | D2  | D3  | D4  | SUPPLY |
|------|-----|-----|-----|-----|--------|
| S1   | 18  | 13  | 13  | 26  | 350    |
| S2   | 16  | 13  | 11  | 24  | 150    |
| S3   | 21  | 24  | 19  | 13  | 200    |
| DEMAND | 100 | 250 | 200 | 150 |      |

```
Use Arrow keys, [Home], [End], [PgUp], [PgDn] to make entries.
[F3] Reverse MAX and MIN,      [F5] Delete Row,        [F6] Add Row
[F9] to accept entries         [F7] Delete Column,     [F8] Add Column
```

**Figure 6.5**    Example 1: Transportation Input

```
OPTIMAL ALLOCATION:

          D1        D2        D3        D4      SUPPLY
      ┌─────────────────────────────────────────────
  S1  │ 0        250       100        0        350
  S2  │ 50        0        100        0        150
  S3  │ 50        0         0        150       200
      └─────────────────────────────────────────────
DEMAND│ 100      250       200       150

SOLUTION VALUE =  9450

Alternate Optimal Solution Exists

            Press any key to continue
```

**Figure 6.6**        Example 1: Transportation Output/Solution

Our optimal solution gives us a total cost of $9,450 with the following allocations:

| | |
|---|---|
| Buffalo to Reading | 250 units |
| Buffalo to N.Y. | 100 units |
| Boston to Orlando | 50 units |
| Boston to N.Y. | 100 units |
| Denver to Orlando | 50 units |
| Denver to San Diego | 150 units |

Note that the solution indicates there are alternate optima.

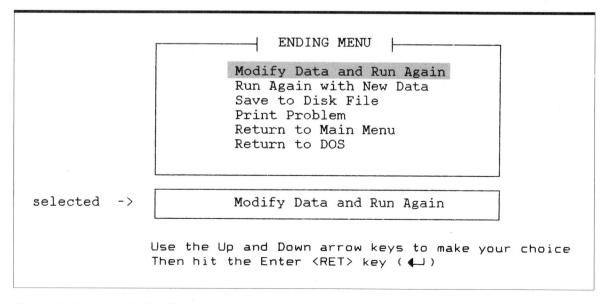

```
            ┤  ENDING MENU  ├
      ┌─────────────────────────────────┐
      │  Modify Data and Run Again      │
      │  Run Again with New Data        │
      │  Save to Disk File              │
      │  Print Problem                  │
      │  Return to Main Menu            │
      │  Return to DOS                  │
      │                                 │
      └─────────────────────────────────┘

selected  ->  ┌─────────────────────────────┐
              │   Modify Data and Run Again │
              └─────────────────────────────┘

      Use the Up and Down arrow keys to make your choice
      Then hit the Enter <RET> key ( ⏎ )
```

**Figure 6.7**        Ending Menu

### Example 2: Transportation—Unacceptable Route

The railroad route from Buffalo to Reading has ceased operation. For now, Dennco cannot ship widgets from Buffalo to meet Reading's demand. What effect does this have on shipping allocations and cost (see Example 1)?

Figure 6.8 shows the input for this problem. The Ending Menu allows us to make changes in the data and run the problem again. When we do that, our original input appears with a message "HERE IS WHAT YOU ENTERED." Notice that we make a change in the Buffalo to Reading cell (cell S1,D2), by entering an M in that cell. We moved to the location using the arrow keys and then typed the M over the 13. We have included both tables: the original entries and the new table with the M. Figure 6.9 shows the new output for this problem.

```
[MIN] HERE IS WHAT YOU ENTERED:


                  D1        D2        D3        D4      SUPPLY

        S1        18        13        13        26       350
        S2        16        13        11        24       150
        S3        21        24        19        13       200
     DEMAND       100       250       200       150

Use Arrow keys, [Home], [End], [PgUp], [PgDn] to make entries.
[F3] Reverse MAX and MIN,       [F5] Delete Row,          [F6] Add Row
[F9] to accept entries          [F7] Delete Column,       [F8] Add Column


[MIN] HERE IS WHAT YOU ENTERED:


                  D1        D2        D3        D4      SUPPLY

        S1        18        M         13        26       350
        S2        16        13        11        24       150
        S3        21        24        19        13       200
     DEMAND       100       250       200       150

Use Arrow keys, [Home], [End], [PgUp], [PgDn] to make entries.
[F3] Reverse MAX and MIN,       [F5] Delete Row,          [F6] Add Row
[F9] to accept entries          [F7] Delete Column,       [F8] Add Column
```

**Figure 6.8**    Example 2: Transportation—Unacceptable Route Input

```
OPTIMAL ALLOCATION:


           | D1        D2        D3        D4        SUPPLY
-----------+----------------------------------------------------
    S1     | 100       0         200       50        350
    S2     | 0         150       0         0         150
    S3     | 0         100       0         100       200
-----------+----------------------------------------------------
  DEMAND   | 100       250       200       150

SOLUTION VALUE =   11350

             Press any key to continue
```

**Figure 6.9**        Example 2: Transportation—Unacceptable Route Output/Solution

Total cost has jumped to $11,350 and shipping allocations have changed to the following:

| | |
|---|---|
| Buffalo to Orlando | 100 |
| Buffalo to N.Y. | 200 |
| Buffalo to San Diego | 50 |
| Boston to Reading | 150 |
| Denver to Reading | 100 |
| Denver to San Diego | 100 |

### Example 3: An Unbalanced Transportation Problem

The Gritty Sand and Gravel Company sells sand to the Michigan Highway Department for use on icy roads. GS&G Co. has three production sites that ship sand monthly to one of three state distribution centers. The production capacities and demands at each distribution center are shown in the following table. Also shown are the shipping costs per ton from each site to each center.

| GS&G Site | Production Capacity | Distribution Center | Monthly Demand |
|---|---|---|---|
| A | 20 | X | 30 |
| B | 40 | Y | 20 |
| C | 30 | Z | 25 |

**Shipping Costs:**

| To: | X | Y | Z |
|---|---|---|---|
| From: | | | |
| A | 4 | 3 | 5 |
| B | 7 | 2 | 4 |
| C | 3 | 6 | 4 |

GS&G wishes to ship in a way which will minimize total shipping costs. What allocations should be made to achieve this objective?

Figures 6.10 and 6.11 show the input and output for this problem. We have changed the variable names in this tableau, using X, Y, Z for destinations and A, B, C, for sources. Notice the messages in the output that identify this as an unbalanced problem and that notify the user that dummies are added by the program:

UNBALANCED SUPPLY AND DEMAND.   SUPPLY EXCEEDS DEMAND.

ADDING A DUMMY COLUMN WITH   . . .   UNITS AND ZERO COST IN EACH CELL.

NEW TABLEAU:

```
TYPE OF PROBLEM:   (MAX/MIN)

HOW MANY ROWS (SOURCES) IN THE TABLEAU ? 3

HOW MANY COLUMNS (DESTINATIONS) IN THE TABLEAU ? 3

[MIN] ENTER THE TABLEAU VALUES:

                D1        D2        D3        SUPPLY
        S1    4         3         5         20
        S2    7         2         4         40
        S3    3         6         4         30
    DEMAND    30        20        25

Use Arrow keys, [Home], [End], [PgUp], [PgDn] to make entries.
[F3] Reverse MAX and MIN,     [F5] Delete Row,        [F6] Add Row
[F9] to accept entries        [F7] Delete Column,     [F8] Add Column
```

**Figure 6.10**   Example 3: Transportation—Unbalanced Problem Input

```
UNBALANCED SUPPLY AND DEMAND.   SUPPLY EXCEEDS DEMAND.

ADDING A DUMMY COLUMN WITH   15   UNITS AND ZERO VALUE IN EACH CELL.

NEW TABLEAU:


          | D1       D2       D3       DUMMY   SUPPLY
   ───────┼──────────────────────────────────────────
     S1   | 4        3        5        0        20
     S2   | 7        2        4        0        40
     S3   | 3        6        4        0        30
   ───────┼──────────────────────────────────────────
   DEMAND | 30       20       25       15


             Press any key to continue



OPTIMAL ALLOCATION:


          | D1       D2       D3       DUMMY   SUPPLY
   ───────┼──────────────────────────────────────────
     S1   | 0        0        5        15       20
     S2   | 0        20       20       0        40
     S3   | 30       0        0        0        30
   ───────┼──────────────────────────────────────────
   DEMAND | 30       20       25       15

SOLUTION VALUE =   235

             Press any key to continue
```

**Figure 6.11**     Example 3: Transportation—Unbalanced Problem Output/Solution

Total cost is minimized at $235 with the following allocations:

| | |
|---|---|
| From A to Z | 5 tons |
| From B to Y | 20 tons |
| From B to Z | 20 tons |
| From C to X | 30 tons |

Of course the 15 tons allocated to be shipped from A to the dummy distribution center represent the excess supply and are not really shipped.

### Example 4: A Maximization Problem

The Prairie Dog Marketing Company has hired 200 market survey poll-sters to conduct a new survey, 65 at its Kansas City office, 100 at its Denver office, and 35 at its Salt Lake City office. The pollsters will be sent to three cities: Cheyenne (50 pollsters), St. Louis (75), and Omaha (75). Based upon revenue and costs, the company estimates the following income for each pollster:

|  | Cheyenne | St. Louis | Omaha |
|---|---|---|---|
| Kansas City | 68 | 90 | 86 |
| Denver | 77 | 62 | 81 |
| Salt Lake | 84 | 59 | 78 |

How should Prairie Dog assign these pollsters if it wishes to maximize its total income on the survey?

Figures 6.12 and 6.13 show the input and solution to this problem. The only difference in our entry is in the initial selection. Be sure to remember to enter it as a maximization problem.

```
TYPE OF PROBLEM:   (MAX/MIN)


HOW MANY ROWS (SOURCES) IN THE TABLEAU ? 3

HOW MANY COLUMNS (DESTINATIONS) IN THE TABLEAU ? 3


[MAX] ENTER THE TABLEAU VALUES:



              |  D1      D2      D3      SUPPLY
         -----+-----------------------------------
         S1   |  68      90      86      65
         S2   |  77      62      81      100
         S3   |  84      59      78      35
         DEMAND|  50      75      75

Use Arrow keys, [Home], [End], [PgUp], [PgDn] to make entries.
[F3] Reverse MAX and MIN,      [F5] Delete Row,        [F6] Add Row
[F9] to accept entries         [F7] Delete Column,     [F8] Add Column
```

**Figure 6.12**      Example 4: Transportation—Maximization Input

**Figure 6.13**
Example 4:
Transportation—
Maximization
Output/Solution

```
OPTIMAL ALLOCATION:

            |  D1       D2       D3       SUPPLY

     S1     |  0        65       0        65
     S2     |  15       10       75       100
     S3     |  35       0        0        35

   DEMAND   |  50       75       75

SOLUTION VALUE =   16640

              Press any key to continue
```

If Prairie Dog uses the following assignments of pollsters, its income will be maximized at $16,640:

65 from Kansas City to St. Louis; 15 from Denver to Cheyenne; 10 from Denver to St. Louis; 75 from Denver to Omaha; and 35 from Salt Lake City to Cheyenne.

## 6.5

**Summary Notes** for the Transportation Program

1. Tableau size: 40 rows (sources), 40 columns (destinations). This restriction does not include dummies, that is, 40 rows and 40 columns are available *before* dummies are added. It is not necessary to add dummy sources or destinations. This is automatically done by the program. The screen displays only 7 columns by 10 rows at a time, but scrolls one column or one row at a time to display more of the tableau.

2. In the output tableaus with more than 7 destinations, the tableau will be segmented because of the 80-character screen width. Output for tableaus with more than 15 sources (approximately) will begin to scroll off the screen, but the screen can be frozen with the [CTRL] and [NUM LOCK] keys.

3. Supply, demand, and cell values are limited to 7 digits; however, scientific notation or scaling can be used to accommodate larger values. Use M (or −M for maximization problems) for an unacceptable route.

4. Default variables for supply and demand are provided (S and D). These can be changed in the table by typing the variable name of choice over the default name. Variable names are limited to 5 characters.

5. Messages in the output identify unbalanced problems (dummies are added by the program) and infeasible problems (a cell identified as unacceptable may be required for an optimal solution).

6. To move around the table: Arrow keys move the cursor right, left, up, down; the [TAB] and the ⟨RET⟩ key emulate the right arrow key; [HOME] moves cursor to left-hand edge of line; [END] moves cursor to right-hand edge of line; [PgUp] moves cursor to first row of cell values section of the tableau; [PgDn] moves cursor to last row of the cell values section.

7. To make changes in tableau size and problem type: [F3] reverses MAX/MIN; [F5] deletes a row (used to eliminate a supply source); [F6] adds a row (used to add a source); [F7] deletes a column (used to eliminate a destination); [F8] adds a column (used to add a destination). Note that rows and columns are added or deleted one at a time. The function key must be used for each addition or deletion.

8. To accept the entries: The [F9] accepts the entries. This key must be pressed to continue the program and achieve a solution. Make sure all entries have been made and verified first. Recall that entries are edited, errors are corrected and/or problem modifications are made *before the [F9] key is pressed to accept the entries.* Entries are changed by typing over an incorrect entry (the entry you wish to change). For a review of editing entries or correcting errors, check Chapter one.

## 6.6

**Problems**

1. Given the following transportation tableau, determine the optimal shipping allocations to minimize total shipping cost. (Per unit shipping costs cannot be represented in the upper right-hand corner of the cell, as they appear in some textbooks. Instead, they appear in the cell itself.)

| From \ To | W | X | Y | Z | SUPPLY |
|---|---|---|---|---|---|
| A | 4 | 3 | 5 | 7 | 50 |
| B | 6 | 5 | 3 | 4 | 80 |
| C | 5 | 4 | 10 | 8 | 40 |
| D | 7 | 8 | 3 | 4 | 90 |
| DEMAND | 75 | 55 | 50 | 80 | |

2. Given this tableau:

| From\To | A | B | C | D | SUPPLY |
|---------|-----|-----|-----|-----|--------|
| 1 | 43 | 37 | 34 | 40 | 300 |
| 2 | 28 | 36 | 32 | 38 | 200 |
| 3 | 40 | 39 | 36 | 44 | 225 |
| DEMAND | 150 | 75 | 325 | 175 | |

determine optimal shipping allocations and cost.

3. Given this tableau:

| From\To | A | B | C | SUPPLY |
|---------|------|------|------|--------|
| 1 | 2.40 | 2.20 | 3.30 | 150 |
| 2 | 2.60 | 2.80 | 2.55 | 200 |
| 3 | 3.10 | 3.70 | 3.10 | 175 |
| 4 | 2.80 | 2.90 | 3.20 | 300 |
| DEMAND | 250 | 300 | 250 | |

determine shipping allocations to achieve the objective of minimizing total shipping costs.

4. Given the following tableau:

| From\To | A | B | C | D | E | F | SUPPLY |
|---------|-----|-----|-----|-----|-----|-----|--------|
| 1 | 3 | 5 | 8 | 12 | 14 | 17 | 50 |
| 2 | 4 | 7 | 10 | 13 | 15 | 18 | 125 |
| 3 | 12 | 10 | 9 | 7 | 4 | 2 | 75 |
| 4 | 6 | 9 | 4 | 5 | 6 | 9 | 100 |
| 5 | 8 | 10 | 12 | 10 | 8 | 6 | 225 |
| 6 | 7 | 5 | 6 | 8 | 10 | 12 | 200 |
| DEMAND | 175 | 50 | 100 | 150 | 250 | 50 | |

   a.  determine optimal shipping allocations to minimize total shipping costs.
   b.  determine what happens to this cost if the routes from 1 to E and 3 to E are closed because of construction.

5. Phillip's Dinettes Plus, Inc. has manufacturing plants in three locations and ships to warehouses in three cities. Given the following tableau, determine optimal shipping allocations to minimize cost:

| From\To | Newark | Atlanta | Topeka | Supply |
|---------|--------|---------|--------|--------|
| Rochester | 5 | 8 | 12 | 150 |
| Fort Wayne | 9 | 7 | 5 | 175 |
| Denver | 15 | 12 | 10 | 250 |
| DEMAND | 200 | 300 | 175 | |

6. Phillips has increased production capacity at both the Rochester and Denver plants and has added an additional warehouse in Phoenix to meet demand at the newly opened market in the Southwest. Demand in Atlanta has been declining. The revised production capacities (supply) and warehouse demand are shown in the following tables.

| Supply | | Demand | |
|---|---|---|---|
| Rochester | 250 dinettes | Newark | 200 |
| Fort Wayne | 175 | Atlanta | 250 |
| Denver | 350 | Topeka | 175 |
| | | Phoenix | 150 |

**Per-Unit Shipping Costs to Phoenix:**

| | | |
|---|---|---|
| Rochester to Phoenix | | 18 |
| Fort Wayne to Phoenix | | 10 |
| Denver to Phoenix | | 5 |

All other per-unit shipping costs remain the same as in problem 5.

**a.** Determine shipping costs and allocations necessary to minimize cost.

**b.** What happens to cost and allocations if the shipping route from Fort Wayne to Atlanta is temporarily unacceptable?

7. This winter has been very severe in Michigan. The Gritty Sand Gravel Company (Example 3) has seen an increase in demand for sand at each of its distribution centers. Given the following production capacities, monthly demand (in tons), and shipping costs, what allocations should Gritty make to minimize costs? What is the total cost?

| GS&G Site | Prod. Capacity | Dist. Center | Monthly Demand |
|---|---|---|---|
| A | 20 | X | 40 |
| B | 40 | Y | 30 |
| C | 30 | Z | 35 |

**Shipping Costs:**

| From\To | X | Y | Z |
|---|---|---|---|
| A | 4 | 3 | 5 |
| B | 7 | 2 | 4 |
| C | 3 | 6 | 4 |

8. ABC, Inc. ships pencils from distribution centers in Buffalo, Syracuse, and Albany to stationery stores in five New York cities: Rochester, Potsdam, Utica, Olean, and Old Forge. Given the following supply, demand, and cost tables, find the optimal allocation to minimize cost.

| Dist. Center | Supply | Stores | Demand |
|---|---|---|---|
| Buffalo | 25 | Rochester | 15 |
| Syracuse | 20 | Potsdam | 10 |
| Albany | 15 | Utica | 12 |
| | | Olean | 8 |
| | | Old Forge | 5 |

**Shipping costs:**

| From\To | Rochester | Potsdam | Utica | Olean | Old Forge |
|---|---|---|---|---|---|
| Buffalo | .25 | .50 | .40 | .30 | .60 |
| Syracuse | .30 | .40 | .10 | .45 | .45 |
| Albany | .40 | .40 | .10 | .60 | .50 |

9. Dennco (Example 1) produces a special widget that is in great demand in only two of its plants. Since this widget is used in different industries, different prices can be charged to different customers. Orders placed by

three customers for these special widgets exceed the manufacturing capacity of these two plants. Dennco must decide how to allocate these widgets to its customers to maximize profit. Given the following matrix showing the plants and their capacities, customers and demand, and profit per unit for each allocation:

| Plant | Customers A | B | C | SUPPLY |
|-------|------|-----|-----|--------|
| Boston | 25 | 28 | 33 | 3,500 |
| Denver | 22 | 19 | 18 | 5,000 |
| Orders | 3,700 | 4,200 | 2,800 | |

a. How many widgets should each plant produce for each customer to maximize profit?
b. Which demand will not be met?

10. If Prairie Dog Marketing Co. (Example 4) decides to send 50 pollsters to each original city and the remaining 50 to San Diego, what changes will be made in the assignment of these people if they still wish to maximize profit? The expected income from pollsters sent to San Diego from each source is summarized below. All other data are the same as in Example 4.

| Kansas City | to San Diego | 55 |
|-------------|--------------|----|
| Denver | to San Diego | 82 |
| Salt Lake City | to San Diego | 80 |

Using the new data given above and the relevant data from Example 4, determine the new assignments and profit.

# Chapter 7

# Assignment

**A**ssignment problems, like transportation problems discussed in the previous chapter, deal with physical allocations (distribution, assignment, transfer). However, assignment problems refer to those specific decision-making situations in which one-to-one allocations or assignments must be made. These problems require determining the most efficient assignment of jobs to machines, people to tasks or projects, and sales people to territories. Assignment problems are, in fact, a special form of transportation problems. The distinguishing feature of assignment problems is the requirement that only one job or worker is assigned to one machine or project. Furthermore, the value (cost, profit, time, etc.) associated with making a particular assignment is known. The manager must determine the assignments that will optimize a stated objective. Most often, this objective is to minimize total costs or time of performance, but it can also be to maximize some objective such as profits.

## 7.1 The Assignment Program

Assignment problems, like transportation problems, can be solved using linear programming. Although it may be computationally inefficient, assignment problems can be solved using a transportation algorithm. However, more efficient, special purpose algorithms have been developed specifically for assignment problems. These methods usually require finding an initial feasible solution and then proceeding iteratively using a matrix reduction procedure until the optimal solution is found. These algorithms achieve the stated objective of the problem, either to minimize or maximize some objective.

This assignment program uses a specialized algorithm which requires only that you identify the problem objective (maximization or minimization); enter the data needed to set up the assignment matrix, that is, the number of rows and columns; and then fill in the table by entering the values associated with each particular assignment in the corresponding cell. The program determines the optimal assignment for either minimization or maximization objectives, automatically adds dummy rows and columns necessary to balance the problem, and solves problems with unacceptable assignments. It is also possible to use this program (and a branch and bound technique) to solve traveling salesman problems, that is, problems necessitating sequential assignments.

Before entering the data for this program, it is a good idea to prepare the problem by setting up the assignment matrix and entering the measure of performance (the value, cost, profit, etc. associated with that assignment) in the corresponding cells. It is a convenient way to summarize the data.

## 7.2 Data Entry

Data entry is a two part procedure nearly identical to the procedure used in the transportation program. Remember, you have the opportunity to retrieve data from a disk file, as discussed in Chapter one and again in Chapter six.

1. Select the problem objective (MAX/MIN) and describe the size of the problem (up to 40 rows by 40 columns) as prompted by the program. Figure 7.1 gives an example entry.

**Figure 7.1**
Initial Assignment
Entries

TYPE OF PROBLEM: MAX/ MIN

HOW MANY ROWS IN THE TABLEAU? 5

HOW MANY COLUMNS IN THE TABLEAU? 5

Recall that after each selection or response to the prompts, the ⟨RET⟩ key must be pressed to complete the entry.

2. Fill in the table. In the assignment matrix provided by the program, enter the value (for example, cost, profit) associated with each specific assignment. Each cell in the body of the table corresponds to

one assignment. Use the cursor movement keys to move through the table. Make entries by typing them. Any entry (including variable names) can be changed by entering a new value, that is, by typing over the value already there. The default variables offered by the program are 1, 2, 3, and so on for both rows and columns. You can use these or type over them to use variable names of your choosing. The designated function keys ([F3], [F5], [F6], [F7], and [F8]) can be used to modify the problem. These keys are summarized later in this section. Entries must be accepted with the [F9] key after all entries have been made and verified. Figure 7.2 shows an example of an assignment matrix.

**Figure 7.2**
Sample
Assignment
Tableau Entry

[MIN] ENTER THE TABLEAU VALUES

|   | 1 | 2 | 3 | 4 | 5 |
|---|---|---|---|---|---|
| 1 | 25 | 27 | 21 | 24 | 29 |
| 2 | 14 | 13 | 18 | 16 | 15 |
| 3 | 19 | 22 | 16 | 20 | 22 |
| 4 | 26 | 23 | 24 | 18 | 25 |
| 5 | 30 | 28 | 27 | 17 | 19 |

Use Arrow keys, [Home], [End], [PgUp], [PgDn] to make entries.
[F3] Reverse MAX and MIN,   [F5] Delete Row,        [F6] Add Row
[F9] to accept entries,              [F7] Delete Column,   [F8] Add Column

The screen can display only 7 columns and 10 rows at a time. When you reach the right edge of the screen, it scrolls horizontally to reveal the next column. As you reach the bottom of the display area, the screen scrolls vertically to allow the next row to be entered. Cell values are restricted to 7-digit numbers (scientific notation can be used). In most problems requiring very large values, you can avoid size difficulties by simply scaling the values down before entering them (be consistent and remember to adjust the scale of the optimal solution value). Numbers do not have to be integer.

## 7.3  Output and Solution

The output for the assignment model includes:

1. The optimal assignment matrix (the assignments are shown in the appropriate cells by a 1). The display of large tableaus (more than 7

columns) will be segmented. Output for tableaus with more than 15 rows will scroll off the screen. To freeze the screen, press [CTRL] and [NUM LOCK]. To continue the display, press any key.

2. The solution value (total cost, distance, profit, etc.). Recall that assignment problems can have alternate optimal solutions. The output will indicate that alternate optima exist, but will not give specific alternate optimal assignments. However, recall that the solution value will be the same regardless of the specific optimal assignments used.

3. Messages in the output identify unbalanced problems and notify the user that dummies are added by the program, for example,

UNBALANCED PROBLEM

ADDING A DUMMY COLUMN WITH ZERO VALUE IN EACH CELL.

NEW TABLEAU:

Figure 7.3 shows the example solution.

**Figure 7.3**
Sample
Assignment
Output/Solution

OPTIMAL ASSIGNMENT

|   | 1 | 2 | 3 | 4 | 5 |
|---|---|---|---|---|---|
| 1 | 0 | 0 | 1 | 0 | 0 |
| 2 | 0 | 1 | 0 | 0 | 0 |
| 3 | 1 | 0 | 0 | 0 | 0 |
| 4 | 0 | 0 | 0 | 1 | 0 |
| 5 | 0 | 0 | 0 | 0 | 1 |

SOLUTION VALUE = 90

Press any key to continue

## 7.4  Examples

### Example 1: Assignment

Job Shop Manufacturing has four jobs it wishes to run. These jobs can be scheduled on any of four available machines. The production costs for each job on each machine are shown in the following table. Job Shop would like to assign jobs to the machines in a manner which will minimize total production costs for these jobs.

| Jobs | Machines | | | |
|------|----|----|----|----|
|      | A | B | C | D |
| 135 | 14 | 18 | 12 | 19 |
| 219 | 36 | 27 | 31 | 34 |
| 186 | 28 | 26 | 26 | 23 |
| 408 | 42 | 44 | 48 | 52 |

What jobs should Job Shop assign to each machine to minimize production costs?

Figure 7.4 shows the input for this problem. Figure 7.5 shows the output or solution to this problem. When we obtain the output we will press any key as directed to continue. That will give us the Ending Menu. We will select the option "Modify Data and Run Again," so that we can use this same problem (with modifications) for the next example. Figure 7.6 shows the Ending Menu.

```
TYPE OF PROBLEM:   (MAX/MIN)

HOW MANY ROWS IN THE MATRIX ? 4

HOW MANY COLUMNS IN THE MATRIX ? 4


[MIN] ENTER THE TABLEAU VALUES:


            |   1       2       3       4
   ---------|--------------------------------
       1    |  14      18      12      19
       2    |  36      27      31      34
       3    |  28      26      26      23
       4    |  42      44      48      52


Use Arrow keys, [Home], [End], [PgUp], [PgDn] to make entries.
[F3] Reverse MAX and MIN,      [F5] Delete Row,        [F6] Add Row
[F9] to accept entries         [F7] Delete Column,     [F8] Add Column
```

**Figure 7.4**    Example 1: Assignment Input

**Figure 7.5**
Example 1:
Assignment
Output/Solution

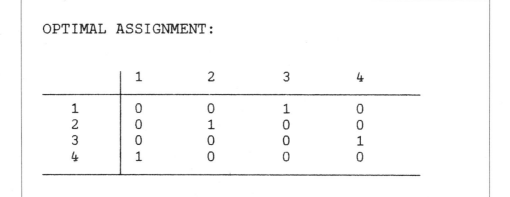

OPTIMAL ASSIGNMENT:

|   | 1 | 2 | 3 | 4 |
|---|---|---|---|---|
| 1 | 0 | 0 | 1 | 0 |
| 2 | 0 | 1 | 0 | 0 |
| 3 | 0 | 0 | 0 | 1 |
| 4 | 1 | 0 | 0 | 0 |

SOLUTION VALUE =   104

Press any key to continue

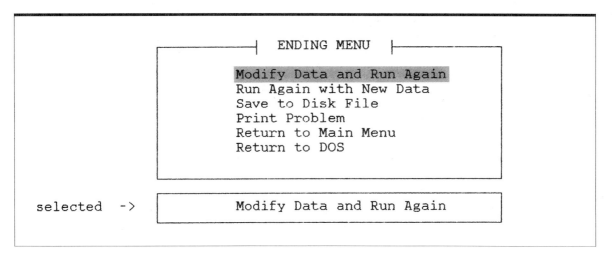

ENDING MENU

Modify Data and Run Again
Run Again with New Data
Save to Disk File
Print Problem
Return to Main Menu
Return to DOS

selected  ->   Modify Data and Run Again

**Figure 7.6**      Ending Menu

This solution assigns job 135 to machine C, job 219 to machine B, job 186 to machine D, and job 408 to machine A. The total cost is minimized at $104.

Now let's go back to this problem and run it again as a maximization problem for Example 2.

### Example 2: A Maximization Problem

Assume that there was a real mix up at Job Shop Manufacturing (Example 1). Someone used the wrong data in the assignment matrix. The costs used were really the profit expected from the assignment of a job to a machine. Now Job Shop would like to use these figures to determine what assignments to make to maximize profit. What assignments would you recommend?

Figure 7.7 shows the input for this problem. It includes the input summary from the original problem, and the new table with the objective changed, using the [F3] key to reverse from MIN to MAX. We then have to accept the entries with the [F9] key. Figure 7.8 shows the output.

```
[MIN] HERE IS WHAT YOU ENTERED:


                1       2       3       4

        1      14      18      12      19
        2      36      27      31      34
        3      28      26      26      23
        4      42      44      48      52

Use Arrow keys, [Home], [End], [PgUp], [PgDn] to make entries.
[F3] Reverse MAX and MIN,      [F5] Delete Row,         [F6] Add Row
[F9] to accept entries         [F7] Delete Column,      [F8] Add Column


[MAX] HERE IS WHAT YOU ENTERED:


                1       2       3       4

        1      14      18      12      19
        2      36      27      31      34
        3      28      26      26      23
        4      42      44      48      52

Use Arrow keys, [Home], [End], [PgUp], [PgDn] to make entries.
[F3] Reverse MAX and MIN,      [F5] Delete Row,         [F6] Add Row
[F9] to accept entries         [F7] Delete Column,      [F8] Add Column
```

**Figure 7.7**    Example 2: Maximization Problem Input—Modifying Data

When this becomes a maximization problem both the assignments and the solution change. Now, job 135 is assigned to B, 219 to A, 186 to C, and 408 to D, and the profit is maximized at $132.

**Figure 7.8**
Example 2:
Maximization
Problem Solution

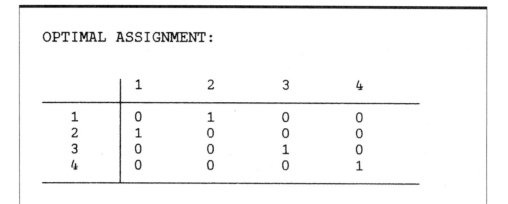

**Example 3: Assignment with Unbalanced Rows and Columns**

The Quick Pick-Up Company picks up packages for shipment from its customers and takes them to the airport. Quick Pick-Up has calls for pick-ups from three customers. The radio dispatcher has determined the current location of the company's four trucks and calculated mileage to the customers' locations. Which truck should be dispatched to which customer to minimize total mileage?

|       | Customer |    |    |
|-------|----|----|----|
| Truck | A  | B  | C  |
| 1     | 19 | 17 | 20 |
| 2     | 8  | 15 | 14 |
| 3     | 10 | 13 | 9  |
| 4     | 22 | 15 | 18 |

Figure 7.9 shows the input for this problem. Figure 7.10 shows the output/solution. The program automatically adds the dummy column, with the zero (0) value in each cell, needed to balance this problem. Note the messages:

UNBALANCED PROBLEM.

ADDING A DUMMY COLUMN WITH ZERO VALUE IN EACH CELL.

If it is necessary to add more than one dummy row or column, the program will do so. However, you will get the message informing you of this, once for each dummy added. When a dummy is added, the output includes a new matrix showing the row(s) or column(s) added.

```
TYPE OF PROBLEM:   (MAX/MIN)


HOW MANY ROWS IN THE MATRIX ? 4

HOW MANY COLUMNS IN THE MATRIX ? 3


[MIN] ENTER THE TABLEAU VALUES:


            |   1       2       3
       _____|_____
         1  |  19      17      20
         2  |   8      15      14
         3  |  10      13       9
         4  |  22      15      18


Use Arrow keys, [Home], [End], [PgUp], [PgDn] to make entries.
[F3] Reverse MAX and MIN,      [F5] Delete Row,        [F6] Add Row
[F9] to accept entries         [F7] Delete Column,     [F8] Add Column
```

**Figure 7.9**          Example 3: Unbalanced Assignment Input

```
UNBALANCED PROBLEM.

ADDING A DUMMY COLUMN WITH ZERO VALUE IN EACH CELL.

NEW TABLEAU:


            |   1         2         3       DUMMY
       _____|_____
         1  |  19        17        20         0
         2  |   8        15        14         0
         3  |  10        13         9         0
         4  |  22        15        18         0


             Press any key to continue            (continued)
```

**Figure 7.10**          Example 3: Unbalanced Assignment Output/Solution

```
OPTIMAL ASSIGNMENT:


              1         2         3        DUMMY
        ─────────────────────────────────────────
    1   │     0         0         0          1
    2   │     1         0         0          0
    3   │     0         0         1          0
    4   │     0         1         0          0
        ─────────────────────────────────────────



SOLUTION VALUE =   32

            Press any key to continue
```

**Figure 7.10**     (continued)

The minimum mileage of 32 miles is achieved by assigning truck 2 to customer A, truck 3 to customer C, and truck 4 to customer B. The matrix shows truck 1 assigned to customer 4, which is nonexistent (dummy), so in reality truck 1 is unassigned.

### Example 4: Traveling Salesman Problem

Maria has recently been hired in sales and assigned a territory with three cities. Since she wishes to minimize her traveling, she would like to plan a tour that will begin at her office and move from city to city. She will visit each city only once before returning to her home office. Using the following table showing cities to visit and mileage, determine the tour that will minimize her mileage and make sure she visits each city once before returning home.

| From \ To | Office | Hogshead | Big Flats | Port City |
|-----------|--------|----------|-----------|-----------|
| Office    | —      | 160      | 135       | 115       |
| Hogshead  | 160    | —        | 55        | 110       |
| Big Flats | 135    | 70       | —         | 125       |
| Port C    | 115    | 110      | 120       | —         |

Figure 7.11 shows the input and initial solution to this problem. We entered an M in each cell that would make the assignment of a city to itself (which is unacceptable). The traveling salesman problem has to be solved using the data modification feature of the ending routine with a branch and bound technique. As you know from your management science textbooks, in branch and bound, the set of feasible solutions is partitioned into smaller subsets (which are mutually exclusive) until the optimal solution is identified.

**Figure 7.11**
Example 4:
Traveling
Salesman
Problem—Input
and Initial Solution

```
TYPE OF PROBLEM:    (MAX/MIN)


HOW MANY ROWS IN THE MATRIX ? 4

HOW MANY COLUMNS IN THE MATRIX ? 4


[MIN] ENTER THE TABLEAU VALUES:
```

|   | 1 | 2 | 3 | 4 |
|---|---|---|---|---|
| 1 | M | 160 | 135 | 115 |
| 2 | 160 | M | 55 | 110 |
| 3 | 135 | 70 | M | 125 |
| 4 | 115 | 110 | 120 | M |

```
OPTIMAL ASSIGNMENT:
```

|   | 1 | 2 | 3 | 4 |
|---|---|---|---|---|
| 1 | 0 | 0 | 0 | 1 |
| 2 | 0 | 0 | 1 | 0 |
| 3 | 0 | 1 | 0 | 0 |
| 4 | 1 | 0 | 0 | 0 |

```
SOLUTION VALUE =   355

              Press any key to continue
```

This initial solution gives two subtours (1–4–1 and 2–3–2) and a lower bound of 355. Selecting the feasible tour of 1–2–3–4–1, in other words, taking the cities in the order given, would result in an upper bound of 455. The initial solution does not represent a complete tour, making it necessary to branch on one of the subtours. Since both subtours involve the same number of cities, we will arbitrarily branch on subtour 1–4–1 (Office–Port City–Office) by making first trip 1–4 and then trip 4–1 unacceptable. (Had the subtours involved differing numbers of cities, we would have chosen the subtour with fewer cities to branch on.) Using the "Modify Data and Run Again" option of the Ending Menu, we will make trip 1–4 unacceptable by replacing the cell 1,4 value (115) with M. In the summary table, you can move to that cell using the arrow key and type the M over the 115. Figure 7.12 shows input and output in the new problem.

**Figure 7.12**
Example 4:
Branch 1 Entries
and Solution

```
[MIN] HERE IS WHAT YOU ENTERED:


                  1          2          3          4

         1        M         160        135         M
         2       160         M          55        110
         3       135         70         M         125
         4       115        110        120         M



OPTIMAL ASSIGNMENT:


              1          2          3          4

     1        0          0          1          0
     2        0          0          0          1
     3        0          1          0          0
     4        1          0          0          0



SOLUTION VALUE =   430

           Press any key to continue
```

The output shows a feasible solution with a tour of 1–3–2–4–1 and a value (lower and upper bound) of 430. Because this matrix is not symmetrical, in other words, the distances between cities are not the same traveling in each direction, we must now solve the second branch as well. We will modify the data again, changing the value of cell 1,4 from M back to 115 and the value of cell 4,1 to M, making 4–1 unacceptable. Figure 7.13 shows the modifications (but not the Ending Menu) and the solution to branch 2.

**Figure 7.13**
Example 4:
Branch 2 Entries
and Solution

```
[MIN] HERE IS WHAT YOU ENTERED:
```

|     | 1   | 2   | 3   | 4   |
| --- | --- | --- | --- | --- |
| 1   | M   | 160 | 135 | 115 |
| 2   | 160 | M   | 55  | 110 |
| 3   | 135 | 70  | M   | 125 |
| 4   | M   | 110 | 120 | M   |

```
OPTIMAL ASSIGNMENT:
```

|     | 1   | 2   | 3   | 4   |
| --- | --- | --- | --- | --- |
| 1   | 0   | 0.  | 0   | 1   |
| 2   | 0   | 0   | 1   | 0   |
| 3   | 1.  | 0   | 0   | 0   |
| 4   | 0   | 1   | 0   | 0   |

```
SOLUTION VALUE =  415

            Press any key to continue
```

This solution is feasible with a tour of 1–4–2–3–1 and a value (lower and upper bound) of 415. Since this value is less than the 430 we achieved with branch 1, this is the optimal tour. Notice that it was necessary to make both changes—to change cell 1,4 to 115 and to change cell 4,1 to M. Figure 7.14 (p. 156) shows the diagram for the branch and bound nodes.

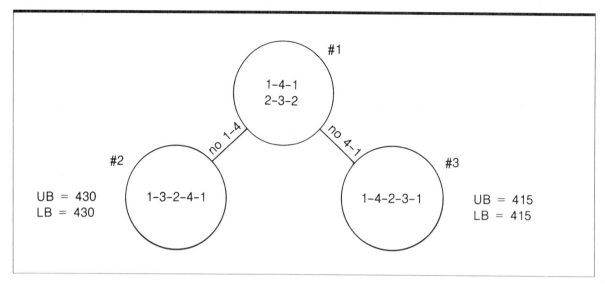

**Figure 7.14**     Example 4: Branch and Bound Diagram

# 7.5

1. Tableau size: 40 rows, 40 columns. It is not necessary to add dummy rows or columns (therefore, these are not counted in the 40). Dummies are added automatically by the program. The screen displays only 7 columns by 10 rows at a time, but scrolls one column or one row at a time to display more of the tableau.

2. In the output, tableaus with more than 7 columns will be displayed in segments because of the 80 character screen width. Output for tableaus with more than 15 rows will scroll off the screen (press [CTRL] and [NUM LOCK] to freeze the screen).

3. Cell values: limited to 7 digits. However, scientific notation or scaling can be used to accommodate larger values. Use M (or −M) for an unacceptable assignment.

4. Variables: default variables (1, 2, 3, etc.) are provided. These can be changed in the table by typing the variable name of choice over the default name. Variable names are limited to 5 characters.

5. Messages in the output will indicate that alternate optima exist (but will not give specific alternate optimal assignments) and will identify unbalanced problems (dummies are added by the program).

6. To move around the table: arrow keys move cursor right, left, up, down; [TAB] and ⟨RET⟩ emulate the right arrow key; [HOME] moves cursor to left-hand edge of line; [END] moves cursor to right-hand edge of line; [PgUp] moves cursor to first row of cell values section

of the tableau; [PgDn] moves cursor to last row of the cell values section.

7. To make changes in tableau size, and problem type: [F3] reverses MAX/MIN; [F5] deletes a row; [F6] adds a row; [F7] deletes a column; [F8] adds a column. Note that rows and columns are added or deleted one at a time. The function key must be used for each addition or deletion.

8. To accept the entries: the [F9] accepts the entries. This key must be pressed to continue the program and achieve a solution. Make sure all entries have been made and verified first. Recall that entries are edited, errors are corrected and/or problem modifications are made *before the [F9] key is pressed to accept the entries.* Entries are changed by typing over an incorrect entry. For a review of editing entries or correcting errors, check Chapter one.

## 7.6

**Problems**

1. Given the following table showing people to be assigned to projects and the attendant cost for each assignment:

| Person \ Project | 1 | 2 | 3 | 4 |
|---|---|---|---|---|
| Weinstein | 35 | 40 | 43 | 38 |
| Garcia | 56 | 61 | 59 | 53 |
| Krammeritsch | 29 | 32 | 37 | 42 |
| Biorn | 28 | 34 | 41 | 49 |

determine the assignments that will minimize total cost.

2. Given the following matrix showing jobs to be assigned to machines and the production cost of each assignment:

| Job \ Machine | A | B | C | D | E | F |
|---|---|---|---|---|---|---|
| 1 | 25 | 27 | 21 | 29 | 24 | 20 |
| 2 | 14 | 11 | 18 | 13 | 16 | 15 |
| 3 | 19 | 24 | 11 | 20 | 22 | 25 |
| 4 | 30 | 32 | 36 | 31 | 18 | 11 |
| 5 | 26 | 23 | 15 | 30 | 12 | 30 |
| 6 | 11 | 16 | 19 | 9 | 35 | 22 |

a. What jobs should be assigned to what machines to minimize production cost?

b. What happens if it is not possible to assign job 1 to machine A or machine F?

3. Using this matrix:

|   | 1 | 2 | 3 |
|---|---|---|---|
| 1 | 365 | 300 | 250 |
| 2 | 200 | 233 | 268 |
| 3 | 245 | 195 | 225 |
| 4 | 175 | 100 | 325 |

determine the assignments that will maximize total value.

4. Job Shop Manufacturing (Example 1) again has four jobs it needs to run. These four jobs must be scheduled on three machines. The following table shows the cost associated with each particular assignment.

| | | Machines | |
|---|---|---|---|
| Job | A | B | C |
| 1 | 10 | 13 | 17 |
| 2 | 15 | 12 | 19 |
| 3 | 21 | 11 | 9 |
| 4 | 12 | 25 | 8 |

   a. What assignments will minimize total production costs?
   b. Which job will not be assigned?

5. Prairie Dog Market Research has just received four new contracts and must now assign project directors to each of them. The time required to complete each project is a function of the experience of the director who is in charge of the project. The following table shows available directors, the project, and the expected time of completion (in days) for that particular assignment.

| | | Project | | |
|---|---|---|---|---|
| Director | 1 | 2 | 3 | 4 |
| Richards | 25 | 21 | 32 | 35 |
| Santiago | 47 | 36 | 19 | 14 |
| Murphy | 24 | 18 | 42 | 17 |
| Jancowski | 18 | 40 | 20 | 25 |

   a. What assignments should be made so that total time to complete all of the projects is minimal?
   b. If Murphy cannot be assigned to project 4, does it make any difference in the assignments and total time?

6. Big School's Library uses student assistants to enter new resources in the library's data base. These five students must enter books, periodicals, and media into separate files in the main data base. Each type of entry requires a different amount of time because of the complexity of the entry, and, of course, student entry or typing time varies. The librarian has made the following estimates of approximate times for each possible assignment. Only one student can be assigned to a specific task to maintain a needed level of consistency.

|         | Data Entry Type | | |
| Student | Books | Periodicals | Media |
|---------|-------|-------------|-------|
| Une-He  | 4     | 5           | 3     |
| Sara    | 2     | 3           | 1     |
| Aaron   | 3     | 6           | 4     |
| Ramon   | 4.5   | 7           | 1.5   |
| Sean    | 2.5   | 5           | 3     |

Which students should be assigned to what data entry task to minimize total time spent on the task? Which students would not be assigned to enter data?

7. Midvale, in upstate New York, wants to renovate five midtown building sites. Three contractors have bid on these jobs, but not all three have bid on every job. The following lists show what companies have bid on which contracts.

| M&M Co. | | D&B, Inc | | S.S.&J. | |
|---------|--------|---------|--------|---------|--------|
| Job 1   | 20,000 | Job 2   | 19,500 | Job 1   | 21,000 |
| Job 2   | 18,000 | Job 3   | 3,900  | Job 2   | 19,000 |
| Job 3   | 4,000  | Job 4   | 37,500 | Job 3   | 4,200  |
| Job 5   | 8,500  | Job 5   | 8,700  | Job 4   | 38,000 |
|         |        |         |        | Job 5   | 9,000  |

   a. If only one job can be awarded to a contractor, which contract should be given to which contractor in order to minimize the cost of the renovation?
   b. Are there any jobs that won't get done with this kind of assignment?

8. In Example 4, Maria had been given a sales route with three cities. Her firm is trying to consolidate territories and has just given Maria two more cities to cover. To minimize her mileage, she has had to revise the tour previously devised. Below is a list of her stops and estimated mileage between cities, including the new cities.

| From \ To | Office | Hogshead | Big Flats | Port City | Rockland | New City |
|-----------|--------|----------|-----------|-----------|----------|----------|
| Office    | —      | 160      | 135       | 115       | 90       | 150      |
| Hogshead  | 160    | —        | 55        | 110       | 75       | 200      |
| Big Flats | 135    | 70       | —         | 125       | 185      | 95       |
| Port City | 115    | 110      | 120       | —         | 115      | 140      |
| Rockland  | 90     | 75       | 175       | 130       | —        | 205      |
| New City  | 150    | 195      | 95        | 140       | 210      | —        |

What new sales route would you recommend to Maria?

9. Rose is a working mother who saves all of her errands for her day off. This time she wants to drop her vacuum cleaner at the repair shop, pick up bagels for the weekend, try the eclairs at the new French Bakery, and stop at the computer center to see some printers. Rose is a very efficient woman and naturally would like to minimize the time she spends in the car. Moreover, it is understood that she wants to stop only once at each address. The following table shows the stops she has to make and the estimated time between stops.

| | | | STOPS | | |
|---|---|---|---|---|---|
| | **Home** | **Bagel shop** | **Repair shop** | **Bakery** | **Computer center** |
| Home | — | 2 | 14 | 7 | 5 |
| Bagel | 2 | — | 9 | 5.5 | 6 |
| Repair | 14 | 9 | — | 2.5 | 4 |
| Bakery | 7 | 5.5 | 2.5 | — | 8 |
| Computer | 5 | 6 | 4 | 8 | — |

What sequence of stops do you recommend for Rose?

Chapter **8**

# Network Flow Models

**N**etwork flow models describe the flow of items through a system. A network is an arrangement of branches (arcs, links, paths) connected at various junction points (nodes), through which items move (flow) from point to point, or source to destination, along the connecting links. A network is graphically represented as a collection of nodes (the junction points) connected by arcs (the branches of the paths). These network flow models are all special applications of 0,1 integer programming and, therefore, must conform to the basic assumptions of IP. However, while such problems can in fact be solved using LP, special purpose algorithms are available that are more efficient and easier to use.

Network models are one of management's most popular and effective analysis techniques. Network models provide a picture of the system being analyzed, thereby allowing better understanding through a visual interpretation. Furthermore, a large number of real life situations can be conceived and constructed as network models. These include such diverse systems as electrical transmission lines, pipelines, communication networks (telephone lines, cable television lines, etc.), and transportation systems (railroad routes, highway systems, airline routes, etc.). In addition, many other kinds of problems can be conceived and analyzed as network problems. Once this network representation has been developed, the special purpose algorithms are used to solve the problem.

In this chapter, we will discuss three types of problems: shortest-route, maximal flow, and minimal spanning tree. A network technique used for project analysis, PERT, will be discussed in Chapter nine.

## 8.1 The Network Flow Models Program

The program allows the user a choice of three models:

1. Shortest-route
2. Maximal flow
3. Minimal spanning tree

Shortest-route determines the shortest distance (route) through the network, or specifically, the shortest route from an originating point to one or more destinations. Since shortest does not refer to physical distance only, it is more descriptive to think of this as finding the least cost path through a network, where cost can be such things as time, money, or distance. The objective, then, is to find the least cost route from a given node to any (or all) of the nodes in the network.

Maximal flow solves problems involving networks whose branches have differing limited flow capacities. The amount of flow through the network is important. The objective is to maximize the total amount of flow from an origin (input or source) to a destination (output or sink) in a given period of time. In other words, the objective is to determine the amount of flow across each arc, in a network composed of capacitated arcs, that will permit the maximum total flow from source to sink in a given amount of time.

The objective of a minimal spanning tree problem is to find the set of arcs that will connect all the nodes in the network in such a way that minimizes the total distance (the sum of the branch lengths).

Before beginning to enter data, it will be helpful to analyze the problem and prepare the data as follows:

1. For each problem, draw the network (limit of 30 nodes and 30 branches).
2. Number the nodes, using consecutive integers from 1 to 30.
3. Label each branch with the value (a nonnegative number) attached to that branch, such as time, distance, or flow, in the direction of the flow. The program automatically assumes that shortest-route and minimal spanning tree are symmetrical, the value is identical in either direction. Maximal flow is not symmetrical. Flow can vary with the direction. Label the branches accordingly.
4. Create a table for all the data, including a branch number (which is useful primarily to construct the table), beginning and ending node, and value. With maximal flow count flow in each direction as a separate branch. As an example, 2 to 3 and 3 to 2 count as two branches. Number each branch to keep track of the number of branches you have.

Once you have prepared your data, you are ready to begin entering it.

## 8.2  Data Entry

Data entry begins with the selection of the network flow model from the menu. Figure 8.1 shows this menu. Selection is made, as directed on screen, by using the up and down arrow keys to highlight the model of choice, and pressing the ⟨RET⟩ key to complete the entry.

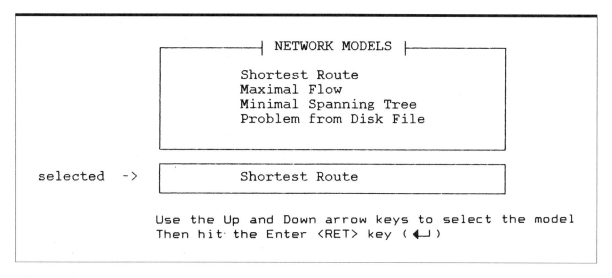

```
                          ┤ NETWORK MODELS ├
                    ┌──────────────────────────────────┐
                    │    Shortest Route                │
                    │    Maximal Flow                  │
                    │    Minimal Spanning Tree         │
                    │    Problem from Disk File        │
                    │                                  │
                    └──────────────────────────────────┘

 selected  ->       ┌──────────────────────────────────┐
                    │          Shortest Route          │
                    └──────────────────────────────────┘

           Use the Up and Down arrow keys to select the model
           Then hit the Enter <RET> key ( ↵ )
```

**Figure 8.1**    Network Flow Models Menu

All three models use the same entry routine, so the information you are required to enter is the same for all models. This makes the program consistent and extremely easy to use. However, as briefly mentioned in the problem preparation discussion, certain assumptions and requirements apply to the data entered for the specific models. Obviously, these affect the problem solution. The hard work for the user, then, is in problem formulation and data preparation.

Data entry is in two steps: an initial prompt, which asks the number of branches, and a tabular input, which describes the network (beginning and ending nodes and branch values).

1. Enter the number of branches, in response to the prompt "NUMBER OF BRANCHES ?" Remember to press ⟨RET⟩ to complete the entry. The program limit is 30 branches.

2. Fill in the table with the network values. The program provides a fill-in-the-blank table. Use the cursor movement keys (Arrow keys, [HOME], [END], [PgUp], [PgDn]) to move through the table and type the required entry. The type of problem and the number of branches can be changed with the function keys, as indicated on

screen and summarized below. After verifying the entries, they must be accepted, using the [F9] key.

For each branch (you have defined the number of branches), enter the beginning node, ending node, and the branch value (time, distance, cost, etc.). The program automatically enters the branch number. For all models, start the description with node 1. For maximum flow, the final node number should be the highest node number. The program limit is 30 nodes. Entries will vary slightly with the program because of certain model assumptions, as stated previously. The program assumes that shortest-route and minimal spanning tree are symmetrical. It is assumed that the branch is the same in either direction. In other words, the value on the branch from one node to another is identical in reverse, for example, a branch from node 4 to node 5 is the same as a branch from 5 to 4. Thus you enter the branch only once. However, maximal flow is assumed to be asymmetrical. The flow from one node to another is not necessarily identical in reverse, thus the branch from node 4 to node 5 may have a flow (capacity or value) of 25 but the flow from 5 to 4 may be 15. As a result, these are each entered as a branch with a beginning and ending node given in the direction of the flow, for example, one branch for the flow from 4 to 5 and another for the flow from 5 to 4. Flows of 0 need not be entered. Figure 8.2 shows an example entry for a shortest-route problem having 10 branches.

**Figure 8.2**
Network Flow
Models Data Entry

| [SHORTEST ROUTE] | | | ENTER NETWORK VALUES: |
|---|---|---|---|
| BRANCH | BEGINNING NODE | ENDING NODE | BRANCH VALUE |
| 1 | 1 | 2 | 40 |
| 2 | 1 | 3 | 20 |
| 3 | 1 | 4 | 36 |
| 4 | 2 | 3 | 12 |
| 5 | 2 | 5 | 48 |
| 6 | 3 | 4 | 26 |
| 7 | 3 | 5 | 58 |
| 8 | 3 | 6 | 32 |
| 9 | 4 | 6 | 30 |
| 10 | 5 | 6 | 16 |

Note that the screen can display only 10 rows at a time. When you reach the bottom of the screen, it scrolls to allow the next row to be entered.

## 8.3 Output and Solution

Output for these models, while similar in form, is tailored to the model and the solution being sought. All are in summary form.

1. For shortest-route, the output shows the shortest path (all branches making up the path) and the branch value for each path in the network, from node 1 to all other nodes. Although this shows the path from node 1 to the destination nodes, it can be used to find the shortest path from any node to any other node by looking at the path column and the branch value column and making the necessary adjustments. It is also possible, when preparing the data, to designate any node as the starting node, that is, node 1. Figure 8.3 shows an example output for a shortest-route problem.

**Figure 8.3**
Sample Shortest-
Route Solution

SOLUTION—SHORTEST ROUTE NETWORK

| BRANCH | BRANCH VALUE | PATH |
|--------|--------------|------|
| 1–2 | 32 | 1–3–2 |
| 1–3 | 20 | 1–3 |
| 1–4 | 36 | 1–4 |
| 1–5 | 68 | 1–3–6–5 |
| 1–6 | 52 | 1–3–6 |

Press any key to continue

2. For maximal flow, output includes a summary of the final flow capacity for each branch, a summary of the flow for each path through the network, and the determination of the total maximal flow. Figure 8.4 shows a sample maximal flow output.

**Figure 8.4**
Sample Maximal
Flow Output

SOLUTION—MAXIMAL FLOW NETWORK

FLOW OVER EACH BRANCH:

| BRANCH | FLOW |
|--------|------|
| 1–2 | 5 |
| 1–3 | 8 |
| 1–4 | 6 |
| 2–6 | 8 |
| 3–2 | 3 |

(continued)

**Figure 8.4**
(continued)

| | |
|---|---|
| 3–5 | 0 |
| 3–6 | 5 |
| 4–5 | 6 |
| 5–6 | 6 |

Press any key to continue.

FLOW THROUGH NETWORK:

| FLOW | PATHS: |
|---|---|
| 5 | 1–2–6 |
| 3 | 1–3–2–6 |
| 5 | 1–3–6 |
| 6 | 1–4–5–6 |

MAXIMAL FLOW THROUGH NETWORK =   19

Press any key to continue.

3. For a minimal spanning tree problem, the output summary shows the branches that will connect all the nodes (such that the total length is minimized), and the corresponding value for each branch. Figure 8.5 shows an example output.

**Figure 8.5**
Sample Minimal
Spanning Tree
Output

SOLUTION--MINIMAL SPANNING TREE

| BRANCH | BRANCH VALUE |
|---|---|
| 1–3 | 3 |
| 3–2 | 4 |
| 3–4 | 5 |
| 4–7 | 3 |
| 7–8 | 2 |
| 2–5 | 6 |
| 5–6 | 3 |

MINIMUM TOTAL SPAN =   26

Press any key to continue.

When, as directed on screen, you press any key to continue, the Ending Menu will appear. You will be able to modify the data and run the problem again if you choose to.

## 8.4  Examples

### Example 1: Shortest-Route

Dennco, Inc. transports widgets by trucks from its main plant in Rochester to six cities in New York, Syracuse, Albany, Watertown, Binghamton, Plattsburgh, and New York City. The shipping manager, Mr. Smith, would like to cut transportation costs by cutting the total distance each truck must travel to reach its destination.

The system of truck routes and the distances between cities are shown in Figure 8.6. We want to determine the shortest routes from the origin, Rochester (node 1), to the six cities (nodes 2–7). Figure 8.7 shows the input for this problem. Note there are 12 branches in this system. Figure 8.8 shows the solution.

**Figure 8.6**
Example 1:
Shortest-Route
Network

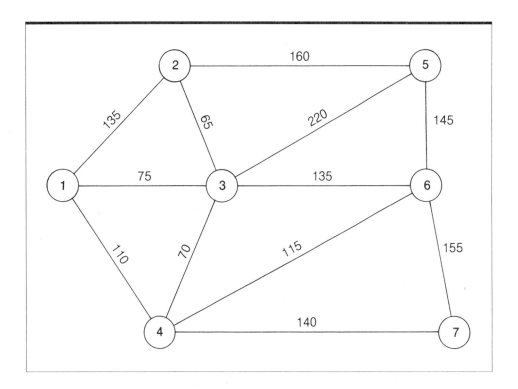

```
NUMBER OF BRANCHES ? 12


[SHORTEST ROUTE]                ENTER NETWORK VALUES:


          BEGINNING      ENDING         BRANCH
BRANCH      NODE          NODE          VALUE

    1   |    1             2             135
    2   |    1             3             75
    3   |    1             4             110
    4   |    2             3             65
    5   |    2             5             160
    6   |    3             5             220
    7   |    3             6             135
    8   |    3             4             70
    9   |    4             6             115
   10   |    4             7             140
   11   |    5             6             145
   12   |    6             7             155



Use Arrow keys, [Home], [End], [PgUp], [PgDn] to make entries.
[F3] Change Model Selected    [F5] Delete Row,         [F6] Add Row
[F9] to accept entries
```

**Figure 8.7**    Example 1: Shortest-Route Input

**Figure 8.8**
Example 1:
Shortest-Route
Output

```
SOLUTION - SHORTEST ROUTE NETWORK

                   BRANCH
BRANCH             VALUE           PATH
------             -----           ----
1 - 2              135             1 - 2
1 - 3              75              1 - 3
1 - 4              110             1 - 4
1 - 5              295             1 - 2 - 5
1 - 6              210             1 - 3 - 6
1 - 7              250             1 - 4 - 7

            Press any key to continue.
```

The solution requires very little explanation. The optimal routes are shown. In the case of a tie, as there is from 1 to 5 using paths 1–3–5 and 1–2–5, each with a total distance of 295, the program arbitrarily selects one (path 1–2–5 in this example).

### Example 2: Maximal Flow

The B-Low Cost Natural Gas Company has a pipeline network which transmits natural gas from its origin to several storage locations. Because of varying pipe sizes, the flow capacities along the network branches vary. The pipe network and the flow capacities (in 1000s of gallons per hour) are shown in Figure 8.9. What is the maximal flow per hour over this system and over each branch?

**Figure 8.9**
Example 2:
Maximal Flow
Network

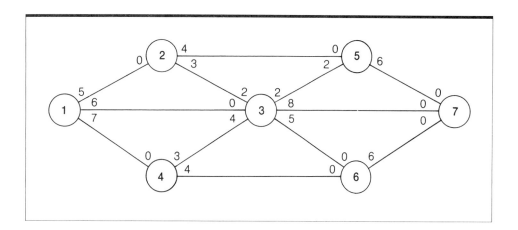

Figure 8.10 shows the input for this problem. There are 15 branches. Note the branches and capacities 2 to 3 and 3 to 2, 3 to 4 and 4 to 3, and 3 to 5 and 5 to 3. Figure 8.11 shows the output for the problem. It takes a while for the calculations to be made. Also the output will scroll off the screen. Recall that the [CTRL]–[NUM LOCK] keys are used to freeze the screen and pressing any key then releases it (see Chapter one).

```
NUMBER OF BRANCHES ? 15


[MAXIMAL FLOW]                    HERE IS WHAT YOU ENTERED:


           BEGINNING    ENDING       BRANCH
BRANCH       NODE        NODE        VALUE
       ┌─────────────────────────────────────
   1   │     1           2             5
   2   │     1           3             6
   3   │     1           4             7
   4   │     2           3             3
   5   │     2           5             4
   6   │     3           2             2
   7   │     3           4             4
   8   │     3           5             2
   9   │     3           6             5
  10   │     3           7             8
  11   │     4           3             3
  12   │     4           6             4
  13   │     5           3             2
  14   │     5           7             6
  15   │     6           7             6



Use Arrow keys, [Home], [End], [PgUp], [PgDn] to make entries.
[F3] Change Model Selected     [F5] Delete Row,          [F6] Add Row
[F9] to accept entries
```

**Figure 8.10**     Example 2: Maximal Flow Input


**Figure 8.11**
Example 2:
Maximal Flow
Output

```
FLOW OVER EACH BRANCH:

    BRANCH          FLOW
    ------          ----
    1 - 2            5
    1 - 3            6
    1 - 4            7
    2 - 3            2
    2 - 5            3
    3 - 5            2
    3 - 6            1
    3 - 7            8
    4 - 3            3
    4 - 6            4
    5 - 7            5
    6 - 7            5

    FLOW THROUGH NETWORK:                    (continued)
```

**Figure 8.11**
(continued)

```
FLOW          PATHS:
----          -----
  6        1 - 3 - 7
  2        1 - 2 - 3 - 7
  3        1 - 2 - 5 - 5 - 7
  2        1 - 4 - 3 - 5 - 7
  1        1 - 4 - 3 - 6 - 7
  4        1 - 4 - 6 - 7

MAXIMAL FLOW THROUGH NETWORK =    18
```

The solution is clearly shown in the output. The maximal flow over this system is 18, over paths 1–3–7, 1–2–3–7, 1–2–5–7, 1–4–3–5–7, 1–4–3–6–7 and 1–4–6–7.

### Example 3: Minimal Spanning Tree

Suburban Cable Company has been awarded the contract to connect 8 villages with cable television service. The 8 villages are connected by the roads and highways (branches) as shown in Figure 8.12. If SCC wishes to run all primary cable lines only along these roads and highways, what is the minimum length of cable (in miles) required to connect all 8 villages? What routes (branches) should be used?

**Figure 8.12**
Example 3:
Minimal Spanning
Tree Network

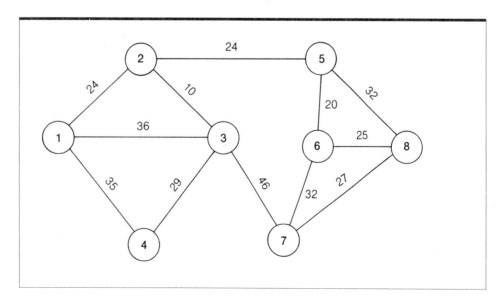

Figure 8.13 shows the input for this problem and Figure 8.14 shows the output. Both are self-explanatory.

```
NUMBER OF BRANCHES ? 12


[MINIMAL SPANNING TREE]        ENTER NETWORK VALUES:



          BEGINNING      ENDING          BRANCH
BRANCH      NODE          NODE           VALUE

    1         1            2              24
    2         1            3              36
    3         1            4              35
    4         2            3              10
    5         2            5              24
    6         3            4              29
    7         3            7              46
    8         5            6              20
    9         5            8              32
   10         6            7              32
   11         6            8              25
   12         7            8              27




Use Arrow keys, [Home], [End], [PgUp], [PgDn] to make entries.
[F3] Change Model Selected     [F5] Delete Row,         [F6] Add Row
[F9] to accept entries
```

**Figure 8.13**     Example 3: Minimal Spanning Tree Input


**Figure 8.14**
Example 3:
Minimal Spanning
Tree Output

```
SOLUTION - MINIMAL SPANNING TREE NETWORK


                  BRANCH
     BRANCH       VALUE
     - - - - -    - - - - -
     1 - 2         24
     2 - 3         10
     2 - 5         24
     5 - 6         20
     6 - 8         25
     8 - 7         27
     3 - 4         29

  MINIMUM TOTAL SPAN =   159

            Press any key to continue.
```

As you can see the minimum length of cable will be 159 miles. It will use branches 1–2, 2–3, 2–5, 5–6, 6–8, 8–7, and 3–4.

## 8.5

**Summary Notes**
for the Network Flow Programs

1. Size: 30 nodes and 30 branches. The screen can display only 10 rows at a time, but scrolls up to allow additional entries.

2. Node numbers must be *consecutive* integers from 1 to 30. For maximal flow, the sink will have the highest node number.

3. Branch values: shortest-route and minimal spanning tree are assumed to be symmetrical (branch value is constant, independent of direction, in other words, branch 4 to 5 is the same as branch 5 to 4). Thus, a branch should be entered only once. Maximal flow is assumed to be asymmetrical (flow can vary with direction), so you must enter branch values for flow in each direction, with a beginning and ending node given in the direction of the flow. Do not enter branches with flows of 0.

4. Moving around the table: Arrow keys move cursor right, left, up, down; [TAB] and ⟨RET⟩ emulate the right arrow key; [HOME] moves cursor to left-hand edge of line; [END] moves cursor to right-hand edge of line; [PgUp] moves cursor to first row of the table; [PgDn] moves cursor to last row.

5. Function keys in entering data: [F3] changes the model selected, rotating through the choices in the order listed in the menu; [F5] deletes a row (used to eliminate a branch); [F6] adds a row (used to add a branch).

6. To accept the entries press the [F9] key. This key must be pressed to continue the program and achieve a solution. Make sure all entries have been made and verified first. Recall that entries are edited, errors are corrected and/or problem modifications are made *before the [F9] key is pressed to accept the entries.* Entries are changed by typing over an incorrect entry. For a review of editing entries or correcting errors, check Chapter one.

## 8.6

**Problems**

1. Given the following network with the distances (in miles) between nodes, determine the shortest route from node 1 to each of the other nodes.

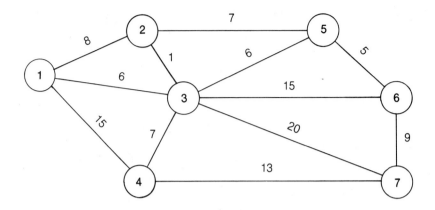

**2.** Given the following network with the distances (in miles) between nodes, determine the shortest route from node 1 to each of the other nodes.

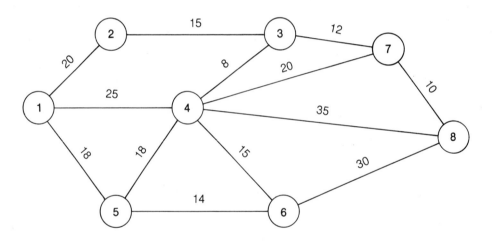

**3.** Given the following network with the distances (in miles) between nodes, determine the shortest route from node 3 to each of the other nodes.

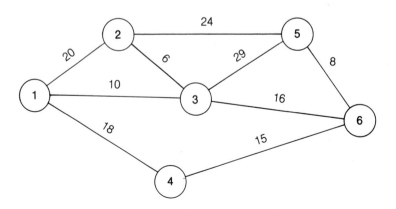

**4.** Downtown Department Store, Inc. makes deliveries from its main store in the city to six suburban stores. The network below represents the location and possible routes (including mileage) connecting each store. If Downtown uses one truck for each suburban store delivery, determine the shortest route to each store. Looking at these routes, decide if it would be possible for Downtown to make deliveries to all stores using these routes and fewer than six trucks.

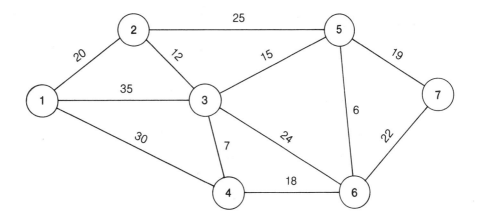

**5.** Given the following network with the flow capacities along each branch, determine the maximum flow from source node 1 to destination node 7 and the flow along each branch.

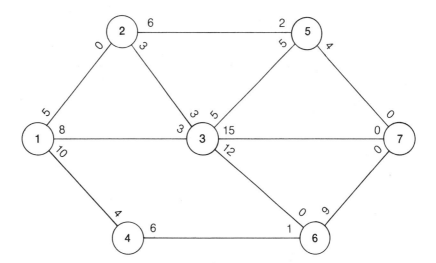

6. Given the following network with the flow capacities along each branch, determine the maximum flow from source node 1 to destination node 11 and the flow along each branch.

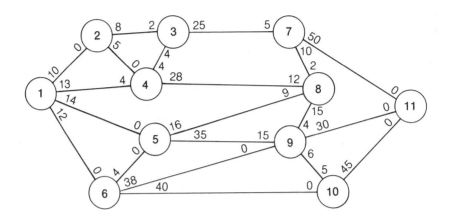

7. At the Bright Day processing plant, liquid ammonia (used in all the home cleaning products manufactured at this plant), is transferred from one part of the plant (source) to another via a network of pipes. The pipe network and flow capacities in gallons per minute are shown below. What is the maximum flow capacity for the system from the source location, node 1, to destination 8? How much ammonia will flow through the section of pipe from node 3 to node 7 (pipe 3–7). If a temporary break occurs on line 2–5, what is the maximal flow to destination 8?

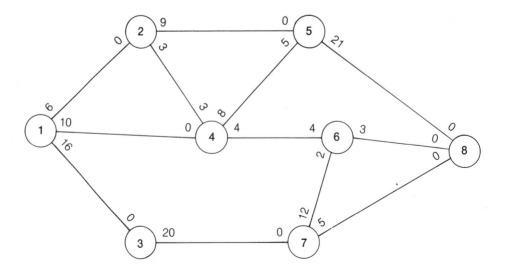

8. Given the following network with the distances between nodes shown, develop a minimal spanning tree.

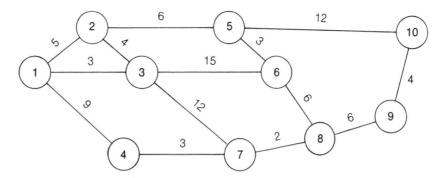

**9.** Given the following network with the distances between nodes shown, develop a minimal spanning tree.

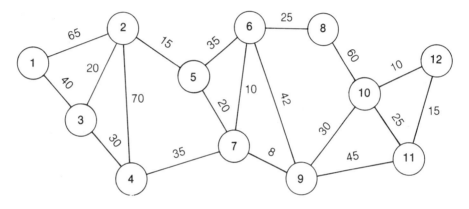

**10.** Pearville Parks and Recreation Department would like to add a bicycle path through Center Park. This path must connect all major recreational areas, tennis courts, playground, bike rental barn, picnic area, snack bar, with the three entrances to the park. The park layout with the proposed bicycle path (with distances in miles between areas) is represented by the network below. Given a very tight rec budget, it is essential to minimize the cost of constructing this path. Determine the minimum length path that can be built and still connect all these locations.

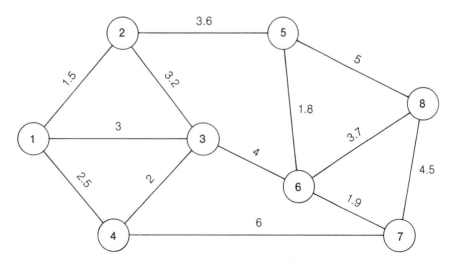

# 9

# Network Scheduling with PERT

**P**ERT (Program Evaluation and Review Technique) is a network analysis technique used to plan, schedule, and control complex projects. Such projects, consisting of a variety of separate but interconnected identifiable activities and their immediate predecessors, require cooperation between numerous individuals and/or departments. They usually contain too much information for one person to remember and control. PERT, with its graphic representation of the problem, enables a manager to schedule and coordinate the various interdependent jobs so that the entire project is completed on time. PERT is used for monitoring progress, highlighting bottlenecks and potential problems, and identifying expected project completion dates and the probability of completing the project within a given time.

Any project in which the separate, identifiable activities and their immediate predecessors can be described may be analyzed by PERT. Often these are projects that have never been done before. PERT is frequently used in such diverse projects as communications system design, transportation system design, new product or process development, large scale construction, and equipment maintenance.

At its simplest level PERT will provide:

1. Expected project completion date.

2. Start and completion date for each activity.

3. Critical activities that must be completed exactly as scheduled to ensure completion on time.

4. Allowable slack time for noncritical activities.

## 9.1 The PERT Program

The object of this program is to determine the project completion time (and variability where applicable) and to identify the activities on the critical path. It computes early and late start times, early and late finish times, and slack time for each activity. It then identifies those activities on the critical path, and determines the completion time, variance, and standard deviation on the critical path, if the problem is probabilistic and has a single critical path. If the problem has more than one critical path, the program identifies this situation, delineates two of the paths, and determines critical path variance for each of those paths.

Because of the differences in textbooks, this program allows the user to describe the PERT network using either beginning and ending node numbers for each activity or identified activities and their immediate predecessors. Either method allows both probabilistic and deterministic time estimates.

Before beginning to enter data for this program, the problem and data have to be prepared. Preparation will vary as described in the following two sections.

### Network Using Beginning and Ending Node Numbers

We suggest that the user draw the network on paper before using the computer.

1. Draw the project network. Include dummy activities with 0 times.

2. Number the nodes using any reasonable integer values, for example, 1, 2, . . . or 10, 20, . . . . There can be no more than 3 digits in each node number.

3. Use capital letters beginning with the letter A for the activities. (After using all twenty-six letters, A–Z, start over using AA, AB, AC, etc.). The activities must be in alphabetical order, that is, activity B must come before C, D, . . . , but after A. If an activity leaving a node has a lower letter than an activity entering a node, an error will result. There is a program limit of 52 activities.

4. Create a table for all the data. For each activity include activity letter, beginning and ending node, and time estimate(s). For a probabilistic problem give optimistic, most likely, and pessimistic time estimates; for a deterministic problem, give the expected time.

### Networks Using Activities and Immediate Predecessors

1. Give each activity in the project an identifying letter of the alphabet. Use capital letters, beginning with the letter A. (After using all

twenty-six letters in the alphabet, A–Z, start over using AA, AB, AC, etc.). There can be no more than 52 activities.

2. Identify for each activity, its immediate predecessor(s), with a limit of 10 per activity. All predecessors must be letters that come before the activity letter, for example, activity E can be preceded by A, B, C, or D, but not by F.

3. Create a table for the data. For each activity include the activity letter, immediate predecessor(s) (using a hyphen [-] to indicate none), and time estimate(s). For a probabilistic problem give optimistic, most likely, and pessimistic time estimates; for a deterministic problem, give the expected time.

## 9.2 Data Entry

The initial data entry step is the selection, from the menu shown here, of the model variation you wish to use. These variations identify the method you are using to describe the PERT network, using either beginning and ending node numbers or immediate predecessors (as discussed previously).

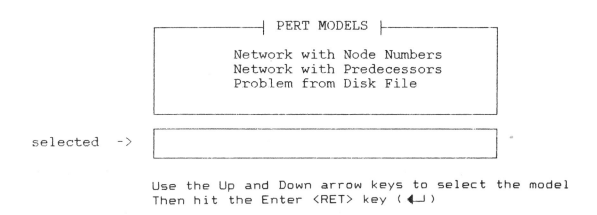

```
                 ──┤ PERT MODELS ├──────────
   ┌─────────────────────────────────────────────┐
   │        Network with Node Numbers            │
   │        Network with Predecessors            │
   │        Problem from Disk File               │
   │                                             │
   └─────────────────────────────────────────────┘

selected  ->  ┌─────────────────────────────────────────────┐
              │                                             │
              └─────────────────────────────────────────────┘

   Use the Up and Down arrow keys to select the model
   Then hit the Enter <RET> key ( ◀┘ )
```

Use the up and down arrow keys to highlight the selection of choice, and complete the entry by pressing ⟨RET⟩ as directed on screen and described in Chapter one.

If you are working from a problem for which a network has been drawn (by you, by someone else, or given in the problem), select "Network with Node Numbers." If you are working from an activities and predecessors list, select "Network with Predecessors." Selecting "Problem from Disk File" has been discussed in Chapter one.

Data entry is from both prompted input, which requires a detailed description of the problem, and from tabular input which defines the network. The tabular entries that you are required to make will depend upon how the problem is being entered (with node numbers or predecessors) and whether the problem is probabilistic or deterministic.

As prompted:

1.  Identify the problem as DETERMINISTIC or PROBABILISTIC. Use the right and left arrow keys to highlight your selection and press ⟨RET⟩ to complete the entry.

2.  Enter the number of activities (integer only; limit 52). Recall that ⟨RET⟩ completes the entry. If you have drawn the network and have any dummy activities, include them in your count.

3.  Fill in the table with the network values. The table that appears on screen in response to your initial entries already includes the activities (letters A, B, etc.). The required entries will vary with the type of problem being solved, which depends, of course, upon your previous choices. These entries are described in the next section.

### Networks Using Beginning and Ending Node Numbers

You are required to enter, for each activity:

1.  The numbers of the beginning and ending nodes (integers, with a 3-digit limit). As discussed earlier in this chapter, the activities (including dummies), must be in alphabetical order.

2.  Times. If the problem is deterministic, you are required to enter only the expected time. If the problem is probabilistic, you must enter optimistic (**OPT**), most likely (**M.L.**), and pessimistic (**PESS**) times. Common sense dictates (and your textbooks confirm) that for the times given, a<m<b, that is, optimistic times are lower than most likely, and most likely times are lower than pessimistic times. An error message occurs if you are inconsistent. Furthermore, time period units must be consistent, for example, all units in days or all units in weeks.

Figure 9.1 shows a sample entry for a probabilistic Pert problem that describes the network using beginning and ending nodes.

**Figure 9.1**
Sample PERT
Network with Node
Numbers Entry

THIS PROBLEM IS (DETERMINISTIC/ PROBABILISTIC )

HOW MANY ACTIVITIES ARE THERE ? 8

ENTER THE NETWORK VALUES BELOW:

| ACT | BEGIN NODE | END NODE | OPT. TIME | M.L. TIME | PESS. TIME |
|-----|-----------|----------|-----------|-----------|------------|
| A | 1 | 2 | 2 | 6 | 10 |
| B | 1 | 3 | 2 | 4 | 6 |
| C | 1 | 4 | 10 | 12 | 20 |
| D | 2 | 3 | 2 | 8 | 14 |
| E | 2 | 6 | 8 | 12 | 18 |
| F | 3 | 5 | 3 | 5 | 7 |
| G | 4 | 5 | 11 | 15 | 23 |
| H | 5 | 6 | 4 | 6 | 12 |

Use Arrow keys, [Home], [End], [PgUp], [PgDn], to make entries.
[F5] Delete Row,   [F6] Add Row,   [F9] Accepts Entries

Note that if this were a deterministic problem, you would have to enter only the expected time of completion (in a column headed EXPECTED TIME).

### Networks Using Predecessors

In this case, you are working from a network in which the immediate predecessor(s) for each activity has been identified. Therefore, you must enter for each activity:

1. Its predecessor(s), using a hyphen (-) or a blank cell to indicate that there are no predecessors and a comma (,) to separate the letters, such as C, D, if there is more than one predecessor. There is a program limit of 52 activities. All predecessors must be letters that come before the activity letter, for example, activity E can be preceded by A, B, C, or D, but not by F. There is a program limit of 10 predecessors for any activity. The program will truncate your entry (if it is over 10 characters) for display purposes only. The actual entry, not the displayed entry, is used in the solution.

2. Times. If the problem is deterministic, you enter only expected times. If the problem is probabilistic, you must enter optimistic, most likely, and pessimistic times. The time periods must be in consistent units

and rational; for instance, the pessimistic time cannot be less than the optimistic time.

Figure 9.2 shows a sample entry for a deterministic PERT problem that is described using immediate predecessors.

**Figure 9.2**
Sample PERT with
Predecessors
Entry

THIS PROBLEM IS ( DETERMINISTIC /PROBABILISTIC)

HOW MANY ACTIVITIES ARE THERE ?   9

ENTER THE NETWORK VALUES BELOW:

| ACT | IMMED PRED | EXPECTED TIME |
|-----|-----------|---------------|
| A | — | 12 |
| B | — | 3 |
| C | A | 12 |
| D | A,B | 12 |
| E | B | 18 |
| F | C | 15 |
| G | C,D | 21 |
| H | E | 9 |
| I | F,G,H | 24 |

Use Arrow keys, [Home], [End], [PgUp], [PgDn], to make entries.
[F5] Delete Row,   [F6] Add Row,   [F9] Accepts Entries

Note that for probabilistic problems, you must enter the optimistic, most likely, and pessimistic times in columns headed OPT. TIME, M.L. TIME, and PESS. TIME.

Error correction is of the tabular entry format. All values entered in the table can be changed (retyped), using the cursor movement keys to move through the table. As directed, it is also possible to add and delete rows to change the size of the problem network. However, it is not possible to change the identification of the problem as probabilistic or deterministic or to change the original menu selection.

## 9.3  Output/Solution

For *all* PERT problems, the solution shows:

1. Each activity: a summary of start and finish times, the calculated slack time, and whether it is on the critical path.

2. The critical path. If multiple critical paths exist, the program notes this. However, it identifies only two. By comparing the activities shown to be on the critical path with your drawing of the network, you should be able to delineate any other critical paths.

3. Network completion time.

*In addition*, for probabilistic problems, the output includes:

1. A summary of the calculated expected times and variances for each activity. Expected times are calculated using the traditional (if somewhat shopworn) $(a+4m+b)/6$ formula still found in most management science textbooks.

2. The variance on the critical path.

3. The standard deviation on the critical path.

Note that the output may be quite lengthy. There is a built-in pause and you may use the [CTRL]–[NUM LOCK] keys to freeze a portion on the screen until you press any key to release it (see Chapter one).

Figure 9.3 shows a sample PERT output. Note that it is for a probabilistic problem. Therefore, the first summary shows the calculated expected times and variances.

**Figure 9.3**
Sample PERT
Output/Solution

| ACTIVITY | BEG NODE | END NODE | EXPECTED (T) | VAR |
|----------|----------|----------|--------------|-----|
| A | 1 | 2 | 6.0 | 1.78 |
| B | 1 | 3 | 4.0 | 0.44 |
| C | 1 | 4 | 13.0 | 2.78 |
| D | 2 | 3 | 8.0 | 4.00 |
| E | 2 | 6 | 12.3 | 2.78 |
| F | 3 | 5 | 5.00 | 0.44 |
| G | 4 | 5 | 15.7 | 4.00 |
| H | 5 | 6 | 6.7 | 1.78 |

Press any key to continue.

| ACT | EARLY START | LATE START | EARLY FINISH | LATE FINISH | SLACK (LS–ES) | CRITICAL PATH |
|-----|-------------|------------|--------------|-------------|---------------|---------------|
| A | 0.0 | 9.7 | 6.0 | 15.7 | 9.7 | |
| B | 0.0 | 19.7 | 4.0 | 23.7 | 19.7 | |
| C | 0.0 | 0.0 | 13.0 | 13.0 | 0.0 | YES |
| D | 6.0 | 15.7 | 14.0 | 23.7 | 9.7 | |
| E | 6.0 | 23.0 | 18.3 | 35.3 | 17.0 | |
| F | 14.0 | 23.7 | 19.0 | 28.7 | 9.7 | |
| G | 13.0 | 13.0 | 28.7 | 28.7 | 0.0 | YES |
| H | 28.7 | 28.7 | 35.3 | 35.3 | 0.0 | YES |

(continued)

**Figure 9.3**
(continued)

CRITICAL PATH: C–G–H

NETWORK COMPLETION TIME = 33.34
VARIANCE ON CRITICAL PATH = 8.56
STANDARD DEVIATION ON CRITICAL PATH = 2.93

Press any key to continue.

Note that after you have examined the solution, if you wish to make any changes in this problem, use the "Modify Data" option in the Ending Menu (which appears when you press any key as directed on screen).

## 9.4 Examples

### Example 1: Network with Node Numbers—Probabilistic Times

Given the network shown in Figure 9.4:

**Figure 9.4**
Example 1:
Network Diagram

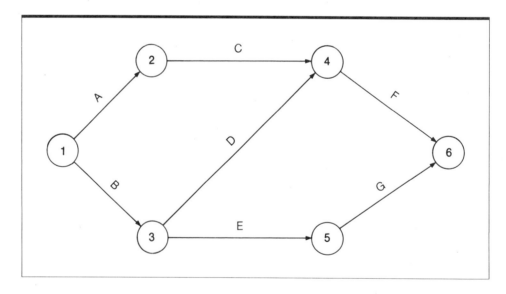

with these probabilistic times (in weeks):

| Activity | Optimistic | Most Likely | Pessimistic |
|----------|-----------|-------------|-------------|
| A | 1 | 2 | 3 |
| B | 2 | 3 | 4 |
| C | 1 | 3 | 5 |
| D | 3 | 6 | 15 |
| E | 3 | 4 | 5 |
| F | 5 | 5 | 5 |
| G | 4 | 6 | 8 |

determine:

1.  Critical path.
2.  Earliest completion time.
3.  Slack times.

Figure 9.5 shows the input for this problem. Figure 9.6 shows the table of calculated expected times and variances. Figure 9.7 gives the solution, including the start and finish times, slack times, completion time, and critical path.

```
THIS PROBLEM IS   (DETERMINISTIC/PROBABILISTIC)


HOW MANY ACTIVITIES ARE THERE (ENTER NUMBER AND PRESS RETURN)?  7


   ENTER NETWORK VALUES BELOW:


           BEGIN       END        OPT.       M.L.       PESS.
   ACT     NODE        NODE       TIME       TIME       TIME
   -------------------------------------------------------------
    A       1           2          1          2          3
    B       1           3          2          3          4
    C       2           4          1          3          5
    D       3           4          3          6          15
    E       3           5          3          4          5
    F       4           6          5          5          5
    G       5           6          4          6          8
   -------------------------------------------------------------


Use Arrow keys, [Home], [End], [PgUp], [PgDn] to make entries.
[F5] Delete Row,         [F6] Add Row,          [F9] Accepts Entries
```

**Figure 9.5**       Example 1: Node Numbers—Probabilistic Input

**Figure 9.6**
Example 1: Node
Numbers—
Probabilistic
Expected Time and
Variance Output

| ACTIVITY | BEG NODE | END NODE | EXPECTED (t) | VAR |
|----------|----------|----------|--------------|------|
| A | 1 | 2 | 2.0 | 0.11 |
| B | 1 | 3 | 3.0 | 0.11 |
| C | 2 | 4 | 3.0 | 0.44 |
| D | 3 | 4 | 7.0 | 4.00 |
| E | 3 | 5 | 4.0 | 0.11 |
| F | 4 | 6 | 5.0 | 0.00 |
| G | 5 | 6 | 6.0 | 0.44 |

Press any key to continue.

```
             EARLY     LATE      EARLY     LATE      SLACK     CRITICAL
    ACT      START     START     FINISH    FINISH    (LS-ES)   PATH
    ---      -----     -----     ------    ------    -------   --------
     A        0.0       5.0       2.0       7.0       5.0
     B        0.0       0.0       3.0       3.0       0.0       YES
     C        2.0       7.0       5.0      10.0       5.0
     D        3.0       3.0      10.0      10.0       0.0       YES
     E        3.0       5.0       7.0       9.0       2.0
     F       10.0      10.0      15.0      15.0       0.0       YES
     G        7.0       9.0      13.0      15.0       2.0

    CRITICAL PATH:  B-D-F

    NETWORK COMPLETION TIME =   15
    VARIANCE ON CRITICAL PATH =   4.11
    STANDARD DEVIATION ON CRITICAL PATH =   2.03

                 Press any key to continue.
```

**Figure 9.7**        Example 1: Node Numbers—Probabilistic Solution

For this problem we have determined that:

1. The critical path is B–D–F.

2. The network completion time is 15 weeks.

3. Using the information available in the table for critical path activities and slack times, we see that noncritical activities A and C each has a slack time of 5 weeks and E and G each has a slack time of 2 weeks.

### Example 2: Network with Node Numbers—Deterministic Times

Given the network shown in Figure 9.8:

**Figure 9.8**
Example 2:
Network Drawing

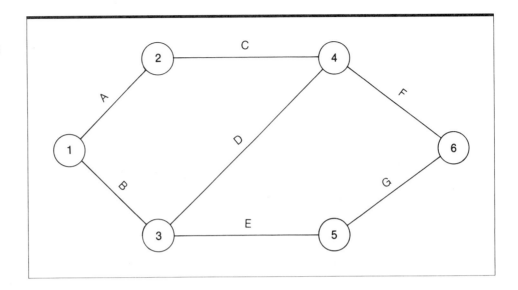

with these expected times (in weeks):

| Activity | Expected Time |
|----------|---------------|
| A | 2 |
| B | 3 |
| C | 3 |
| D | 7 |
| E | 4 |
| F | 5 |
| G | 8 |

determine:

1. Critical path.

2. Network completion time.

Notice that these times are identical to the expected times calculated in the probabilistic problem (Example 1, Figure 9.6) except that the time for activity G has been changed to create a situation where there are multiple critical paths.

Figure 9.9 (p. 190) shows the entries for this problem. Figure 9.10 shows the output/solution. Note that since this is a deterministic problem, there is no table of expected time and variation calculations. The output goes directly to the table of start, finish, and slack times, and the determination of the critical path activities and network completion time. Notice also that the program alerts us to the existence of multiple critical paths.

For this problem we have determined that:

1. There are multiple critical paths. The program identifies two, B–D–F and B–E–G. Since each activity on a critical path is identified *in the solution summary*, you have only to look at the network you have

```
THIS PROBLEM IS   (DETERMINISTIC/PROBABILISTIC)


HOW MANY ACTIVITIES ARE THERE (ENTER NUMBER AND PRESS RETURN)? 7


      ENTER NETWORK VALUES BELOW:


            BEGIN       END         EXPECTED
   ACT      NODE        NODE        TIME
   _____

    A        1           2           2
    B        1           3           3
    C        2           4           3
    D        3           4           7
    E        3           5           4
    F        4           6           5
    G        5           6           8
   _____


Use Arrow keys, [Home], [End], [PgUp], [PgDn] to make entries.
[F5] Delete Row,          [F6] Add Row,          [F9] Accepts Entries
```

**Figure 9.9**　　　　Example 2: Node Numbers—Deterministic Input

```
         EARLY     LATE      EARLY     LATE      SLACK     CRITICAL
   ACT   START     START     FINISH    FINISH    (LS-ES)   PATH
   ---   -----     -----     ------    ------    -------   --------
    A     0.0       5.0       2.0       7.0       5.0
    B     0.0       0.0       3.0       3.0       0.0       YES
    C     2.0       7.0       5.0      10.0       5.0
    D     3.0       3.0      10.0      10.0       0.0       YES
    E     3.0       3.0       7.0       7.0       0.0       YES
    F    10.0      10.0      15.0      15.0       0.0       YES
    G     7.0       7.0      15.0      15.0       0.0       YES

MULTIPLE CRITICAL PATHS

    B-D-F
    B-E-G


NETWORK COMPLETION TIME =   15

              Press any key to continue.
```

**Figure 9.10**　　　　Example 2: Node Numbers—Deterministic Solution

drawn to determine each critical path—an excellent reason for first drawing the network.

2. The network completion time is 15 weeks.

### Example 3:  A Probabilistic Problem with Entry from Predecessors

Given this list of activities and predecessors:

| Activity | Immediate Predecessors |
|----------|------------------------|
| A | — |
| B | — |
| C | A |
| D | B |
| E | B |
| F | C,D |
| G | E |

with these probabilistic times (in weeks):

| Activity | Optimistic | Most Likely | Pessimistic |
|----------|------------|-------------|-------------|
| A | 1 | 2 | 3 |
| B | 2 | 3 | 4 |
| C | 1 | 3 | 5 |
| D | 3 | 6 | 15 |
| E | 3 | 4 | 5 |
| F | 5 | 5 | 5 |
| G | 4 | 6 | 8 |

determine:

1. Critical path.

2. Earliest completion time.

3. Slack times.

Figure 9.11 (p. 192) shows the input, Figure 9.12 shows the expected times and variances calculated for each activity, and Figure 9.13 gives the solution for this problem.

For this problem we have determined that:

1. The critical path is B–D–F.

2. The network completion time is 15 weeks.

3. Using the information available in the table for critical path activities and slack times, we see that noncritical activities A and C each has a slack time of 5 weeks and E and G each has a slack time of 2 weeks.

```
THIS PROBLEM IS  (DETERMINISTIC/PROBABILISTIC)

HOW MANY ACTIVITIES ARE THERE (ENTER NUMBER AND PRESS RETURN)? 7

        ENTER NETWORK VALUES BELOW:


        IMMED       OPT.      M.L.      PESS.
  ACT │ PRED        TIME      TIME      TIME
──────┼──────────────────────────────────────────
   A  │             1         2         3
   B  │             2         3         4
   C  │ A           1         3         5
   D  │ B           3         6         15
   E  │ B           3         4         5
   F  │ C,D         5         5         5
   G  │ E           4         6         8
──────┴──────────────────────────────────────────

Use Arrow keys, [Home], [End], [PgUp], [PgDn] to make entries.
[F5] Delete Row,          [F6] Add Row,          [F9] Accepts Entries
```

**Figure 9.11**      Example 3: Predecessors—Probabilistic Input

```
              IMMEDIATE      EXPECTED
  ACTIVITY    PREDECESSOR      (t)           VAR
  --------    -----------    ---------      -----
     A                         2.00         0.11
     B                         3.00         0.11
     C           A             3.00         0.44
     D           B             7.00         4.00
     E           B             4.00         0.11
     F           C,D           5.00         0.00
     G           E             6.00         0.44

              Press any key to continue.
```

**Figure 9.12**      Example 3: Predecessors—Probabilistic Expected Times and Variances Output

```
                EARLY    LATE    EARLY    LATE     SLACK    CRITICAL
        ACT     START   START   FINISH   FINISH   (LS-ES)    PATH
        ---     -----   -----   ------   ------   -------   --------
         A      0.0     5.0     2.0      7.0      5.0
         B      0.0     0.0     3.0      3.0      0.0       YES
         C      2.0     7.0     5.0      10.0     5.0
         D      3.0     3.0     10.0     10.0     0.0       YES
         E      3.0     5.0     7.0      9.0      2.0
         F      10.0    10.0    15.0     15.0     0.0       YES
         G      7.0     9.0     13.0     15.0     2.0

        CRITICAL PATH: B-D-F

        NETWORK COMPLETION TIME =   15
        VARIANCE ON CRITICAL PATH =   4.11
        STANDARD DEVIATION ON CRITICAL PATH =   2.03

                    Press any key to continue.
```

**Figure 9.13**     Example 3: Predecessors—Probabilistic Solution

## Example 4: A Deterministic Problem with Entry from Predecessors

Given this list of activities, predecessors, and expected times:

| Activity | Immediate Predecessor | Expected Time |
|---|---|---|
| A | — | 2 |
| B | — | 3 |
| C | A | 3 |
| D | B | 7 |
| E | B | 4 |
| F | C,D | 5 |
| G | E | 8 |

determine:

1. Critical path.

2. Earliest completion time.

Figure 9.14 (p. 194) shows the entries required for this problem. Figure 9.15 shows the output/solution. Note that multiple critical paths exist. Those activities lying on a critical path are identified in the table with a YES.

```
THIS PROBLEM IS  (DETERMINISTIC/PROBABILISTIC)


HOW MANY ACTIVITIES ARE THERE (ENTER NUMBER AND PRESS RETURN)? 7


       ENTER NETWORK VALUES BELOW:


            IMMED       EXPECTED
     ACT  | PRED        TIME

      A   |               2
      B   |               3
      C   |    A          3
      D   |    B          7
      E   |    B          4
      F   |    C,D        5
      G   |    E          8



Use Arrow keys, [Home], [End], [PgUp], [PgDn] to make entries.
[F5] Delete Row,          [F6] Add Row,          [F9] Accepts Entries
```

**Figure 9.14**     Example 4: Predecessors—Deterministic Input

```
            EARLY     LATE      EARLY     LATE      SLACK     CRITICAL
     ACT    START     START     FINISH    FINISH    (LS-ES)   PATH
     ---    -----     -----     ------    ------    -------   --------
      A     0.0       5.0       2.0       7.0       5.0
      B     0.0       0.0       3.0       3.0       0.0       YES
      C     2.0       7.0       5.0       10.0      5.0
      D     3.0       3.0       10.0      10.0      0.0       YES
      E     3.0       3.0       7.0       7.0       0.0       YES
      F     10.0      10.0      15.0      15.0      0.0       YES
      G     7.0       7.0       15.0      15.0      0.0       YES

MULTIPLE CRITICAL PATHS

B-D-F
B-E-G


NETWORK COMPLETION TIME =   15

            Press any key to continue.
```

**Figure 9.15**     Example 4: Predecessors—Deterministic Solution

For this problem, we have determined:

1.  There are multiple critical paths. Referring to the predecessors and the solution (Figure 9.15), we can determine that these paths are B–D–F and B–E–G.

2.  The network completion time is 15 weeks.

## 9.5

**Summary Notes** for the PERT Programs

1.  Size limitations: 52 activities; node numbers can be no more than 3 digits; maximum of 10 predecessors for any given activity. Note that the table cannot display this many. Your entry may be truncated. However, the program remembers and uses what you entered.

2.  Node numbers must be integers. Activities must be in alphabetical order, that is, an activity leaving a node must have a letter greater than an activity entering the node.

3.  For problems entered using predecessors, the predecessor letters have to be less than the activity letter, in other words, for each activity its predecessors must be letters that come before it.

4.  When entering predecessors, use a hyphen (-) or make no entry if there are no predecessor activities for a given activity. Use a comma to separate letters when there is more than one predecessor for a given activity.

5.  For probabilistic problems, the times must be $a<m<b$, such that optimistic times are lower than most likely times and most likely times are lower than pessimistic times. Time period units must be consistent, for example, all in days or weeks.

6.  Moving around the table: Arrow keys move cursor right, left, up, down; [HOME] moves cursor to left-hand edge of line; [END] moves cursor to right-hand edge of line; [PgUp] moves cursor to first row of the table; [PgDn] moves cursor to last row of the table.

7.  Function keys in entering data: [F5] deletes a row (used to eliminate an activity); [F6] adds a row (used to add an activity); [F9] accepts the entries. The [F9] key must be pressed to continue the program and achieve a solution.

8.  Output indicates when there are multiple critical paths and identifies two such paths. The existence of additional critical paths is so noted. Moreover, the output summary indicates when an activity lies on a critical path.

## 9.6

**Problems**   1.  Given the following information, determine the expected time required to complete the project and the variance on the critical path.

| Activity | Immediate Predecessor | Optim Time | M. L. Time | Pessim Time |
|----------|----------------------|------------|------------|-------------|
| A | — | 2 | 3 | 4 |
| B | — | 1 | 2 | 6 |
| C | A | 3 | 5 | 7 |
| D | B | 4 | 5 | 6 |
| E | C,D | 8 | 10 | 15 |
| F | C,D | 1 | 7 | 19 |
| G | E | 2 | 2 | 2 |
| H | F | 4 | 5 | 6 |

2.  The Atlas Construction Company is about to bid on a new project. Given the project activities and completion times shown below, how long should it take Atlas to complete the project? What is the critical path for this project?

| Activity | Immediate Predecessor | Time (weeks) |
|----------|----------------------|--------------|
| A | — | 4 |
| B | — | 1 |
| C | — | 4 |
| D | B | 4 |
| E | A | 6 |
| F | C,D | 5 |
| G | E | 7 |
| H | E | 2 |
| I | H | 3 |
| J | F | 8 |

3.  Given the following network:

| Activity | Time | Activity | Time |
|----------|------|----------|------|
| 1–2 | 17 | 3–6 | 15 |
| 1–3 | 20 | 4–6 | 26 |
| 1–4 | 12 | 5–7 | 13 |
| 2–5 | 18 | 6–7 | 7 |
| 4–3 | 14 | 7–8 | 16 |
| 3–5 | 8 | | |

   a.  Determine the project completion time.
   b.  Identify the critical path.
   c.  If activity 1–2 can be reduced to 14 days, what will be the impact on the project completion time?
   d.  If the following time reductions are also achieved, will the solution to this problem change? What will be the new solution?

| Activity | New Time |
|----------|----------|
| 2–5 | 14 |
| 1–4 | 10 |
| 7–8 | 9 |

4. MacMillan Research Corporation has just signed a contract on the following project:

| Activity | Immediate Predecessor | a | m | b |
|---|---|---|---|---|
| A | — | 1 | 2 | 3 |
| B | — | 2 | 3 | 5 |
| C | A | 8 | 9 | 11 |
| D | A,B | 4 | 7 | 10 |
| E | B | 5 | 7 | 9 |
| F | C | 2 | 6 | 10 |
| G | C,D | 2 | 8 | 16 |
| H | E | 3 | 5 | 9 |
| I | F,G,H | 3 | 7 | 11 |

What is the expected completion time on this project? What is the probability that this project will be completed within 27 days? How much slack is there on activity F? How much slack is there on activity G?

5. Given the following project network and information:

| Activity | a | b | c |
|---|---|---|---|
| 1–2 | 1 | 3 | 5 |
| 1–3 | 1 | 2 | 3 |
| 2–4 | 5 | 6 | 13 |
| 3–5 | 1 | 4 | 7 |
| 3–6 | 1 | 1 | 1 |
| 4–8 | 5 | 8 | 11 |
| 5–7 | 1 | 2 | 9 |
| 6–7 | 4 | 5 | 6 |
| 7–8 | 4 | 6 | 8 |
| 8–9 | 3 | 4 | 5 |

a. Determine the expected project completion time.
b. What is the probability this project will be completed within 20 weeks?

6. Given the following network:

| Activity | Opt a | M–Lkly b | Pess c |
|---|---|---|---|
| 1–2 | 2 | 3 | 4 |
| 1–3 | 2 | 5 | 8 |
| 1–4 | 7 | 8 | 12 |
| 2–5 | 6 | 7 | 9 |
| 2–6 | 3 | 10 | 12 |
| 3–4 | 2 | 2 | 2 |
| 4–6 | 2 | 4 | 8 |
| 5–7 | 4 | 7 | 9 |
| 6–8 | 5 | 9 | 19 |
| 7–8 | 3 | 5 | 15 |

a. Determine the expected completion time for this project.
b. Determine the critical path.
c. Determine the standard deviation on the critical path.

7.  Denneco Construction is preparing to bid on a construction contract. They have developed a PERT network and have gathered the following time estimates (in weeks).

| Activity | a | m | b |
|---|---|---|---|
| 1–2 | 1 | 2 | 4 |
| 2–3 | 1 | 3 | 5 |
| 2–4 | 2 | 5 | 8 |
| 3–5 | 5 | 6 | 7 |
| 4–6 | 3 | 4 | 7 |
| 6–7 | 6 | 8 | 10 |
| 6–8 | 5 | 6 | 13 |
| 7–9 | 3 | 3 | 3 |
| 8–9 | 2 | 5 | 14 |
| 8–10 | 1 | 2 | 3 |
| 9–11 | 4 | 5 | 8 |
| 10–11 | 5 | 7 | 9 |

a.  What is the expected completion time on this project?

b.  If there is a penalty clause in the contract for non-completion within 33 weeks, what is the probability Denneco will have to pay the penalty if they get the contract?

8.  Given the following network:

| Activity | Immediate Predecessor | Expected Time |
|---|---|---|
| A | — | 17 |
| B | — | 4 |
| C | — | 5 |
| D | B | 2 |
| E | C | 4 |
| F | D,E | 6 |
| G | D,E | 8 |
| H | G | 3 |
| I | H | 5 |
| J | F | 7 |
| K | F | 10 |
| L | A,J | 20 |
| M | A,J | 14 |
| N | H | 6 |
| O | N | 9 |
| P | I,K,M | 11 |

a.  Determine the critical path.

b.  Determine the expected project completion time.

**9.** Given the following network:

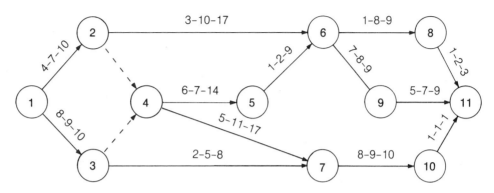

**a.** Identify the critical path.
**b.** Determine the expected completion time for this project.
**c.** How much slack time is associated with activity 4–7? 6–9?
**d.** What is the standard deviation on the critical path?
**e.** What is the probability this project will be completed within 34 weeks? 37 weeks?

Chapter **10**

# Forecasting

Forecasts are predictions of the future or estimates that help managers plan and prepare for the future by reducing uncertainty and providing fairly reliable decision-making guidelines. A wide variety of forecasting techniques are in use, both qualitative and quantitative, ranging from the very simple to the extremely complex. No one technique is perfect; no one method is always superior. They all have some degree of inaccuracy. Moreover, each has its own special use; each works best for a particular kind of problem, under a specific set of circumstances. Therein lies one of the problems with forecasting. All managers, all firms forecast in some fashion; choosing the best method for a particular problem is one of the initial (and difficult) decisions that must be made. However, it should be recognized that all forecasting techniques are based on the same assumption: the same underlying pattern or relationship that existed in the past will continue into the future. Furthermore, it is generally acknowledged that as the time period covered by the forecast increases, accuracy decreases, and that actual results will be different from the predicted values.

The variety of available forecasting techniques just mentioned is echoed in the treatment of forecasting in current textbooks. A quick reading of several texts will reveal little agreement in selected methodology, terminology, or nomenclature. In this chapter we have chosen to include models and variations using two quantitative approaches: 1. those that are based on an extension of past history, that is, time series, where patterns over a period of time are detected and then projected into the future; and 2. those that are based on a recognized linear relationship between two variables (one dependent and one independent), that is, causal models where the identified relationship, in the form of a linear equation, is used to predict the future. It should be noted that the distinction between time series and causal models is sometimes blurry, especially in the case where the independent variable is time and/or a trend line is being projected over time. The term associative models is sometimes used to describe recognized linear relationships between variables and may be more descriptive.

In general one or another of these forecasting methods can be used to: 1. project the past into the future, smoothing out random fluctuations; 2. make forecasts that allow adjustments for trends; 3. derive a forecasting equation to show the linear relationship; 4. use a linear equation to make predictions; 5. evaluate the relationship between two variables (the degree of strength of the linear relationship); and/or 6. make seasonal adjustments.

## 10.1 The Forecasting Program

The primary objective of the various forecasting models is to make accurate and reliable predictions about the future and consequently enable them to be used as the basis for management planning and decision making. The models based on past history (moving averages and exponential smoothing) use past values to calculate averages. They also use some form of weighting system to determine a forecast and to determine mean absolute deviation (MAD) as an error measurement. The model based on an identifiable linear relationship between two variables (linear regression or least squares regression analysis) uses the data points of the dependent and independent variables to derive the regression equation and then uses that relationship to determine the forecast values. This model will also determine the standard deviation of regression and the correlation coefficient.

The forecasting program allows the user a choice of three basic models with variations:

1. Moving averages—simple and weighted

2. Exponential smoothing—simple and trend adjusted

3. Linear regression—simple and seasonally adjusted

## 10.2 Data Entry

Since there are three forecasting models included in the program, the first step in entering data is to select from the forecasting models menu the model you wish to run. This menu is shown here.

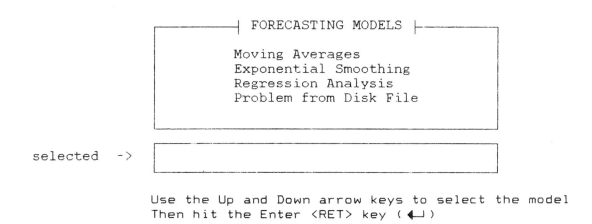

Use the up and down arrow keys to make a selection. Press ⟨RET⟩ to complete the entry. Note that entry from disk file is always an option and has
been discussed fully in Chapter one.

Data entry for each of these models is from both prompted input and
tabular input. The required entries will be presented in the following sections, which discuss the specific model.

Error correction for these models is in the tabular entry format, therefore, cursor movement keys are used to move to the error, the entry is retyped, and the [F9] key is used to accept the entries. Recall that this has
been discussed in Chapter one.

## 10.3  Moving Averages

Moving averages are averages that are continually updated as time passes
and new information becomes available. This model allows you to solve
problems using either simple or weighted averages.

### Data Entry

First, you must describe the problem, for example, number of periods. Then
you simply enter the value for each period and the weights (if weighted) in
a table provided by the program.

Thus, as prompted:

1.  Enter the number of periods (limit 100 periods). (Note: ⟨RET⟩
    completes the entry.)

2. Enter the number of periods used in the moving average (limit 20 periods). It must be an integer. Recall that in projecting the past into the future, a moving average tries to smooth out the fluctuations in a pattern by removing some of the random variations in the data. However, such averages do not react quickly to changing patterns in the data. The speed of the response to such changes is partly controlled by adjusting the number of periods included in the averages. Remember, the larger the number, the slower the reaction to change.

3. Describe whether or not the problem is a weighted average problem. Respond to the prompt IS THIS A WEIGHTED AVERAGE PROBLEM ? If the response is YES, you will later be given the opportunity to enter the weights. Recall that in a simple moving average (not weighted) each period is weighted equally. Weights are added in an attempt to make the forecast more accurate. Generally the recent periods are weighted more heavily. It is also another way of controlling the speed of adjustment to change.

4. Fill in the table. Note that the table is one long column in which you enter the values and the weights. Therefore, it is possible to modify or change any of the entries that you have made in the table, as long as it is done before you press the [F9] key to accept the entries. You are able to change the number of periods and the number of periods in the moving average, the entry describing the problem as weighted or not, and the weights. Use the up and down arrow keys and the [PgUp] and [PgDn] keys to move through the table. Enter:
   a. The actual values for the corresponding time periods. For large problems the column will scroll off the screen. Recall that you can use the [PgUp] key or the up arrow key to see the initial entries.
   b. The weights. Note that the table indicates the periods in the moving average and whether or not it is a weighted average (with a YES or NO). For weighted problems, the table includes a labeled line for each weight (W1, W2, etc.). At the label W1, enter the weight for the earliest period—the first period. The weight for the most recent time period is entered last. For instance, if you are using the months January, February, and March, the first period is January (W1); and March is the most recent period (W3). Weights are normalized before any calculations are done—so you may enter decimal values or integer values.

Figure 10.1 shows a sample entry for a weighted moving average problem.

### Output and Solution

The output summary includes:

1. A table showing the actual values, the moving average forecast, and the error (the difference between actual and forecast).

**Figure 10.1**
Sample Moving
Average Entry
(Weighted)

MOVING AVERAGE

NUMBER OF PERIODS TO BE ENTERED ?   5

NUMBER OF PERIODS USED IN THE MOVING AVERAGE ?   2

IS THIS A WEIGHTED AVERAGE PROBLEM ? ( YES /NO)

ENTER THE ACTUAL VALUES:

| NUMBER | 5 |
|--------|---|
| 1 | 14 |
| 2 | 17 |
| 3 | 15 |
| 4 | 21 |
| 5 | 20 |
| PDS/AVG | 2 |
| WEIGHTS | YES |
| W 1 | 1 |
| W 2 | 2 |

Use Arrow keys, [PgUp], [PgDn] to make entries.
[F9] Accepts entries

**Figure 10.2**
Sample Moving
Averages Output

OUTPUT SUMMARY:

| PERIOD | ACTUAL | FORECAST | ERROR |
|--------|--------|----------|-------|
| 1 | 14.00 | | |
| 2 | 17.00 | | |
| 3 | 15.00 | 16.00 | −1.00 |
| 4 | 21.00 | 15.67 | 5.33 |
| 5 | 20.00 | 19.00 | 1.00 |
| 6 | | 20.33 | |

FORECAST FOR PERIOD 6 =   20.33

MEAN ABSOLUTE DEVIATION (MAD) =   2.44

MEAN SQUARED ERROR (MSE) =   10.15

Press any key to continue.

2. The forecast for the next period that identifies the next period number.

3. Mean absolute deviation (between the actual and forecast)—MAD.

4. Mean squared error—MSE.

Figure 10.2 shows the sample output.

Recall that it is possible to return to the problem to make changes in and run the problem again, using the Ending Menu "Modify Data . . ." selection.

### Example 1: Moving Average

Given the following sales figures from the L&T Novelty Shop, use a three-month period to compute a simple moving average, and then forecast sales for the month of December.

| Month | Sales | Month | Sales |
|---|---|---|---|
| January | 85 | July | 82 |
| February | 88 | August | 76 |
| March | 93 | September | 75 |
| April | 87 | October | 83 |
| May | 77 | November | 85 |
| June | 75 | | |

What is the MAD for your forecasts?

Figure 10.3 shows the input and Figure 10.4 shows the output (solution) for this problem. We will want to change this to a weighted average in the next example for comparison, so we will use the "Modify Data" option in the Ending Menu.

MOVING AVERAGE

NUMBER OF PERIODS TO BE ENTERED ? 11

NUMBER OF PERIODS USED IN THE MOVING AVERAGE ? 3

IS THIS A WEIGHTED AVERAGE PROBLEM ? (YES/NO)

(continued)

**Figure 10.3**    Example 1: Simple Moving Average Input

```
     ENTER THE ACTUAL VALUES:


    NUMBER    |   11
       1      |   85
       2      |   88
       3      |   93
       4      |   87
       5      |   77
       6      |   75
       7      |   82
       8      |   76
       9      |   75
      10      |   83
      11      |   85
    PDS/AVG   |    3
    WEIGHTS   |   NO


 Use Arrow keys, [PgUp], [PgDn] to make entries.
 [F9] Accepts entries
```

**Figure 10.3**    (continued)

**Figure 10.4**
Example 1:
Simple Moving
Average Output

```
 OUTPUT SUMMARY:

   PERIOD        ACTUAL       FORECAST          ERROR
   ------        ------       --------        ----------
      1          85.00
      2          88.00
      3          93.00
      4          87.00        88.67            -1.67
      5          77.00        89.33           -12.33
      6          75.00        85.67           -10.67
      7          82.00        79.67             2.33
      8          76.00        78.00            -2.00
      9          75.00        77.67            -2.67
     10          83.00        77.67             5.33
     11          85.00        78.00             7.00
     12                       81.00
```

                                              (continued)

**Figure 10.4**
(continued)

```
FORECAST FOR PERIOD  12  =  81

MEAN ABSOLUTE DEVIATION (MAD) =           5.50

MEAN SQUARED ERROR (MSE) =          45.33

                    Press any key to continue.
```

The forecast for December is identified as 81 and the mean absolute deviation is 5.5. You will have to decide if it is acceptable.

At the Ending Menu, which appears when you press any key as directed, select the "Modify Data" option. We will modify this data in the next example.

### Example 2: Weighted Moving Average

Mr. Jones, manager of the L&T Novelty Shop, was not satisfied with the forecasts made using moving average as shown in the previous example. He decided to try a weighted average to make the forecast more responsive to changes. Using the values from the first example, but using weights of 1, 1, and 3, prepare a new forecast for December.

Figure 10.5 shows the Ending Menu from the previous problem, with the "Modify Data" selection; Figure 10.6 shows the change made in the input data (the NO for weights is changed to YES and the weights are entered). Figure 10.7 shows the output for the problem.

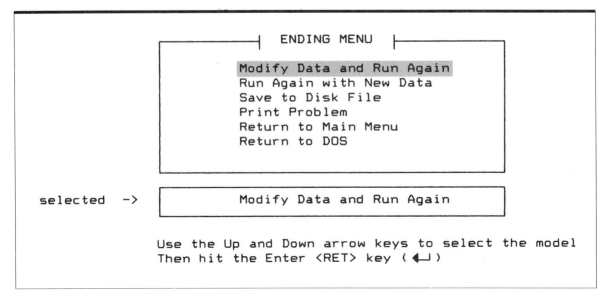

**Figure 10.5**    Example 2: Modify Data Selection from Ending Menu

**Figure 10.6**
Example 2:
Weighted Moving
Average Data
Change

```
         HERE IS WHAT YOU ENTERED:


   NUMBER     │   11

      1       │   85
      2       │   88
      3       │   93
      4       │   87
      5       │   77
      6       │   75
      7       │   82
      8       │   76
      9       │   75
     10       │   83
     11       │   85
   PDS/AVG    │   3
   WEIGHTS    │   YES
    W 1       │   1
    W 2       │   1
    W 3       │   3


 Use Arrow keys, [PgUp], [PgDn] to make entries.
 [F9] Accepts entries
```

**Figure 10.7**
Example 2:
WeightedMoving
Average Output

```
OUTPUT SUMMARY:

   PERIOD        ACTUAL        FORECAST          ERROR
   -------       -------       --------        --------
      1           85.00
      2           88.00
      3           93.00
      4           87.00         90.40           -3.40
      5           77.00         88.40          -11.40
      6           75.00         82.20           -7.20
      7           82.00         77.80            4.20
      8           76.00         79.60           -3.60
      9           75.00         77.00           -2.00
     10           83.00         76.60            6.40
     11           85.00         80.00            5.00
     12                         82.60

                                              (continued)
```

**Figure 10.7**
(continued)

```
FORECAST FOR PERIOD   12  =   82.6

MEAN ABSOLUTE DEVIATION (MAD) =            5.40

MEAN SQUARED ERROR (MSE) =            36.74

                        Press any key to continue.
```

As you can see, the new forecast for December is 82.6 and the MAD is 5.4. This MAD indicates a slightly greater accuracy for the weighted moving average than the simple moving average previously used. The MSE also changed from 45.33 to 36.74. Note that because MSE uses squared values, a few large errors will have a greater impact on MSE than on MAD.

### Seasonal Indices

Seasonal indices may be determined using moving averages, as the following example will demonstrate.

### Example 3: Calculating Seasonal Indices

Given the following data:

|      | Quarter | Sales |
|------|---------|-------|
| 1985 | 1       | 12.5  |
|      | 2       | 12    |
|      | 3       | 11.5  |
|      | 4       | 16    |
| 1986 | 1       | 21.5  |
|      | 2       | 20    |
|      | 3       | 17.5  |
|      | 4       | 24    |

Determine the seasonal index (SI) for each of the four quarters.

Figure 10.8 shows the input of values for this problem. The quarters are numbered sequentially as periods 1–8. We will calculate the moving averages over four periods. Figure 10.9 shows the output from these calculations.

```
NUMBER OF PERIODS TO BE ENTERED ? 8

NUMBER OF PERIODS USED IN THE MOVING AVERAGE ? 4

IS THIS A WEIGHTED AVERAGE PROBLEM ? (YES/NO)

      ENTER THE ACTUAL VALUES:

    _____
    NUMBER   |    8
      1      |   12.5
      2      |   12
      3      |   11.5
      4      |   16
      5      |   21.5
      6      |   20
      7      |   17.5
      8      |   24
    PDS/AVG  |    4
    WEIGHTS  |   NO
    _____


Use Arrow keys, [PgUp], [PgDn] to make entries.
[F9] Accepts entries
```

**Figure 10.8**    Example 3: Seasonal Indices Input

We now have five moving averages for the eight periods (see Figure 10.9, p. 212). The moving average for the first four quarters is shown as the forecast for period 5. Since we are calculating our moving average over an even number of periods, however, this average is really centered between periods (quarters) 2 and 3. Likewise, the second forecast (shown for period 6), is centered between periods 3 and 4. But we need moving averages centered on a particular period for this problem. Therefore, we will run the model again, using the results as inputs and averaging over two periods. This will have the effect of centering the averages on particular periods. Figure 10.10 shows the input and output for this second pass.

**Figure 10.9**
Example 3:
Seasonal Indices
Output

```
OUTPUT SUMMARY:

    PERIOD        ACTUAL       FORECAST           ERROR
    ------        ------       --------        ----------
       1          12.50
       2          12.00
       3          11.50
       4          16.00
       5          21.50         13.00             8.50
       6          20.00         15.25             4.75
       7          17.50         17.25             0.25
       8          24.00         18.75             5.25
       9                        20.75

FORECAST FOR PERIOD   9   =   20.75

MEAN ABSOLUTE DEVIATION (MAD) =            4.69

MEAN SQUARED ERROR (MSE) =            30.61

                     Press any key to continue.
```

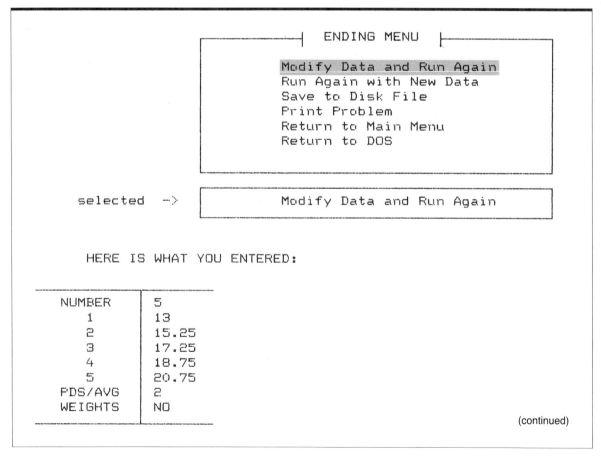

**Figure 10.10**   Example 2: Seasonal Indices Input and Output

```
Use Arrow keys, [PgUp], [PgDn] to make entries.
[F9] Accepts entries




OUTPUT SUMMARY:

    PERIOD         ACTUAL      FORECAST               ERROR
    -------        ------      --------            ----------
       1           13.00
       2           15.25
       3           17.25        14.13               3.13
       4           18.75        16.25               2.50
       5           20.75        18.00               2.75
       6                        19.75

FORECAST FOR PERIOD  6  =  19.75

MEAN ABSOLUTE DEVIATION (MAD) =             2.79

MEAN SQUARED ERROR (MSE) =              7.86

                 Press any key to continue.
```

**Figure 10.10**    (continued)

This output gives us four forecasts. They are interpreted in the following manner: the forecast for period 3 is the moving average centered on quarter 3 (1985); the forecast for period 4 the average for quarter 4 (1985); the forecast for period 5 the average for quarter 1 (1986); and the forecast for period 6 the average for quarter 2 (1986). We can now use these forecasts to determine seasonal indices for the four quarters. The seasonal index for each quarter can be calculated by dividing the actual figure for that quarter by the moving average for the quarter, as shown in the following table.

| Quarter | Actual | Moving Average | Seasonal Index |
|---------|--------|----------------|----------------|
| 3 | 11.5 | 14.13 | 0.81 |
| 4 | 16 | 16.25 | 0.98 |
| 1 | 21.5 | 18.00 | 1.19 |
| 2 | 20 | 19.75 | 1.01 |

Obviously, we would feel more comfortable with these figures if we had more data and consequently, did not have to rely on only one calculation figure.

## 10.4 Exponential Smoothing

Exponential smoothing is a superior weighted moving average technique, using a single smoothing factor that weights recent values more heavily. It eases both the record keeping and computational burden of weighted moving averages. However, it does not respond quickly to trends. This model gives you the opportunity to make an adjustment for trend.

**Data Entry**

With this program, data entry is primarily from tabular input. An initial prompt requires you to describe the size of the problem, that is, the number of periods. Then, you fill in the table provided by the program, entering the actual value for each period used, the forecast for the initial period, and the smoothing factor (alpha). If you are adjusting for trend, you must also enter the smoothing constant for trend (beta) and the trend forecast for period 1 (if one is given).

1. As prompted, enter the number of periods (from 1 to 100).
2. Fill in the table. The table identifies the number of periods (as entered previously). Enter, on the designated line:
   a. The actual value (demand, sales, etc.) for each period.
   b. The forecast for the initial period. If you are not given a beginning forecast, use the actual value used in period 1.
   c. Alpha (0<ALPHA<1). Alpha is the smoothing constant. It must be entered as a decimal value between 0 and 1, such as .3, .5, or .2. The program will not accept a value out of this range. Forecasting accuracy and responsiveness to changes are dependent on the value of this smoothing factor. A low value for alpha gives more weight to older data and a slow response to changes. Conversely, a high alpha value gives more weight to recent data and a faster response to change.
   d. Beta (0<BETA<1). Beta must be entered as a decimal between 0 and 1. Beta is the smoothing constant for trend. If you are not adjusting for trend leave this blank. Like alpha, beta is determined subjectively. There are several ways to make adjustments for trends. Unfortunately, they do not all produce the same answer to a given problem. For this model, we have chosen to add a trend adjustment factor to our exponential smoothing formula. The adjusted forecast is equal to the exponentially smoothed forecast + an exponentially smoothed trend factor (using beta) that has been multiplied by a factor $(1-\beta)/\beta$ to adjust for lag. Again, different authors treat this adjustment differently. Some authors also ignore initial differences. This model does not. Be aware that if the variation you are using differs from the above model, you will have to complete these calculations yourself.
   e. Trend forecast for period 1. If you have a trend forecast given, enter it. If there is none, leave it blank.

Figure 10.11 shows a sample of this input. Note that there is no trend adjustment (beta and the initial trend are left blank).

**Figure 10.11**
Sample
Exponential
Smoothing Entry

EXPONENTIAL SMOOTHING

HOW MANY PERIODS DO YOU HAVE ?   7

ENTER THE ACTUAL VALUES:

| NUMBER | 7 |
|---|---|
| 1 | 67 |
| 2 | 78 |
| 3 | 84 |
| 4 | 75 |
| 5 | 72 |
| 6 | 79 |
| 7 | 91 |
| FCST 1 | 65 |
| ALPHA | .3 |
| BETA | |
| TREND 1 | |

Use Arrow keys, [PgUp], [PgDn] to make entries.
[F9] Accepts entries

**Output and Solution**

The output for this model includes:

1. A table of calculation results showing alpha, actual values for each period, forecasted values and the error, that is, the difference between them.
2. Mean squared error (MSE).
3. Mean absolute deviation.
4. Tracking signal.
5. The forecast for the next period.
6. The opportunity to change alpha and/or beta in the problem you have been solving.
7. A search option which varies alpha and beta automatically in steps of .1 and attempts to minimize MSE.

Figure 10.12 shows the output for the sample, with no change in alpha/beta and without use of the search option.

**Figure 10.12**
Sample
Exponential
Smoothing Output

CALCULATION RESULTS:

ALPHA = .3

| PERIOD | ACTUAL | FORECAST | ERROR |
|--------|--------|----------|-------|
| 1 | 67.00 | 65.00 | 2.000 |
| 2 | 78.00 | 65.60 | 12.400 |
| 3 | 84.00 | 69.32 | 14.680 |
| 4 | 75.00 | 73.72 | 1.276 |
| 5 | 72.00 | 74.11 | −2.107 |
| 6 | 79.00 | 73.47 | 5.525 |
| 7 | 91.00 | 75.13 | 15.868 |
| 8 | | 79.89 | |

| | | |
|--|--|--|
| MSE | = | 94.520 |
| MAD | = | 7.694 |
| TRACKING SIGNAL | = | 6.452 |

FORECAST FOR PERIOD   8   =   79.89

DO YOU WISH TO CHANGE ALPHA AND/OR BETA ? (YES/ NO )

DO YOU WANT TO USE THE SEARCH OPTION TO FIND THE BEST VALUE FOR ALPHA AND/OR BETA ? (YES/ NO )

### Example 4: Exponential Smoothing

Dennco produces a stereo component that has had the following sales records for the past several months:

| Month | Sales |
|-------|-------|
| June | 190 |
| July | 205 |
| August | 200 |
| September | 210 |
| October | 242 |
| November | 234 |

Using a smoothing constant of .3, determine the forecast for December. What is the MSE for your forecast?

Figures 10.13 and 10.14 show the input and the output for this problem.

```
                              ┌─────────────────────────────────────┐
                              │                                     │
                              │     EXPONENTIAL SMOOTHING           │
                              │                                     │
                              └─────────────────────────────────────┘



HOW MANY PERIODS DO YOU HAVE ? 6


     ENTER THE ACTUAL VALUES:


     ─────────────────────────────────
        NUMBER      │      6
          1         │     190
          2         │     205
          3         │     200
          4         │     210
          5         │     242
          6         │     234
        FCST 1      │     190
        ALPHA       │      .3
        BETA        │
        TREND  1    │
     ─────────────────────────────────


Use Arrow keys, [PgUp], [PgDn] to make entries.
[F9] Accepts entries
```

**Figure 10.13**    Example 4: Exponential Smoothing Input

With an alpha of .3, the forecast for December is 219.17 units with a MSE of 439.069. Obviously, they cannot sell parts of a unit. The model does not round to the nearest whole number, but you can.

Example 5 demonstrates the trend adjustment for exponential smoothing. Since we will be using the same data, we will use the "Modify Data" option in the Ending Menu to return to the table to make the necessary change.

```
CALCULATION RESULTS:

ALPHA = .3
  PERIOD      ACTUAL       FORECAST            ERROR
  --------    --------     ---------         ---------

     1        190.00       190.00             0.000
     2        205.00       190.00            15.000
     3        200.00       194.50             5.500
     4        210.00       196.15            13.850
     5        242.00       200.30            41.695
     6        234.00       212.81            21.187
     7                     219.17

        MSE              =              439.069
        MAD              =               16.205
        TRACKING SIGNAL  =                6.000


FORECAST FOR PERIOD   7 =      219.17

DO YOU WISH TO CHANGE ALPHA AND/OR BETA ? (YES/NO)

DO YOU WANT TO USE THE SEARCH OPTION TO FIND THE
BEST VALUE FOR ALPHA AND/OR BETA ? (YES/NO)
```

**Figure 10.14**    Example 4: Exponential Smoothing Output

## Example 5: Exponential Smoothing with Trend Adjustment

After examining the sales records and the forecast for December, Dennco has decided that the forecast is not picking up what looks like an upward trend in sales for this component. Using the sales figures from the previous example and the same alpha, .3, we will do another forecast, this time adjusting for trend by using a beta of .5. When we obtain the solution using these factors, we will answer YES to the question "DO YOU WANT TO USE THE SEARCH OPTION TO FIND THE BEST VALUE FOR ALPHA AND/OR BETA ?"

Figure 10.15 shows the data modification and solution to this problem. Figure 10.16 (p. 220) shows the result of the calculation to determine the "best" alpha and beta. It takes the program a while to do this, since it must calculate all values for 81 different combinations of alpha and beta. Alpha and beta are varied from 0.1 to 0.9 in steps of 0.1.

Adjusting for trend using a beta of .5 gives us a December forecast of 226.24 with a MSE of 341.69. When we search for the "best" alpha and

```
        HERE  IS  WHAT  YOU  ENTERED:


     NUMBER    |  6
       1       |  190
       2       |  205
       3       |  200
       4       |  210
       5       |  242
       6       |  234
     FCST  1   |  190
     ALPHA     |  .3
     BETA      |  .5
     TREND  1  |


Use Arrow keys, [PgUp], [PgDn] to make entries.
[F9] Accepts entries


CALCULATION RESULTS:

ALPHA = .3        BETA =  .5
                                                  ADJUSTED
  PERIOD    ACTUAL    FORECAST       ERROR    TREND  FORECAST    ERROR

     1      190.00    190.00        0.000    0.000   190.00      0.00
     2      205.00    190.00       15.000    0.000   190.00     15.00
     3      200.00    194.50        5.500    2.250   196.75      3.25
     4      210.00    196.15       13.850    1.950   198.10     11.90
     5      242.00    200.30       41.695    3.052   203.36     38.64
     6      234.00    212.81       21.187    7.780   220.59     13.41
     7                219.17                 7.068   226.24

       MSE           =        439.069                   341.690
       MAD           =         16.205                    13.700
       TRACKING SIGNAL =        6.000                     6.000

FORECAST FOR PERIOD   7 =     219.17    ADJUSTED FORECAST =    226.24

DO YOU WISH TO CHANGE ALPHA AND/OR BETA ? (YES/NO)

DO YOU WANT TO USE THE SEARCH OPTION TO FIND THE
BEST VALUE FOR ALPHA AND/OR BETA ? (YES/NO)
```

**Figure 10.15**    Example 5: Exponential Smoothing Data Modification and Output

beta, we get an alpha of .4 and a beta of .1, which gives a forecast of 251.23 with a MSE of 196.935.

## 10.5  Linear Regression

Linear regression is a causal forecasting technique that looks at the relationship between related variables using the independent variable to

```
SEARCH OPTION:


CALCULATION RESULTS:

ALPHA = .4        BETA =  .1
                                                  ADJUSTED
   PERIOD   ACTUAL    FORECAST       ERROR     TREND   FORECAST     ERROR
   ------   ------    --------     ----------  -----   --------   ----------
     1      190.00    190.00         0.000     0.000    190.00       0.00
     2      205.00    190.00        15.000     0.000    190.00      15.00
     3      200.00    196.00         4.000     0.600    201.40      -1.40
     4      210.00    197.60        12.400     0.700    203.90       6.10
     5      242.00    202.56        39.440     1.126    212.69      29.31
     6      234.00    218.34        15.664     2.591    241.65      -7.65
     7                224.60                   2.958    251.23

       MSE              =         365.939                          196.935
       MAD              =          14.417                            9.910
       TRACKING SIGNAL  =           6.000                            4.173

FORECAST FOR PERIOD    7 =     224.60     ADJUSTED FORECAST =      251.23

                 Press any key to continue.
```

**Figure 10.16**    Example 5: Best Alpha and/or Beta Calculation

predict values of the dependent variable (the one we are interested in). Essentially, this relationship is expressed in an equation that is developed to summarize the observed relationship. The independent variable becomes the predictor variable. In simple linear regression, which we are concerned with here, this equation, if plotted, would yield a straight line (of best fit). The objective is to develop an equation for this line which minimizes the sum of squares of the vertical deviations of the plotted points around the line, that is, the difference between the actual observed points and the estimated points on the line. Obviously, the further away the point is from the line, the more serious is the error. This is frequently referred to as least squares regression. The equation, as you know (described in terms of its slope and y intercept), is Y (hat) = a + bX.

### Data Entry

Data entry consists of an initial prompted input defining the size of the problem (number of paired values) and tabular input to enter the actual X and Y values. Be aware that some texts define any relationship involving time as a form of time series. Some acknowledge time series analysis as a special category of least squares regression. Regardless of how it is defined or what it is called, if the problem can be stated as the linear relationship between two variables, it can be solved with this program. You may wish to plot the given values first to see if a linear model is reasonable—do they scatter around a straight line. Data entry requires that you:

1. Enter the number of paired values in the problem, the number of points you will plot on this line (the limit is 100 pairs).

2. Enter the corresponding X and Y values in the table provided: X is the independent variable and Y is the dependent variable. Use the cursor movement keys to move throughout the table. Note that any entry in the table can be changed, including the number of pairs. Do not enter the variable for which you are trying to forecast. You will have the opportunity to make a forecast later in the program. These variables must be entered in pairs. If time is the independent variable, most texts (in an effort to simplify computations) require you to change the year given to values that sum to zero (0). If you wish, you may continue to do so. However, the computer can do the calculations using the time as given faster than you can zero them and without making careless errors, so there is no need for you to zero them (unless you choose to).

Figure 10.17 shows a sample entry for regression analysis.

**Figure 10.17**
Sample
Regression
Analysis Entry

REGRESSION ANALYSIS

NUMBER OF PAIRED VALUES GIVEN ?   6

ENTER THE ACTUAL VALUES:

|        | X  | Y  | VALUES |
|--------|----|----|--------|
| NUMBER | 6  |    |        |
| 1      | 4  | 7  |        |
| 2      | 6  | 6  |        |
| 3      | 9  | 11 |        |
| 4      | 13 | 16 |        |
| 5      | 14 | 15 |        |
| 6      | 17 | 20 |        |

Use Arrow keys, [PgUp], [PgDn] to make entries.
[F9] Accepts entries

**Output and Solution**

Output includes:

1. A summary (in tabular format) of the computations using the X and Y values, i.e., X*Y, X^2 (X-squared), Y^2 (Y-squared) and the

summations of these columns necessary to develop the regression equation.

2. The regression equation.
3. The standard deviation of regression.
4. The correlation coefficient.
5. The opportunity, in response to a prompt, to see the trend line points, that is, the Y (hats). By answering YES, you will see the points, as generated by the regression equation, that will draw the straight line (as compared with the observed values you used to develop the equation). You may in fact wish to plot these points (observed and then generated) on a scatter diagram to compare them.
6. The opportunity to forecast using the equation. To forecast:
   a. Respond YES to the prompt "DO YOU WISH TO FORECAST USING THE EQUATION ?".
   b. As directed, enter the value for X (the independent variable) immediately after the arrow.
   c. To signal to the program that you are finished making forecasts at this time, enter a zero (0) or simply ⟨RET⟩.

Figure 10.18 shows the sample output for the regression analysis. The output may generate long lists. The screen can be frozen using [Ctrl]–[NumLock] as described in Chapter one.

**Figure 10.18**
Sample Linear
Regression
Computations

OUTPUT SUMMARY:

| X | Y | X*Y | X^2 | Y^2 |
|---|---|---|---|---|
| 4.00 | 7.00 | 28.00 | 16.00 | 49.00 |
| 6.00 | 6.00 | 36.00 | 36.00 | 36.00 |
| 9.00 | 11.00 | 99.00 | 81.00 | 121.00 |
| 13.00 | 16.00 | 208.00 | 169.00 | 256.00 |
| 14.00 | 15.00 | 210.00 | 196.00 | 225.00 |
| 17.00 | 20.00 | 340.00 | 289.00 | 400.00 |
| 63.00 | 75.00 | 921.00 | 787.00 | 1,087.00 |

Press any key to continue.

THE REGRESSION EQUATION IS

Y =  1.331  +  1.064 X

STANDARD ERROR OF THE ESTIMATE, S(e):
S(e) =  1.368

(continued)

**Figure 10.18**
(continued)

```
CORRELATION COEFFICIENT, R:
R = .975          (R^2 =   .95 )

DO YOU WISH TO SEE THE TREND LINE POINTS (Y HATS) ? ( YES /NO)

                        X          Y(HAT)
                       ─────────────────────
                       4.00        5.586
                       6.00        7.713
                       9.00       10.904
                      13.00       15.159
                      14.00       16.223
                      17.00       19.414

DO YOU WISH TO FORECAST USING THE EQUATION ? ( YES /NO)

INPUT A VALUE FOR X (TO STOP ENTER A ZERO (0) OR 〈RET〉 ->
? 7.5

   WHEN X =   7.5       Y = 9.309

INPUT A VALUE FOR X (TO STOP ENTER A ZERO (0) OR 〈RET〉 -> ? 10

   WHEN X =   10        Y = 11.968

INPUT A VALUE FOR X (TO STOP ENTER A ZERO (0) OR 〈RET〉 -> ?
```

If you wish to run the problem again with modified data, to correct a mistake, or to do postoptimality analyses, use the "Modify Data" option in the Ending Menu (which has been discussed previously).

## Example 6: Linear Regression

Dennis Donuts has donut shops located in several small suburban villages. The manager of shop number 1 believes his sales of specialty donuts are directly related to the amount of money he spends on promotion in the local weekly newspaper and shopping guides. He has accumulated the following data:

| Advertising | Sales |
| --- | --- |
| 70 | 1,500 |
| 60 | 1,300 |
| 40 | 1,200 |
| 140 | 2,500 |
| 160 | 2,700 |
| 150 | 2,700 |
| 145 | 2,500 |
| 200 | 4,000 |

```
                    ┌─────────────────────────────────────────┐
                    │                                         │
                    │          REGRESSION ANALYSIS            │
                    │                                         │
                    └─────────────────────────────────────────┘


   NUMBER OF PAIRED VALUES GIVEN ? 8


         ENTER THE ACTUAL VALUES:
                  X       Y     VALUES
    -----------------------------------------
         NUMBER  │    8
            1    │   70      1500
            2    │   60      1300
            3    │   40      1200
            4    │  140      2500
            5    │  160      2700
            6    │  150      2700
            7    │  145      2500
            8    │  200      4000
    -----------------------------------------


   Use Arrow keys, [PgUp], [PgDn] to make entries.
   [F9] Accepts entries
```

**Figure 10.19**    Example 6: Linear Regression Input

```
OUTPUT SUMMARY:

       X              Y              X*Y             X^2            Y^2
    --------       ----------      -----------      ----------     -------------
      70.00        1,500.00        105,000.00        4,900.00      2,250,000.00
      60.00        1,300.00         78,000.00        3,600.00      1,690,000.00
      40.00        1,200.00         48,000.00        1,600.00      1,440,000.00
     140.00        2,500.00        350,000.00       19,600.00      6,250,000.00
     160.00        2,700.00        432,000.00       25,600.00      7,290,000.00
     150.00        2,700.00        405,000.00       22,500.00      7,290,000.00
     145.00        2,500.00        362,500.00       21,025.00      6,250,000.00
     200.00        4,000.00        800,000.00       40,000.00     16,000,000.00
    --------       ----------      -----------      ----------     -------------
     965.00       18,400.00      2,580,500.00      138,825.00     48,460,000.00


            Press any key to continue.
```

**Figure 10.20**    Example 6: Linear Regression Output

Develop a regression equation for this data. Determine the coefficient of correlation. Does a relationship exist? If he wants to spend $175 next week, what sales can he expect?

Figure 10.19 shows the input for this example, and Figures 10.20, 10.21, and 10.22 show the various outputs for the example.

**Figure 10.21**
Example 6:
Regression
Equation Output

```
THE REGRESSION EQUATION IS:

    Y  =   357.895   +   16.1 X


STANDARD ERROR OF THE ESTIMATE, S(e):

    S(e)  =   233.729


CORRELATION COEFFICIENT, R:

    R  =   .973            (R^2  =   .947 )
```

```
DO YOU WISH TO SEE THE TREND LINE POINTS (Y HATS) ? (YES/NO)
      X              Y(HAT)
  ----------      ----------
    70.00          1484.920
    60.00          1323.916
    40.00          1001.909
   140.00          2611.944
   160.00          2933.951
   150.00          2772.948
   145.00          2692.446
   200.00          3577.965


DO YOU WISH TO FORECAST USING THE EQUATION ? (YES/NO)


INPUT A VALUE FOR X (TO STOP ENTER A ZERO (0) OR <RET>) -> ? 175

         WHEN X  =   175     Y = 3175.456


INPUT A VALUE FOR X (TO STOP ENTER A ZERO (0) OR <RET>) -> ?
```

**Figure 10.22**    Example 6: Regression Forecast Points

From the output, you can see that the regression equation is:

$$Y = 357.896 + 16.1 \; X$$

The correlation coefficient is:

$$R = .973$$

which indicates that an extremely strong relationship exists. If the manager spends $175, he should expect sales of around $3,175.

## 10.6

**Summary Notes** for the Forecasting Programs

1. Size limits: 100 periods for moving averages and exponential smoothing problems; 20 periods included in the moving average; 100 pairs (of X and Y values) for regression analysis problems.

2. With a weighted moving average, enter the weight for the most recent time period last. Enter weights as decimal values or integer values (weights are normalized before any calculations are done).

3. Alpha and beta (exponential smoothing) are entered as decimal values between 0 and 1.

4. For the initial period forecast (exponential smoothing) use the actual period 1 value if no beginning forecast is given.

5. In regression analysis, X (independent variables) and Y (dependent variables) have to be entered in pairs; do not enter the variable for which you are forecasting.

6. It is not necessary to zero the years if time is the independent variable (regression analysis).

7. Since there may be long lists of output generated by these programs, the data output to the screen will scroll off the screen before you have a chance to examine it fully. Each program has a routine built into it which causes output generation to pause slightly after each 15 lines (approximately). If you want to further examine the data on the screen, press the [Ctrl]–[Num Lock] keys simultaneously to freeze the output on the screen until you press another key.

8. Use the designated cursor movement keys to move up and down the column to make and edit entries. Up and down arrow keys move cursor up and down one line at a time; left and right arrow keys (regression only) move one column left or right; [PgUp] moves cursor to first line in the column; [PgDn] moves cursor to last line of the column. You can modify any entry in the column.

9. Use the [F9] key to accept the entries. You must press this key to continue the program and achieve a solution.

## 10.7

**Problems**

1. Over the past 18 buying periods, Sara's Sewing Shoppe has recorded the following demand for a certain craft kit: 13, 15, 17, 13, 16, 21, 19, 14, 20, 22, 25, 29, 16, 18, 16, 20, 20, 18. Using a three-period moving average, what demand do you forecast for the next period? What is the mean absolute deviation?

2. What is the difference in the forecast if you use a six-period moving average? How does this change the MAD?

3. Sara has decided to try a weighted three-period moving average, using weights of 1, 2, and 3. How will this affect her forecast for period 19? Which method do you think will work best for Sara?

4. The Career Guidance Center wants to forecast the number of individuals who will enroll in their basic career planning workshops during the next fiscal year. Given the figures shown below:

| Year | Enrollment |
|------|-----------|
| 1 | 356 |
| 2 | 400 |
| 3 | 389 |
| 4 | 432 |
| 5 | 467 |
| 6 | 450 |
| 7 | 459 |

compute an exponentially smoothed forecast for year 8, using an alpha = .2. Assume a forecast of 350 for year 1.

5. Using the same data, compute a trend adjusted forecast using alpha = .2 and beta = .1. After you have arrived at a forecast for next year, use the search option to find the best alpha and beta. Assume a beginning trend of 10.

6. From 1977–1984, Leo's Moving and Storage has recorded the following tonnage moved: 4,300, 4,200, 4,500, 5,000, 5,400, 4,900, 5,300, 5,500. Using an alpha of .2, calculate exponentially smoothed forecasts using these values, and forecast the tonnage they can expect to move in 1985. What is the MAD?

7. Using the figures from the previous problem, use trend adjusted exponential smoothing with a beta of .2 and forecast again for 1985. How does this affect the MAD? Which forecast would you recommend?

8. Mr. Mateo has a small suburban appliance store. He has noticed that the large AM/FM stereo cassette radios (boom boxes) have become a large seller. He has recorded the following sales for the past year:

| Month | Sales |
|---|---|
| January | 35 |
| February | 29 |
| March | 39 |
| April | 42 |
| May | 51 |
| June | 56 |
| July | 42 |
| August | 37 |
| September | 41 |
| October | 49 |
| November | 55 |
| December | 64 |

Using trend adjusted exponential smoothing with an alpha of .3 and a beta of .2 forecast sales for next January. Use a guess of 32 for the initial forecast. What is the MAD for this forecast? Do you think Mr. Mateo could get a more accurate forecast using a different alpha and/or beta? Use the search option to find the best forecast.

9. A garden center in western New York state has noticed a relationship between sales of snowblowers and the annual snowfall predicted for the region by the *Farmer's Almanac*. They have accumulated the following data:

| Prediction (inches) | Sales (in 000s) |
|---|---|
| 85 | 5 |
| 125 | 12 |
| 130 | 12 |
| 90 | 8 |
| 75 | 5 |
| 140 | 15 |
| 135 | 13 |
| 100 | 10 |

Do a scatter diagram of these points to see if a visible linear relationship exists. Develop a regression equation for this data. What is the correlation coefficient? If the almanac predicts 145 inches of snow for the coming winter, what can the center expect in sales?

10. Given the following records for sales of convertibles by Joe's Used Cars,

| 1986 Quarter | Number Sold |
|---|---|
| 1 | 3 |
| 2 | 7 |
| 3 | 10 |
| 4 | 5 |

| 1987 Quarter | Number Sold |
|---|---|
| 1 | 7 |
| 2 | 9 |
| 3 | 14 |
| 4 | 7 |

determine the seasonal indices.

11. The local savings and loan has noticed that applications for new home loans increase in the month following the announcement of the amount of Dabco's Employee Bonus. The following data have been recorded:

| Bonus (per 000/yr) | Applications |
| --- | --- |
| 15 | 6 |
| 21 | 9 |
| 19 | 7 |
| 25 | 12 |
| 22 | 11 |
| 18 | 10 |
| 30 | 15 |

Develop a regression equation to show this relationship. What is the standard error of the estimate? Is there a linear relationship? How do you know? Dabco just announced a bonus of $17 per thousand for every year of employment. How many new home loan applications can the savings and loan expect in the next month?

# Chapter 10 Supplement

# Formulas Used in Exponential Smoothing

While most of the formulas used in this book are fairly standard among traditional management science and quantitative methods textbooks, there is some variation in the formulas used to calculate trend adjusted exponentially smoothed forecasts. For this reason, the formulas used by the model are given below.

The exponentially smoothed forecast was determined using the formula

$$F_{t+1} = \alpha A_t + (1 - \alpha)F_t$$

where $F_{t+1}$ = exponentially smoothed forecast for next period
$\alpha$ = weighting factor $(0 =< \alpha <= 1)$
$A_t$ = actual demand for this period
$F_t$ = exponentially smoothed forecast for this period

The trend component of the trend adjusted forecast was determined using the formula

$$T_{t+1} = \beta(F_{t+1} - F_t) + (1 - \beta)T_t$$

where $T_{t+1}$ = exponentially smoothed trend factor for next period
$\beta$ = weighting factor $(0 =< \beta <= 1)$
$T_t$ = exponentially smoothed trend factor for this period

The trend adjusted forecast for next period is then determined by the formula

$$\text{Adj } F_{t+1} = F_{t+1} + ((1 - \beta)/\beta)T_{t+1}$$

# Chapter 11

# Computer Simulation

Simulation is a mathematical technique that provides information about the system under study which will enable a manager to make better decisions. Unlike most of the other models in this book, simulation does not use an optimizing algorithm. It does not attempt to determine an optimal solution to a problem, but rather describes the performance of the system given a set of input parameters. Simulation is used when the system under study is too complex, dynamic, and/or probabilistic in nature to permit the development of an optimization model. While most of the models in this book represent a system mathematically, simulation attempts to imitate the expected behavior of the system. By conducting a number of simulations using the computer, managers can gather information about the behavior of the system. This information can then be used as the basis for making better decisions regarding the system. Simulation also allows decision makers to test alternative decisions and to observe the results without suffering the possible negative consequences that would result from such tests on the actual system.

The accuracy of simulation results are obviously dependent upon how well the model, which imitates the actual system, is constructed, and the model is highly dependent upon the data gathered on the real system. Most simulations are based upon historical data, which provide the range of possible results and the probabilities that those results will occur (often described by one of the common statistical probability distributions, such as Poisson, exponential, or uniform).

Computer simulation has been used in inventory control, production scheduling, queuing, marketing, system maintenance, health-care planning, and public service operations. In general, it can be applied to stochastic situations which are too complex to be described by one of the more common optimizing models.

## 11.1 The Simulation Program

This program gives users the opportunity to perform simple simulations through the use of the Monte Carlo technique. There are three different models in the program: Monte Carlo, an inventory simulator, and a queuing simulator.

The Monte Carlo model allows discrete distributions to be entered in the form of observed values (expected occurrences) and the probabilities associated with each occurrence. It then determines a cumulative probability distribution which is used in conjunction with randomly generated numbers to simulate a number of expected occurrences.

The inventory simulation is a discrete, time independent simulation that allows users to make decisions regarding the reorder quantity and reorder point for an inventory system with stochastic demand. Lead time can be constant or variable. The objective of the simulation is to establish a reorder quantity and reorder point which will reduce the total cost of the inventory system, including carrying cost, ordering cost, and stockout cost. Users may define a discrete demand distribution, use a uniform distribution, or use a distribution built into the program.

The queuing simulation is a discrete, time dependent simulation that illustrates the operation of a service facility with stochastic arrivals and service times. The program generates random interarrival times using a preset distribution. As customers arrive, a second distribution determines the service time required. Balking (customers leaving when the line is too long) may be included as desired. The program has two built-in service distributions: fast and normal. Output is in the form of a minute-by-minute description of the system and summary statistics.

Since example problems in any of these simulation models would be similar to the sample problems given, examples have been omitted.

## 11.2 Data Entry

The first step in the data entry process is the selection of the desired model from the menu shown below. Select the model using the arrow keys to highlight your choice and then press the ⟨RET⟩ key to complete the entry.

Data entry for these models is in the form of prompted input, with the exception of the discrete distribution, which is in a modified tabular form. Entry from a disk file was discussed fully in Chapter one.

If you make a mistake while typing an entry, use the backspace/erase key and retype it. If you discover a mistake after you have completed the entry (pressed ⟨RET⟩), you can make corrections after all input entries have been made. When typing entries into the discrete distribution table,

```
                  ┌────────────┤  SIMULTION MODELS  ├────────────┐
                  │                                              │
                  │    Monte Carlo Simulation                    │
                  │    Inventory Simulation                      │
                  │    Queuing  Simulation                       │
                  │    Problem  from Disk File                   │
                  │                                              │
                  │                                              │
                  └──────────────────────────────────────────────┘


selected   ->     ┌──────────────────────────────────────────────┐
                  │                                              │
                  │                                              │
                  └──────────────────────────────────────────────┘
```

press the ⟨RET⟩, (or [TAB]) key to complete the entry and move to the next position in the table. It is *not* possible to use the left or up arrow keys to return to previous entries. You can make corrections in the "HERE IS WHAT YOU ENTERED" data modification part of the program.

Because the entries for each simulation differ, the required entries are discussed within the section on that simulation. All models have certain entries in common, however. The Monte Carlo simulation requires—and inventory simulation optionally permits—you to enter a discrete distribution table. To do so, you must first enter the number of different occurrences or observed values (the number of rows in the table). You will then be asked, for each occurrence (row), to first enter the observed value and then enter the frequency of occurrence or the probability associated with each value. It is not necessary to convert frequencies to probabilities; the program will do so automatically. Complete each entry with the ⟨RET⟩ or [TAB] key.

The general form of these entries is shown below:

NUMBER OF DIFFERENT OBSERVED VALUES ? 4

ENTER EACH OBSERVED VALUE, PRESS ⟨RET⟩ OR [TAB], & ENTER FREQUENCY OF OCCURRENCE (OR PROBABILITY)

OBS #    VALUE    FREQUENCY

If you make any mistakes entering these values, you can still correct them before running the simulation. The discrete distribution will be displayed in the "HERE IS . . ." format and you will be asked if you want to modify the data.

Additional "HERE IS . . ." displays are used to summarize other simulation inputs, but if you make a mistake in any of your other responses, you will have to go through the prompted sequence again, since many of the inputs are conditional upon other responses.

Each simulation will also require you to answer the following prompts:

HOW MANY PERIODS DO YOU WANT TO SIMULATE ?

REPEATABLE SEQUENCE OF RANDOM NUMBERS ? (YES/NO)

The first prompt requires you to enter the number of periods you want to simulate. The second determines whether you want a repeatable sequence of random numbers, so that each time you run the simulation it begins with the same random number and uses the same sequence. If you choose NO, the simulation uses a random starting point and a nonrepeatable sequence of random numbers. You should note, however, that if you choose a nonrepeatable sequence and then choose to print results from the Ending Menu, the results that are printed will differ from those on the screen because the random numbers will change. If you want the printed output to match the screen output, you must use a repeatable sequence of random numbers.

## 11.3  Monte Carlo Simulation

### Data Entry

As prompted, you are required to make the following entries:

1.  The number of different observed values or expected occurrences. This value determines the number of entries that will be made in the discrete distribution table. The maximum number of values is limited to 30.

2.  The observed value and either the frequency of occurrence or the probability associated with it for each value in the discrete distribution table.

3.  The number of periods you wish to simulate. The maximum number of periods is 1,000; the minimum is 1.

4.  Select either a repeatable or new sequence of random numbers by highlighting YES for a repeatable sequence or NO for a random (new) sequence and pressing the ⟨RET⟩ key.

Figure 11.1 shows sample Monte Carlo entries.

### Output

The program begins by producing a table summarizing the input values and showing the cumulative probability distribution. It then displays a table which shows the random number and simulated value for each pe-

**Figure 11.1**
Sample Monte
Carlo Simulation
Input

NUMBER OF DIFFERENT OBSERVED VALUES ? 4

ENTER EACH OBSERVED VALUE, PRESS ⟨RET⟩ OR [TAB], & ENTER
FREQUENCY OF OCCURRENCE (OR PROBABILITY)

| OBS # | VALUE | FREQUENCY |
|-------|-------|-----------|
| 1 | 1 | 1 |
| 2 | 2 | 1 |
| 3 | 3 | 1 |
| 4 | 4 | 1 |

HOW MANY PERIODS DO YOU WANT TO SIMULATE ? 6

REPEATABLE SEQUENCE OF RANDOM NUMBERS ? (YES/ NO )

**Figure 11.2**
Sample Monte
Carlo Simulation
Output

| OBSERVED VALUE | FREQUENCY | PROBABILITY | CUMULATIVE PROBABILITY |
|----------------|-----------|-------------|------------------------|
| 1 | 1 | 0.250 | 0.250 |
| 2 | 1 | 0.250 | 0.500 |
| 3 | 1 | 0.250 | 0.750 |
| 4 | 1 | 0.250 | 1.000 |

Press any key to continue.

| PERIOD | RANDOM NUMBER | SIMULATED VALUE |
|--------|---------------|-----------------|
| 1 | .931 | 4 |
| 2 | .949 | 4 |
| 3 | .042 | 1 |
| 4 | .511 | 3 |
| 5 | .301 | 2 |
| 6 | .034 | 1 |

SUMMARY:

| SIMULATED VALUE | FREQUENCY | OBSERVED PROBABILITY | EXPECTED PROBABILITY |
|-----------------|-----------|----------------------|----------------------|
| 1 | 1 | 0.333 | 0.250 |
| 2 | 1 | 0.167 | 0.250 |
| 3 | 1 | 0.167 | 0.250 |
| 4 | 1 | 0.333 | 0.250 |

Press any key to continue.

riod. A summary table comparing observed probabilities of occurrence with expected (input) probabilities is then displayed. Output for the sample problem is shown in Figure 11.2.

## 11.4    Inventory Simulation

### Assumptions

The inventory simulation makes the following assumptions. Demand for the period is known (learned) at the beginning of the period. Orders are placed as soon as demand is known. Orders are received at the end of the period. The automatic reorder point does not initiate an order unless the total number of units on hand plus the number of units on order falls below the reorder point. Carrying costs are based upon the average inventory for the period which is calculated as the average of the beginning inventory and the ending inventory. Stockouts are not backordered. Should you choose to use the preset system parameters, the following figures apply:

```
Carrying cost per unit per year      = $ 2.60
Cost of placing an order             =   26.00
Cost of being out of stock per unit  =   16.50
Average use per period (units)       = 250
```

### Data Entry

The inventory simulation has a number of prompts, many of them conditional upon prior responses. Thus, all prompts are discussed in the following list entries. Figure 11.3 shows sample input for an inventory simulation, and Figure 11.4 shows a flow chart that illustrates which prompts will be encountered and in what order.

1. Respond YES or NO to the prompt regarding an automatic reorder quantity and reorder point. Selecting YES allows you to establish a set reorder quantity and reorder point. Whenever the inventory level (on-hand plus on-order) falls below the specified point, an order will be placed for the reorder quantity. Responding NO will result in period-by-period prompts, asking if you want to place an order, and if so, for how many units.

   If you chose the automatic feature (YES), enter the reorder quantity and reorder point you want the computer to use.

2. Enter the system parameters. Select PRESET or USER DEFINED.
   a. If you select USER DEFINED enter, as prompted, the carrying cost per unit per year, the cost of placing an order, and the per

unit stockout cost. Then select DISCRETE or UNIFORM demand distribution.

    **b.** If you select DISCRETE enter, as prompted, the number of occurrences, and the observed value and frequency of occurrence for each observation (identical to the Monte Carlo input).

    **c.** If you select UNIFORM enter, as prompted, the lowest and highest demand value limits. This establishes a range for the uniform distribution.

**3.** Select a CONSTANT or VARIABLE lead time. CONSTANT lead times do not change; orders are received 4 weeks after they are placed. Orders are received at the end of a week, after new orders have been placed. VARIABLE lead times vary between 3 and 5 weeks.

**4.** Enter the number of periods you wish to simulate. The minimum number of periods is 1, the maximum 104 (two years).

**5.** Select either a repeatable or new sequence of random numbers by highlighting YES for a repeatable sequence or NO for a nonrepeatable sequence and pressing the ⟨RET⟩ key.

**Figure 11.3**
Sample Inventory
Simulation Input

AUTOMATIC REORDER QUANTITY AND REORDER POINT ? ( YES /NO)

WHAT REORDER QUANTITY DO YOU WANT TO USE ?　800

WHAT REORDER POINT DO YOU WANT TO USE ? 1300

SYSTEM PARAMETERS:

PRESET OR USER DEFINED DISTRIBUTIONS ?　　( PRESET /USER DEFINED)

CONSTANT OR VARIABLE LEAD TIME ? (CONSTANT/ VARIABLE )

HOW MANY PERIODS DO YOU WANT TO SIMULATE ? 8

REPEATABLE SEQUENCE OF RANDOM NUMBERS ? ( YES /NO)

## Output

Output for the inventory simulation begins with a statement of the system parameters, including costs, average inventory for preset or uniform distribution, and beginning inventory. It then continues with period-by-period simulation results including beginning inventory, weekly demand, ending inventory, units short, orders placed or received. Once the simula-

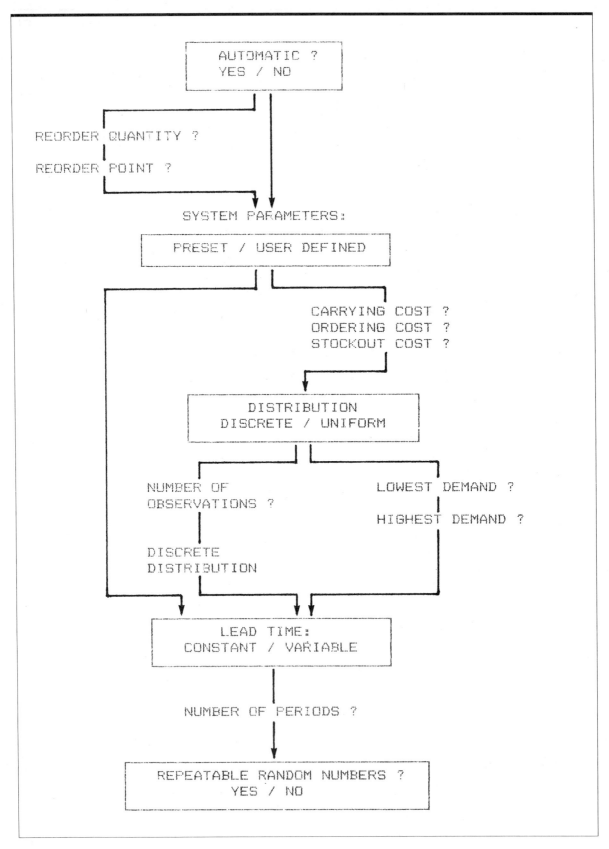

**Figure 11.4**    Flowchart of Inventory Simulation Prompts

tion has been completed, a simulation summary is given. Sample output for this simulation is shown in Figure 11.5.

---

SYSTEM INFORMATION:

CARRYING COST PER UNIT = $ 2.60
COST TO PLACE AN ORDER = $ 26
STOCKOUT COST PER UNIT = $ 16.5
BEGINNING INVENTORY = 1545   UNITS

SIMULATION RESULTS:

| WEEK | BEGINNING INVENTORY | WEEKLY DEMAND | ENDING INVENTORY | UNITS SHORT |
|---|---|---|---|---|
| 1 | 1,545 | 200 | 1,345 | |
| 2 | 1,345 | 250 | 1,095 | |

ORDER PLACED FOR 800 UNITS

| | | | | |
|---|---|---|---|---|
| 3 | 1,095 | 200 | 895 | |
| 4 | 895 | 325 | 570 | |
| 5 | 570 | 175 | 395 | |

ORDER PLACED FOR 800 UNITS

| | | | | |
|---|---|---|---|---|
| 6 | 395 | 325 | 70 | |
| 7 | 70 | 225 | 0 | 155 |

ORDER # 1 RECEIVED AT END OF PERIOD 7—800 UNITS

| | | | | |
|---|---|---|---|---|
| 8 | 800 | 275 | 525 | |

Press any key to continue.

SIMULATION SUMMARY:

NUMBER OF PERIODS =   8   (weeks)
AVERAGE INVENTORY = 725.6   (units)          CARRYING COST = $   290.25
ORDERS          =   2                        ORDERING COST =      52.00
STOCKOUTS       = 155.0   (units)            STOCKOUT COST =   2,557.50
AVERAGE DEMAND  = 246.9   (units)            TOTAL COST    = $ 2,899.75
AVERAGE LEAD TIME =   5   (weeks)

Press any key to continue.

---

**Figure 11.5**    Sample Inventory Simulation Output

The average demand figure is calculated from the simulated demand for each period and may not correspond to the expected average demand.

## 11.5 Queuing Simulation

### Assumptions

The queuing simulation makes the following assumptions. The number of periods simulated represent hours. Times are in minutes. Interarrival times are random with the arrival taking place at the beginning of the minute. Service times are random with the length of service determined when the service begins. Service starts at the beginning of a minute and concludes at the end of the appropriate minute. If balking is allowed, customers leave immediately if the line is too long. If, at the end of the number of simulated periods, a customer is in the process of being serviced, the simulation is extended until the service is completed. Customers in line at the end of the simulation are *not* serviced, however.

### Data Entry

1. Respond YES or NO to the prompt, "IS BALKING ALLOWED ?". YES results in customers leaving if the waiting line is too long. NO allows the line to become very long (theoretically infinite, practically around 8,000).

2. If balking is allowed, enter the maximum line length before balking occurs. If an arriving customer sees a line shorter than this maximum line length, he/she joins the line, otherwise he/she leaves.

3. Select preset or user defined distributions. If you select user defined, you will be prompted to enter two discrete distributions, one for interarrival times and one for service times. If you select preset distributions, you will be asked to select a fast or normal service time distribution. The normal distribution has service times of 2 (35 percent), 4 (50 percent) and 5 (15 percent) minutes, the fast distribution has service times of 1 (35 percent), 2 (30 percent), 3 (20 percent), 4 (10 percent) or 5 (5 percent) minutes.

4. Respond YES or NO to the prompt on initializing the system. Responding NO begins the simulation with no customers in the system. Since it frequently requires a period of time for a simulation to stabilize, summary statistics may be understated when a system in continuous operation is treated as having a discrete starting point. To minimize this effect, responding YES to this prompt simulates

two hours of operation time *before* beginning to display output and record data.

5. Because the computer can simulate results and output them faster than they can be read from the screen, the program inserts a one-second pause between the display of each period. Thus, it takes one real-time minute to display each hour of the simulation. If you are only concerned with the summary figures, respond YES to the prompt to suppress the time delay between figures. Press ⟨RET⟩ to complete the entry.

6. Enter the number of periods (hours) you wish to simulate and press ⟨RET⟩. The maximum number of hours is 8, the minimum 1.

7. Select either a repeatable or new sequence of random numbers by highlighting YES for a repeatable sequence or NO for a nonrepeatable sequence and pressing the ⟨RET⟩ key.

Figure 11.6 shows input for a sample problem.

**Figure 11.6**
Sample Queuing
Simulation Input

IS BALKING ALLOWED ?    ( YES /NO)

MAXIMUM NUMBER WAITING BEFORE BALKING OCCURS ? **4**

SERVICE TIME DISTRIBUTION:   FAST/ NORMAL

DO YOU WANT TO INITIALIZE SYSTEM ?   (YES/ NO )

SUPPRESS TIME DELAY ON SCREEN OUTPUT ? (YES/ NO )

HOW MANY PERIODS DO YOU WANT TO SIMULATE ? **1**

REPEATABLE SEQUENCE OF RANDOM NUMBERS ? ( YES /NO)

**Output**

The output for this simulation gives the minute-by-minute results showing whether an arrival occurred, the interarrival time until the next arrival, the service time (when service begins), the number in line, whether a customer was lost due to balking, and the service status (IDLE if no customers, BUSY if a customer is in the system, and COMPLETED if a service is completed in this minute). Note that even if the status is COMPLETED, the system is still busy if there are any customers in line. Figure 11.7 (p. 242) shows sample output for this simulation.

**Figure 11.7**
Sample Queuing
Simulation Output

SIMULATION RESULTS:

| PERIOD | ARRIVAL? | NEXT IAT | SERVICE TIME | NO. IN LINE | CUSTOMER LOST ? | SYSTEM STATUS |
|--------|----------|----------|--------------|-------------|-----------------|---------------|
| 1 | | | | 0 | | IDLE |
| 2 | YES | 2 | 4 | 0 | | BUSY |
| 3 | | | | 0 | | BUSY |
| 4 | YES | 5 | | 1 | | BUSY |
| 5 | | | | 1 | | COMPLETED |
| 6 | | | 2 | 0 | | BUSY |
| 7 | | | | 0 | | COMPLETED |

.
.

SIMULATION SUMMARY:

| | | TOTAL | HOURLY AVERAGE | PERCENT |
|---|---|-------|----------------|---------|
| TOTAL ARRIVALS | = | 26 | 26.0 | |
| NUMBER SERVED | = | 15 | 15.0 | 57.7% |
| NUMBER BALKING (LOST) | = | 7 | 7.0 | 26.9% |
| NUMBER STILL IN LINE | = | 4 | | 15.4% |

AVERAGE LENGTH OF SERVICE   =   3.7 minutes

AVERAGE TIME SPENT WAITING   =   6.8 minutes

AVERAGE NUMBER IN LINE   =   2.0

AVERAGE INTERARRIVAL TIME   =   2.4 minutes

Press any key to continue.

# 11.6

**Summary
Notes**
for the Simulation
Programs

1. The discrete distribution table is limited to a maximum of 30 observations, that is, 30 observed values and 30 corresponding frequencies of occurrence or probabilities.

2. The Monte Carlo simulation is limited to the simulation of 1,000 periods; the inventory simulation to 104 periods (two years); and the queuing simulation is limited to 8 hours, each hour containing 60 simulated minutes.

3. Selecting a repeatable sequence of random numbers always begins the simulation with the same random number and generates the same sequence of random numbers; responding NO to the prompt causes the computer to generate a different sequence of random numbers each time the simulation is run.

4. When you choose a nonrepeatable sequence of random numbers, and you later choose to send the output to a printer or DOS text file, the results will differ from those displayed on the screen because a new sequence of random numbers is used.

## 11.7

**Problems**

1. The Willard Company has observed the following sales frequencies over the past 30 days:

| Sales | Number of days |
|-------|----------------|
| 150 | 3 |
| 160 | 5 |
| 170 | 7 |
| 180 | 8 |
| 190 | 4 |
| 200 | 3 |

Using the above distribution, simulate sales for the next 30 days.

2. Using the above distribution, simulate six 30 day periods. How does the average sales figure vary from period to period?

3. James Smithson sells insurance policies door to door. Over the past year, he has collected the following data: the probability that somebody is home and is willing to buy a policy is 74 percent. If he sells a policy, the dollar amount sold can be described by the following distribution.

| $ Amount Sold | Probability |
|---------------|-------------|
| $ 10,000 | .10 |
| 20,000 | .15 |
| 30,000 | .25 |
| 40,000 | .30 |
| 50,000 | .10 |
| 60,000 | .10 |

Simulate calls on 100 houses.
   a. At how many of the houses were people home and willing to buy a policy?
   b. What is the dollar amount of insurance sold at the houses found in part (a)?

4. Run the inventory simulation with an automatic reorder quantity of 1,500 and a reorder point of 1,000 with the following user defined inputs:
   a. Carrying cost = 3.50
      Ordering cost = 48
      Stockout cost = 35

  **b.** The following discrete distribution:

| Observation | Frequency |
|:-----------:|:---------:|
| 200 | 10 |
| 250 | 20 |
| 300 | 40 |
| 350 | 20 |
| 400 | 10 |

  **c.** Constant lead time
  **d.** 52 periods
  **e.** Repeatable sequence of random numbers
  Observe the total costs incurred.

5. Run the inventory simulation given in Problem 4, changing the reorder quantity to 2,000 and the reorder point to 1,800. All user defined inputs remain unchanged. How do the total costs differ?

6. Run the inventory simulation given in Problem 4, changing the distribution (part b) from discrete to uniform with a lowest demand of 200 and a highest demand of 400. All other entries remain unchanged. How do the total costs differ? How is the average demand figure affected?

7. Using the figures given in Problem 4, vary the order quantity and reorder point and attempt to minimize total costs.

8. Run the queuing simulation with the following parameters:
  **a.** Balking is not allowed
  **b.** Preset distributions—normal service times
  **c.** No initialized system
  **d.** No time lag
  **e.** 3 hours
  **f.** A repeatable sequence of random numbers
  Observe the results.

  Change part a to allow balking, set a balking limit of 4, and rerun the simulation. How many people are lost due to balking?

9. Rerun Problem 8 with the system initialized and a balking limit of 4. How does this change the results of the simulation?

10. Rerun Problem 9 with balking allowed and a balking limit of 2. How does this change in the balking limit affect the results of the simulation?

11. Rerun Problem 9 with preset distributions and fast service times. How does this change affect the results of the simulation?

# Chapter 12

# Deterministic Inventory

Inventories are a necessary and important factor in the overall efficient functioning of a firm. They often represent a very substantial part of the cost of doing business. Because of this large investment and its importance to the efficient functioning of a firm, it is essential that good inventory management be practiced. This means resolving the dual problem of minimizing inventory costs while maintaining sufficient inventories to meet demand. It requires determining the best ordering pattern (how much to order and when) to minimize annual inventory costs.

Deterministic inventory models, in general, are based upon the assumption that, given deterministic and/or static information about costs and usage, the overall costs associated with inventory can be minimized by making better decisions on how often to order and how many units to order. This basic "how many to order" determination is made in its simplest form by the EOQ model.

The economic order quantity (EOQ) is a mathematical model that determines the order size that minimizes total inventory costs (holding or carrying costs + ordering costs). It is applicable when certain assumptions are met:

1. The entire quantity ordered arrives in the inventory at the same time.

2. Daily demand for the item has a constant or nearly constant rate.

3. Annual demand is known.

4. Shortages are not allowed (the variation of the model allowing this is discussed later).

5. Ordering and holding costs are constant and known.

6. Lead time is either zero (0) or constant and known.

There are a number of variations of this model allowing for different conditions. Each of these has additional assumptions:

1. The production lot size model for finding the economic production run (lot) size. It is used for manufacturing of the intermittent type and assumes a constant supply (production) rate with the production rate being greater than demand or use rate. Ordering cost is now setup cost. (This model is also known as the noninstantaneous receipt model and can be used to determine the order quantity when the units are received from a supplier at a constant rate over time.)

2. The planned shortages (backorder) model assumes that the customer does not cancel an order that cannot be filled, but will wait for the next shipment to arrive. It further assumes that each backordered item incurs a fixed cost when placed on backorder.

3. The EOQ model can also be used to determine whether an offered quantity discount is a viable option. With it you can determine whether the savings offered from volume buying with its resulting lower average ordering costs balance the increased carrying costs.

The EOQ model and its variations will provide:

1. The optimal order quantity which is the size order that minimizes total inventory costs.

2. The annual holding cost, annual ordering costs, and total annual inventory cost.

3. The maximum inventory level.

4. The number of orders per year and cycle time (time between orders).

5. The backorder quantity and cost for the planned shortages model.

6. The order size when a quantity discount is offered.

7. The reorder point (this is not really part of the model but is an essential component of inventory management and is answered in the program).

## 12.1  The Deterministic Inventory Program

The primary goal of this program is to find the order size that minimizes total inventory cost. The program will determine this order quantity and identify the reorder point, thereby answering both the "how much?" and "when?" questions of inventory management. It will calculate total annual inventory cost and its component parts, carrying (holding) and ordering costs. Total inventory cost (TC) = carrying costs + ordering costs + item costs. Since the item cost is a constant in all but the quantity discount version, it will be included only in the total cost figures for that particular version. The program will also determine the number of orders per year and the cycle time. Depending on the variation, it will identify maximum inventory, quantity to order when a quantity discount is offered, or backorder quantity and cost.

This program offers the user a choice of models:

1.  EOQ.

2.  Production lot size.

3.  EOQ with backorders.

4.  Quantity discount.

Very little data preparation is required before using this program. In most cases the program does little more than prompt for inputs and then use those inputs in the equations found in most management science or operations management texts. (The quantity discount model is an exception.) However, it will be necessary for you to identify, depending upon the model chosen, the annual demand in units, ordering or set up costs, carrying costs (either a cost per unit or as percentage of inventory value), production rate, cost of backorders, and prices and minimum quantities for discounts. It is imperative that you keep time, money, and quantity units (dimensions) identical throughout.

## 12.2 Data Entry

The first step in data entry for this program is the selection, from the menu shown here, of the model to be run. Select the model, using the arrow keys to highlight your choice, and then press ⟨RET⟩ to complete the entry.

```
 ┌──┤ DETERMINISTIC INVENTORY MODELS ├──┐
 │                                      │
 │      EOQ                             │
 │      Production Lot Size             │
 │      EOQ with Backorders             │
 │      Quantity Discount               │
 │      Problem from Disk File          │
 │                                      │
 └──────────────────────────────────────┘

selected  ->  ┌──────────────────────────────────────┐
              │                                      │
              └──────────────────────────────────────┘
```

Data entry for these models is from prompted input. This means that you must respond to a series of on-screen questions, which require that you describe the problem. Your responses provide the program with the data necessary to solve the problem. Entry from disk file is an option which has been discussed fully in Chapter one.

If you make a mistake while typing an entry use the backspace/erase key and retype it. If you discover a mistake after you have completed an entry (pressed ⟨RET⟩), you can make corrections after all input entries have been made. As discussed in Chapter one, this is an input summary routine, which allows you to make only one modification at a time, as shown here:

HERE IS WHAT YOU ENTERED:
DO YOU WANT TO MODIFY THE DATA ? ( YES /NO)
WHICH LINE DO YOU WISH TO CHANGE ?

## 12.3 EOQ

### Data Entry

As prompted, you are required to make the following entries (entries must be completed by pressing ⟨RET⟩):

1. The annual demand in units. Note, do not use commas in numbers.

2. The cost of placing an order. Do not use dollar ($) signs.

3. Carrying cost. Entering carrying cost is a two step procedure.
   a. First you describe how carrying cost is expressed in this problem. Carrying cost can be entered either as a dollar/unit value or as percentage of average inventory value (depending upon how it is expressed in the specific problem). You are given a choice. Highlight your choice and press ⟨RET⟩.
   IS THE CARRYING COST EXPRESSED AS:

   $ (Dollar/unit) or % (Percent of inventory value)? ( $ / % )
   b. Next you are prompted to enter carrying cost in the form that corresponds to the way carrying cost is expressed—either as a dollar ($) value or as a percent (%) of average inventory value. This is shown in the next step.
   c. In response to $ you are asked "WHAT IS THE CARRYING COST IN DOLLARS AND CENTS?". Enter carrying cost as a dollar value. No dollar ($) signs. Whole dollar amounts may be entered without a decimal, for example, 6 instead of 6.00.
   d. In response to % you have to answer two questions. First, "WHAT IS THE PRICE PER UNIT OF THE ITEM ?" and then

"CARRYING COST IS WHAT PERCENT OF THE INVENTORY VALUE ?". After the first prompt, enter the unit price of the item. After the second, enter the percent. Enter 10 percent as 10, not .10. Do not use the percent (%) symbol (it is understood).

4. Lead time. Enter the number of days it takes to receive an order after an order has been placed. This information is needed to determine when to reorder. If the problem you are trying to solve is not asking you to find the reorder point and no lead time is given, press ⟨RET⟩ and no reorder point will be determined.

5. Working days in a year. The default value is 365 days. To accept this just press ⟨RET⟩. If the number is different, enter it. If you are not looking for the reorder point, press ⟨RET⟩.

Figure 12.1 shows an example EOQ entry. Note that carrying cost is expressed as a dollar per unit value.

**Figure 12.1**
Sample EOQ
Data Entry

WHAT IS THE ANNUAL DEMAND IN UNITS ?   4500

WHAT IS THE COST OF PLACING AN ORDER ? 25

IS CARRYING COST EXPRESSED AS:

  $ (Dollar/unit) or % (Percent of inventory value)? ( $ / % )

WHAT IS THE CARRYING COST IN DOLLARS AND CENTS?   .70

WHAT IS THE LEAD TIME IN DAYS (IF NONE, HIT ⟨RET⟩) ? 6

HOW MANY WORKING DAYS PER YEAR
     (HIT ⟨RET⟩ FOR 365)   ?   260

**Output and Solution**

The output for this program, shown in Figure 12.2 (p. 250), includes:

1. The EOQ value.
2. Annual costs (carrying cost, ordering cost, total cost, excluding item cost).
3. Reorder point.
4. Number of orders per year.
5. Ordering cycle (cycle length).

**Figure 12.2**
Sample EOQ
Output

THE OPTIMAL EOQ VALUE =   566.95 UNITS

ANNUAL COSTS (EXCLUDING ITEM COSTS):

CARRYING COST  =   $198.43
ORDERING COST  =   $198.43
TOTAL COSTS  =   $396.86

THE REORDER POINT IS   103.85 UNITS

THE NUMBER OF ORDERS PER YEAR IS   7.94

THE CYCLE TIME IS   32.76   DAYS

Press any key to continue.

Values are rounded to the nearest hundredth (costs are rounded to the nearest cent). Since very few people order or use fractions of parts, you will probably have to round the results to whole numbers. Once the problem has been solved, you can use the Ending Menu to modify the data and run the problem again. This is very useful if you wish to do sensitivity analyses, such as comparing results using different costs or demands.

### Example 1: EOQ

Suppose S&R Beverage Company has a fruit drink product that has a constant annual demand of 4,200 cases. A case of this fruit drink costs S&R $3.50. If it costs $25.00 to place an order and inventory carrying costs are charged at 20 percent, what is the economic order quantity and cycle time in days for this product? Given a lead time of 7 days, what is the inventory level at which this product should be reordered?

Figure 12.3 shows the input required for this problem. Note that carrying cost is expressed as a percent of inventory value. Thus, we have to enter both the per unit price of the item and also the percentage of the average inventory value that the carrying cost represents. The input summary shows that we do not wish to make any modifications (a NO response to "DO YOU WANT TO MODIFY THE DATA ?"). Figure 12.4 shows the output/solution to the problem.

For this problem, we are told that the economic order quantity is 547.72 units, which we might round to 548; the cycle time is 47.6 days; and when inventory reaches 80.55 (81) units, it is time to reorder.

```
WHAT IS THE ANNUAL DEMAND IN UNITS ? 4200

WHAT IS THE COST OF PLACING AN ORDER ? 25

IS THE CARRYING COST EXPRESSED AS:

    $ (Dollar/unit) or % (Percent of inventory value) ?  ( $ / % )

WHAT IS THE PRICE PER UNIT OF THE ITEM ? 3.5

CARRYING COST IS WHAT PERCENT OF THE INVENTORY VALUE ? 20

WHAT IS THE LEAD TIME IN DAYS (IF NONE, HIT <RET> ) ? 7

HOW MANY WORKING DAYS PER YEAR
          (HIT <RET> FOR 365) ?


HERE IS WHAT YOU ENTERED:

(1) ANNUAL DEMAND                    4200
(2) COST OF PLACING AN ORDER       $ 25
(3) CARRYING COST                    20 % OF $ 3.5  OR $ .7
(4) NUMBER OF DAYS PER YEAR          365
(5) LEAD TIME IN DAYS                7

DO YOU WANT TO MODIFY THE DATA ? (YES/NO )
```

**Figure 12.3**    Example 1: EOQ Input

**Figure 12.4**
Example 1: EOQ
Output/Solution

```
THE OPTIMAL EOQ VALUE =  547.72  UNITS

ANNUAL COSTS (EXCLUDING ITEM COSTS):

     CARRYING COST =      $191.70
     ORDERING COST =      $191.70
     TOTAL COSTS   =      $383.40

THE REORDER POINT IS  80.55  UNITS

THE NUMBER OF ORDERS PER YEAR IS  7.67


THE CYCLE TIME IS  47.6  DAYS

            Press any key to continue.
```

## 12.4 Production Lot Size

This model, also known as economic lot size, is the production run equivalent to the EOQ. The basic premise of the model is that there is an optimum number of batches or runs that will minimize total annual setup and inventory costs for manufacturing. (It is understood that manufacturing in this case is of the batch or intermittent type.) It is also used for determining order quantities when units are received from a supplier at a constant rate over time instead of all at one time (replacing setup cost with ordering costs). Many of the prompts are the same as for the standard EOQ model.

### Data Entry

As in the basic EOQ model, after selecting the model to be run, you must enter (as prompted) the annual demand, carrying cost, lead time and number of working days in a year. The entries that are unique to the production lot size model are:

1. The cost of setting up a production run (or placing an order). This is essentially the same as the ordering cost entry of the EOQ model. Enter setup cost if this is for a production run or ordering cost if it is for an order received from a supplier at a constant rate over time.

2. The demand or use rate. Average inventory used in this model is figured differently than in the EOQ model. Since the production lot size model assumes simultaneous production and sales, with first a gradual buildup of inventory as goods are produced faster than they are sold, and then a decline in inventory when production ceases but sales continue, you must enter the rate of demand which is needed to determine the average inventory level and thus average carrying costs. You may use demand for any time period, but that time period must be consistent with the time period used for the production rate.

3. Production (or delivery) rate. Enter the rate at which items are produced (or delivered if this is a noninstantaneous receipt problem). Be very sure you have entered production and demand rates in the same unit of time, for instance, daily, monthly, or annually. Production rate must be greater than the demand or use rate.

Figure 12.5 shows a sample entry for this model.

### Output and Solution

The output for this program, shown in Figure 12.6, is self-explanatory. It identifies:

**Figure 12.5**
Sample Production
Lot Size Entry

WHAT IS THE ANNUAL DEMAND IN UNITS ?   16000

WHAT IS THE COST OF SETTING UP A PRODUCTION RUN (OR
   PLACING AN ORDER) ?   70

IS THE CARRYING COST EXPRESSED AS:

   $ (Dollar/unit) or % (Percent of inventory value)? ( $ / % )

WHAT IS THE CARRYING COST IN DOLLARS AND CENTS?   1.25

WHAT IS THE DEMAND OR USE RATE ?   460

WHAT IS THE PRODUCTION (OR DELIVERY) RATE
      (SAME UNIT OF TIME AS USE RATE) ?   1000

WHAT IS THE LEAD TIME IN DAYS (IF NONE, HIT ⟨RET⟩ ) ?   6

HOW MANY WORKING DAYS PER YEAR
      (HIT ⟨RET⟩ FOR 365)?   260

**Figure 12.6**
Sample Production
Lot Size
Output/Solution

THE OPTIMAL LOT SIZE = 1821.68 UNITS

ANNUAL COSTS (EXCLUDING ITEM COSTS):

      CARRYING COST =   $614.82
      SET UP COST    =   $614.82
      TOTAL COSTS    =   $1,229.64

MAXIMUM INVENTORY =   983.71

THE NUMBER OF PRODUCTION RUNS PER YEAR IS   8.78

THE CYCLE TIME IS   29.6   DAYS

THE REORDER POINT IS   369.23   UNITS

Press any key to continue.

1.  Optimal lot size.
2.  Annual costs.
3.  Cycle time.

4. Reorder point.

5. The number of production runs per year.

6. Cycle time.

Costs are rounded to the nearest cent, other figures to the nearest hundredth. Recall that when you have checked the output, and pressed any key to continue, you are in the Ending Menu and can modify the data and run the problem again if you wish to do postoptimality analyses.

### Example 2: Production Lot Size

Shiney Bright, a special tooth powder, is produced on a production line with a weekly capacity of 1,300 cases. The annual demand is estimated at 32,000 cases (640 per week). The demand rate is fairly constant throughout the year. Preparing, cleaning, and setting up the production line costs approximately $140. It costs $4.25 to manufacture each case and the annual inventory carrying cost is 24 percent. It takes one work week (5 days) lead time to schedule and set up a production run, and the company works 260 days per year. What do you recommend as the optimum production lot size? How frequently should we plan a production run? What will be the maximum inventory level?

The input and output/solution for this problem are shown in Figures 12.7 and 12.8. Note that there is no error correction routine shown with this example.

```
WHAT IS THE ANNUAL DEMAND IN UNITS ? 32000

WHAT IS THE COST OF
  SETTING UP A PRODUCTION RUN (OR PLACING AN ORDER) ? 140

IS THE CARRYING COST EXPRESSED AS:

   $ (Dollar/unit) or % (Percent of inventory value) ?   ( $ / % )

WHAT IS THE PRICE PER UNIT OF THE ITEM ? 4.25

CARRYING COST IS WHAT PERCENT OF THE INVENTORY VALUE ? 24

WHAT IS THE DEMAND OR USE RATE ? 640

WHAT IS THE PRODUCTION (OR DELIVERY) RATE
            (SAME UNIT OF TIME AS USE RATE) ? 1300

WHAT IS THE LEAD TIME IN DAYS (IF NONE, HIT <RET> ) ? 5

HOW MANY WORKING DAYS PER YEAR
            (HIT <RET> FOR 365) ? 260
```

**Figure 12.7**    Example 2: Production Lot Size Input

```
THE OPTIMAL LOT SIZE =  4159.62  UNITS

ANNUAL COSTS (EXCLUDING ITEM COSTS):

     CARRYING COST =      $1,077.02
     SET UP COST   =      $1,077.02
     TOTAL COSTS   =      $2,154.04

MAXIMUM INVENTORY =  2111.81

THE NUMBER OF PRODUCTION RUNS PER YEAR IS  7.69


CYCLE TIME IS  33.8  DAYS

THE REORDER POINT IS  615.38  UNITS

              Press any key to continue.
```

**Figure 12.8**    Example 2: Production Lot Size Output/Solution

As you can see, the solution is clearly defined. We are told that the optimum number of cases to produce each run is 4,159.62, which we would probably round to 4,160. We should schedule a run about every 33.8 working days or when the inventory on hand drops to 615.38 cases. Maximum inventory level is 2,111.81 (2,112) cases.

## 12.5  EOQ with Backorders

The backorder model allows for stockouts or planned shortages, recognizing that there are cases when it is desirable to plan for and allow shortages in order to minimize total inventory cost. This usually occurs when carrying costs are very high (often because of a very high unit cost). It is essentially a trade-off in costs.

### Data Entry

Once again, you are prompted to make the necessary entries. Only one entry is unique to this model: the backorder cost. The others—annual demand, ordering cost, carrying cost, lead time, and working days in a year—have been explained in the basic EOQ model. As prompted, enter

1. The backorder cost (including labor, delivery, and goodwill). The backorder cost is a per unit cost. Do not use dollar signs.

**Output and Solution**

The output is presented in the same self-explanatory summary form previously shown. It identifies the EOQ with backorders; annual inventory costs and component parts; the number backordered (number short); maximum inventory; number of orders per year; cycle time; and reorder point (if lead time given).

Figure 12.9 shows a sample entry, and Figure 12.10 shows the output for the backorder model. Note that in this sample, since carrying cost is expressed as a percent of inventory value, it is necessary to give both the percentage and the per unit price. Note also that we gave no lead time and accepted the default of 365 working days.

**Figure 12.9**
Sample EOQ with
Backorders Entry

---

WHAT IS THE ANNUAL DEMAND IN UNITS ?   2400

WHAT IS THE COST OF PLACING AN ORDER ?   22

IS CARRYING COST EXPRESSED AS:

$ (Dollar/unit) or % (Percent of inventory value)? ($ / % )

WHAT IS THE PRICE PER UNIT OF THE ITEM ?   545

CARRYING COST IS WHAT PERCENT OF THE INVENTORY VALUE ?   15

WHAT IS THE LEAD TIME IN DAYS (IF NONE, HIT ⟨RET⟩ )?

HOW MANY WORKING DAYS PER YEAR
    (HIT ⟨RET⟩ FOR 365) ?

WHAT IS THE COST OF BACKORDERS ?   35

---

**Example 3: EOQ with Backorders**

The D&M Hobby and Craft Company has a miniature locomotive for which it allows backorders. Information obtained from the company is as follows:

Annual demand = 2,000 units
Ordering cost = $25/order
Carrying cost = 20% of the average inventory value
Cost of the item = $50 per unit
Backorder cost = $30 per unit per year (based on average shortage level)

**Figure 12.10**
Sample EOQ with
Backorders
Output/Solution

```
THE OPTIMAL EOQ WITH BACKORDERS =    65.64    UNITS

ANNUAL COSTS (EXCLUDING ITEM COSTS):

    CARRYING COST    =   $241.14
    ORDERING COST    =   $804.36
    BACKORDER COST =   $563.23
    TOTAL COSTS      =   $1,608.73

NUMBER BACKORDERED =   45.96

MAXIMUM INVENTORY =   19.68

THE NUMBER OF ORDERS PER YEAR IS   36.56

THE CYCLE TIME IS   9.98   DAYS

Press any key to continue.
```

```
WHAT IS THE ANNUAL DEMAND IN UNITS ? 2000

WHAT IS THE COST OF PLACING AN ORDER ? 25

IS THE CARRYING COST EXPRESSED AS:

   $ (Dollar/unit) or % (Percent of inventory value) ?   ( $ / % )

WHAT IS THE PRICE PER UNIT OF THE ITEM ? 50

CARRYING COST IS WHAT PERCENT OF THE INVENTORY VALUE ? 20

WHAT IS THE LEAD TIME IN DAYS (IF NONE, HIT <RET> ) ?

HOW MANY WORKING DAYS PER YEAR
          (HIT <RET> FOR 365) ?

WHAT IS THE COST OF BACKORDERS ? 30
```

**Figure 12.11**     Example 3: EOQ with Backorders Input

What is the total annual inventory cost for this product? What is the optimal EOQ with backorders? What is the maximum number of units allowed on backorder?

Figure 12.11 shows the input for this problem (no error correction routine shown). Figure 12.12 (p. 258) shows the output/solution.

```
THE OPTIMAL EOQ WITH BACKORDERS =  115.47   UNITS

     CARRYING COST   =      $324.76
     ORDERING COST   =      $433.01
     BACKORDER COST  =      $108.25
     TOTAL COSTS     =      $866.02

NUMBER BACKORDERED =  28.87

MAXIMUM INVENTORY =  86.6

THE NUMBER OF ORDERS PER YEAR IS   17.32


CYCLE TIME IS   21.07   DAYS

            Press any key to continue.
```

**Figure 12.12**    Example 3: EOQ with Backorders Output/Solution

With backorders allowed, the optimal EOQ is 115.47 units and total cost is $866.02.

## 12.6  Quantity Discount Model

Since suppliers often provide a quantity discount as an incentive for large purchases, this model allows you to determine whether the offered discount is really a viable option. In other words, do the savings in unit cost and the lower ordering costs of the offered discount balance the increase in carrying costs? With this model, you can determine the optimal order quantity with consideration given to the quantity discount. When figuring total cost, you will now have to include unit cost.

### Data Entry

Again the model prompts you to make the necessary entries. All but one of these is identical to the entries for Model 1 EOQ—annual demand, ordering cost, carrying cost, lead time, and number of working days/year—which makes sense since it is the EOQ model with additions to help you compare total costs). For the discount model you will also have to enter

1. Quantity discount information. This requires indicating how many prices are being compared (limit of 20 prices total) and the minimum quantity that must be purchased at each price in order to get the discount, as shown here:

   ```
   HOW MANY PRICES ARE THERE ?
   PRICE ( 1 ) = ?        MINIMUM QUANTITY = 0

   PRICE ( 2 ) = ?        MINIMUM QUANTITY ?
   ```

   Enter the total number of prices being compared. If there are different discount prices at different order quantities each one has to be counted. For example, if one price is given for an order of 1,000 units, and another for an order of 1,500 or more you have three prices: the unit price for orders less than the discount quantity and two at discounts. You are limited to a total of 20 prices. At the prompt for price, enter the price and press ⟨RET⟩. Thus, following the prompt, enter the minimum quantity (the quantity which must be purchased in order to qualify for the discount). The original cost or price is entered first, with an assumed minimum quantity of zero (0) that is entered automatically. Moreover, if you had entered a unit price in response to the carrying cost as percent of inventory prompt, the initial price is also entered automatically.

Figure 12.13 shows the sample input for this model.

**Figure 12.13**
Sample Quantity
Discount Entry

```
WHAT IS THE ANNUAL DEMAND IN UNITS ?   750

WHAT IS THE COST OF PLACING AN ORDER ?   15

IS CARRYING COST EXPRESSED AS:

  $ (Dollar/unit) or % (Percent of inventory value)? ( $ / % )

WHAT IS THE CARRYING COST IN DOLLARS AND CENTS ?   2.50

WHAT IS THE LEAD TIME IN DAYS (IF NONE, HIT ⟨RET⟩ )?

HOW MANY WORKING DAYS PER YEAR
      (HIT ⟨RET⟩ FOR 365) ?

HOW MANY PRICES ARE THERE ? 2
PRICE ( 1 ) = ? 10                    MINIMUM QUANTITY = 0
PRICE ( 2 ) = ?  8                    MINIMUM QUANTITY = 125
```

### Output and Solution

For the quantity discount model output includes:

1. A total cost summary for each price available.

2. A recommendation or suggestion to purchase a specific number of units at a given price based on total cost. If a price at a certain quantity is not a realistic purchase—purchasing that quantity would automatically qualify for a lower price—it is so identified with the message "THIS PRICE/QUANTITY NOT FEASIBLE".

3. The number of orders to place per year.

Figure 12.14 shows the sample output for this model.

**Figure 12.14**
Sample Quantity
Discount Output

```
TOTAL COST SUMMARY FOR EACH PRICE AVAILABLE:

CAT   PRICE   QUANT   CARRY   ORDER    ITEM       TOTAL
 1    10.00    95     118.75  118.42   7,500.00   7,737.17
 2     8.00   125     156.25   90.00   6,000.00   6,246.25

PURCHASE 125   UNITS AT A PRICE OF $ 8

THE NUMBER OF ORDERS PER YEAR IS   6

THE CYCLE TIME IS   60.83   DAYS

Press any key to continue
```

### Example 4: Quantity Discount

Given the following information, determine whether or not the quantity discount should be taken:

> Demand is 500 units/year
> Ordering cost is $12/order
> Carrying costs are $2.45/unit
> Price of the item is $12/unit

If the company purchases 100 units at a time, the discount price will be $10.

Figure 12.15 shows the input for this problem. Note that there is no error correction routine shown. Figure 12.16 shows the output summary for this problem. We will go back later to change the discount quantity, so you will see the Ending Menu with the selected option to "Modify Data and Run Again" in Figure 12.17 (p. 262).

```
WHAT IS THE ANNUAL DEMAND IN UNITS ? 500

WHAT IS THE COST OF PLACING AN ORDER ? 12

IS THE CARRYING COST EXPRESSED AS:

   $ (Dollar/unit) or % (Percent of inventory value) ?   ( $ / % )

WHAT IS THE CARRYING COST IN DOLLARS AND CENTS ? 2.45

WHAT IS THE LEAD TIME IN DAYS (IF NONE, HIT <RET> ) ?

HOW MANY WORKING DAYS PER YEAR
            (HIT <RET> FOR 365) ?

HOW MANY PRICES ARE THERE ? 2
PRICE ( 1  ) = ? 12                MINIMUM QUANTITY = 0
PRICE ( 2  ) = ? 10                MINIMUM QUANTITY ? 100
```

**Figure 12.15**     Example 4: Quantity Discount Input

```
TOTAL COST SUMMARY FOR EACH PRICE AVAILABLE:

CAT   COST   QUANT       CARRY         ORDER         ITEM          TOTAL
---   ----   -----       -----         -----         ----          -----
 1    12.00    70         85.75         85.71        6,000.00      6,171.46
 2    10.00   100        122.50         60.00        5,000.00      5,182.50

PURCHASE  100   UNITS AT A PRICE OF $ 10

THE NUMBER OF ORDERS PER YEAR IS   5


THE CYCLE TIME IS   73   DAYS

            Press any key to continue.
```

**Figure 12.16**     Example 4: Quantity Discount Output/Solution

Obviously with a total cost difference of nearly $1,000, the company should choose the quantity discount and purchase 100 units at a time.

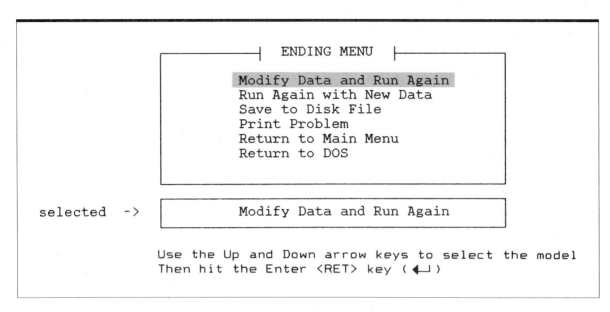

┤ ENDING MENU ├

Modify Data and Run Again
Run Again with New Data
Save to Disk File
Print Problem
Return to Main Menu
Return to DOS

selected -> | Modify Data and Run Again |

Use the Up and Down arrow keys to select the model
Then hit the Enter <RET> key ( ↵ )

**Figure 12.17**    Ending Menu

### Example 5: Quantity Discount

What decision would you recommend the company make if instead of a discount at 100 units, the company is offered a discount for any purchase of 60 units or more? Figure 12.18 shows the change made in the data. Figure 12.19 shows the output/solution using the new data.

Notice that now the $12 price is identified as not realistic (feasible). The EOQ at $12 exceeds the minimum quantity for the discount. Ordering at this EOQ would automatically qualify the firm for the discounted price. Therefore, the firm uses the EOQ for the $10 price (still 70 units because carrying cost per unit is a constant in this problem).

A final note on quantity discounts: when carrying costs are given as a percent of inventory value, total carrying cost will vary with the price. Some textbooks use this approach; others use a carrying cost which is equal to a percentage of the nondiscount price in every case (that is, a constant dollar amount). While the difference in the total carrying cost caused by these different approaches could be small, you should be aware that this model uses the former approach. Each carrying cost is calculated using a percentage of each of the discounted prices. When carrying cost is given as a dollar value, there is no difference in carrying costs or EOQ.

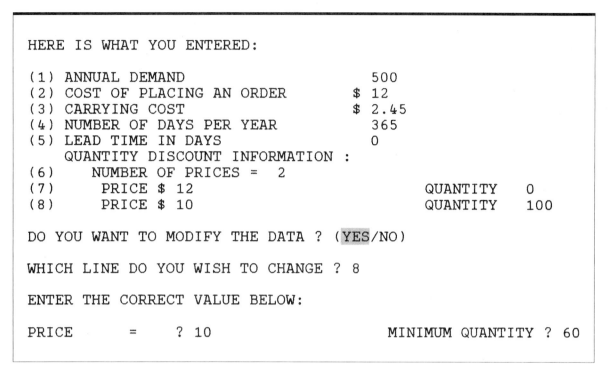

```
HERE IS WHAT YOU ENTERED:

(1) ANNUAL DEMAND                        500
(2) COST OF PLACING AN ORDER        $ 12
(3) CARRYING COST                   $ 2.45
(4) NUMBER OF DAYS PER YEAR           365
(5) LEAD TIME IN DAYS                  0
    QUANTITY DISCOUNT INFORMATION :
(6)    NUMBER OF PRICES =   2
(7)      PRICE $ 12                         QUANTITY   0
(8)      PRICE $ 10                         QUANTITY   100

DO YOU WANT TO MODIFY THE DATA ? (YES/NO)

WHICH LINE DO YOU WISH TO CHANGE ? 8

ENTER THE CORRECT VALUE BELOW:

PRICE      =    ? 10                   MINIMUM QUANTITY ? 60
```

**Figure 12.18**    Example 5: Quantity Discount Data Modification

```
TOTAL COST SUMMARY FOR EACH PRICE AVAILABLE:

CAT   COST   QUANT        CARRY        ORDER        ITEM        TOTAL
---   ----   -----        -----        -----        ----        -----
 1        THIS PRICE/QUANTITY NOT FEASIBLE
 2   10.00     70         85.75        85.71      5,000.00    5,171.46

PURCHASE  70  UNITS AT A PRICE OF $ 10

THE NUMBER OF ORDERS PER YEAR IS  7.14


THE CYCLE TIME IS  51.1  DAYS

          Press any key to continue.
```

**Figure 12.19**    Example 5: Quantity Discount Output/Solution

## 12.7

1. After each prompted entry the ⟨RET⟩ key must be pressed to complete the entry.

2. When entering values, enter numbers only (no commas, $ or % characters). Costs may be entered as whole dollar amounts without a decimal, for example, 10 instead of 10.00.

3. Since carrying cost can be expressed either as a dollar/unit value or as a percentage of inventory value, data entry is in two prompted steps. The first part describes the way the carrying cost is expressed ( $ / % ). The second entry depends upon the method of expression—either

   WHAT IS THE CARRYING COST IN DOLLARS AND CENTS?

   or

   WHAT IS THE PRICE PER UNIT OF THE INVENTORY VALUE?

   followed by

   CARRYING COST IS WHAT PERCENT OF THE INVENTORY VALUE ?

4. Production lot size model. Production and demand rate have to be in the same unit of time, such as daily or weekly. Any time period can be used as long as it is used consistently throughout the problem.

5. EOQ with backorders model. It is not possible to use a zero (0) backorder cost to show no backorder cost. This model can be used only if there is a backorder cost.

6. Quantity discount model. There is a limit of 20 prices (price ranges) that can be compared. This number (prices being compared) includes the unit price for orders less than the discount quantities. This original price/cost is entered first. The minimum quantity of zero (0) is entered automatically. If the program already knows this unit price (entered as part of carrying cost entry), it is also entered automatically by the program as PRICE 1.

## 12.8

1. Great Sounds sells 10,000 walk-around cassette players each year. If each radio costs them $20, carrying costs are $.60 per item and the cost of placing an order is $30 (per order), what is the economic order quantity? Given a lead time of 8 days, what is the reorder point? (Assume Great Sounds is open 7 days a week.) How many times a year should they place an order?

2. Suppose Great Sounds sells an audio component with a constant annual demand of 5,400. Each component costs them $75. If ordering costs are $30 and inventory holding costs are charged at 25 percent of average inventory value, what is the EOQ and the cycle time in days for this component? What is the total inventory cost associated with it?

3. ABC Candy Store purchases 75,000 cartons of candy sticks annually. Each order costs $15 and carrying costs are .25 per carton. What is the optimal order quantity? Determine the annual inventory costs on the candy sticks. There are 260 working days per year and lead time is 7 days. Find the reorder point.

4. Dennco manufactures an item with an annual demand rate of 35,000 units and an annual production rate of 50,000 units. If setup costs are $35 and carrying cost/unit is $2.50, what is the optimal production lot size?

5. Given the following values:

   | | |
   |---|---|
   | Annual demand | = 2,500 units |
   | Setup cost | = $15 |
   | Carrying costs | = $.10/unit/yr. |
   | Daily production rate | = 12 units |
   | Daily demand rate | = 9 units |
   | Lead time | = 5 days |

   determine optimal production lot size, number of production runs per year, and the reorder point.

6. Shiney Bright (Example 2) also produces a toothpaste which has an annual demand of 125,000 cases. The annual production capacity is 175,000 cases. Setup costs are approximately $140. It costs $4.00 to manufacture each case and carrying costs are 24 percent of the average inventory value. It takes one work week (5 days) lead time to schedule and set up a production run and the company works 260 days per year. What do you recommend as the optimum production lot size? What are the total inventory costs associated with this product? What is the maximum inventory level?

7. Given the following information:

   | | |
   |---|---|
   | Annual demand | = 8,800 |
   | Ordering costs | = $45 |
   | Holding costs | = 20% |
   | Item cost | = $95 |
   | Backorder costs | = $50/unit/yr |

   determine
   a. Total annual inventory cost for this product.
   b. Optimal EOQ with backorders.
   c. The number of units backordered.

8. D&B's Garden Center allows backorders on its leaf blowers. The annual demand for the 8 horsepower blower is 150. It costs $12 to place an order, annual carrying cost is $6 per year per unit, and the blower costs D&B's $300. Backordering costs are $15/unit. What is the optimal order quantity with backorders and the total inventory cost? If D&B's did not allow backorders, what order quantity would you recommend? What would total inventory cost be in that case?

9. Given the following information, determine whether or not the quantity discount should be taken:

   Demand is 750 units per year
   Ordering costs are $25 per order
   Carrying costs are $3.60 per unit
   The unit price is $18

   If the company purchases a minimum of 150 units per order, the discount price will be $17.75.

10. Referring to Problem 9, suppose a second discounted price of $17.90 is offered for purchases over 125 units. What difference does this make in your answer?

11. Using the information given in Problem 1 for Great Sounds and its walk-around cassette player, consider these discount offers. If the company purchases bimonthly, it will get a discount price of $19.50. If it purchases quarterly, the price will be $19.40. Determine the optimal order quantity and the total cost.

# Chapter 13

# Probabilistic Inventory

The inventory models presented in the previous chapter assume that demand is always constant and known. Realistically, of course, exact future demand is seldom known or predictable. The inventory models presented in this chapter can be used when demand can be described only in probabilistic terms. The models are still attempting to aid in the "how much" and "when to" order decisions. They may be used in conjunction with the deterministic models. Annual demand can frequently be estimated with some accuracy, and economic order quantity and the number of orders to place per year can be determined using one of the previous models. Therefore, probabilistic inventory models are primarily concerned with determining the inventory level at which to reorder (reorder point) when demand during the lead time is not constant or known. Because demand during this time is not constant, there is a possibility of a stockout occurring when demand during lead time is above average. Consequently, stockout cost, which may or may not be known, becomes an issue. To minimize or avoid these costs, the concept of a safety stock is introduced into probabilistic inventory models. ROP changes from the constant demand $\times$ lead time to demand $\times$ lead time + safety stock. The objective is still to minimize total costs and improve the efficiency of inventory management.

We should note that several probabilistic models and approaches have been developed to help determine when to reorder. Each of these has its own limitations and problems. Not all texts in management science or operations management agree on which models to include, nor even on the usage of the models they agree on. The models selected for this program offer a representative sampling of the choices available.

In general these models are applicable when:

1. The entire quantity ordered arrives in inventory at the same time.

2. Lead time is constant and known.

3. Annual demand is known and average demand per order period can be estimated.

4. Demand during lead time can be described by a probability distribution.

These models will provide one or more of the following:

1. The optimal safety stock that will minimize total costs.

2. The safety stock that will achieve a desired service level.

3. The reorder point that includes the optimal safety stock.

4. The optimum quantity to stock for single-period inventory problems.

5. The service level that will be achieved at a given reorder point.

## 13.1 The Probabilistic Inventory Program

The primary objectives of the various probabilistic models are either to minimize total inventory cost under conditions of uncertainty or to achieve a certain service level. For problems with a discrete demand distribution, the program will determine the optimal safety stock and reorder point that will minimize the sum of stockout cost and safety stock carrying cost. For problems with a continuous demand distribution, the program will either calculate the probability of being out of stock at a given reorder point (the service level achieved with that reorder point) or it will determine the safety stock and the reorder point necessary to achieve a desired service level. For single-period inventory problems, it will identify the stocking level (order quantity) that maximizes expected profits using marginal analysis.

This program offers the user a choice of models:

1. Discrete demand distribution—ROP determination

2. Continuous demand distribution—mean and standard deviation of use known

3. Single period model—marginal analysis

## 13.2 Data Entry

Data entry begins with the selection from the following menu of the probabilistic inventory model to be run.

```
                    ┤ PROBABILISTIC INVENTORY MODELS ├

                        Discrete Demand (ROP)
                        Continuous Demand
                        Single Period - Marginal
                        Problem from Disk File
```

selected  ->  

Use the up and down arrow keys to make a selection. Press ⟨RET⟩ to complete the entry. Note that entry from disk file is always an option and has been discussed fully in Chapter one.

From this point on, as with the deterministic models, data entry is prompted input. Each probabilistic model is unique and is described in the next section.

If you discover a mistake while typing an entry, use the backspace and retype it. If you discover a mistake after you have entered it, you can make corrections (one at a time) after all the input has been completed,

```
HERE IS WHAT YOU ENTERED:
DO YOU WANT TO MODIFY THE DATA ? ( YES/ NO)
WHICH LINE DO YOU WISH TO CHANGE ?
```

as discussed in Chapter one.

## 13.3 Discrete Demand Distribution—ROP Determination

### Data Entry

The data entry prompts are self-explanatory. You are prompted to enter:

1. Mean daily demand. The program is trying to determine the average demand during the reorder period around which the other demands or usages are distributed. Time units must be consistent. However, it is not necessary that they be expressed in days if they are known (given in the problem) in another time frame. If demand *and* lead time are given in weeks or months rather than days, there is no need

to convert to days—just enter the figures given—as long as the time units are consistent. If average demand during lead time is given, you may enter that value as the mean demand per day if you use a lead time of 1. Since lead time demand is the product of mean demand per day and lead time in days, the result will be the same.

2.  Daily lead time. This is the companion question to the mean demand per day. Be consistent; if you used daily demand, enter *daily* lead time in days. Remember, if you used mean demand for the reorder period, then you have to enter a lead time of 1.

3.  The per unit cost of a stockout. Since this model determines the safety stock level that minimizes the sum of the stockout cost and the cost of holding the safety stock, you need to know the per unit stockout being considered. If you do not have this cost (and realistically it is not always available on a per unit basis), you cannot use this model.

4.  Annual per unit carrying cost. Maintaining a buffer inventory (safety stock) is not without cost. This has to be entered as a dollar cost.

5.  Number of orders placed per year. The danger of being out of stock is greatest during the reorder period when inventory is at its lowest point. This will happen each time an order is placed. In figuring total cost, you need to consider the number of times a year this might occur, that is, the number of orders that will be placed per year.

6.  Number of different quantities used during reorder periods. It is necessary to establish a probability distribution for the lead time demand for the various quantities (up to 20) that have been used during the reorder period. It is a two-part entry. First, enter the number of different quantities that have been used (an integer). These quantities have to be entered in *ascending* order. Next, enter the quantities and frequency for each level of usage, pressing ⟨RET⟩ after each entry

QUANTITY        FREQUENCY

Frequency can be recorded as a whole number (for the number of times that quantity was used) or as a probability of occurrence using a decimal representation. However, you must be consistent. Note that if you use a decimal representation of the probability of occurrence, and the decimal values do not add to one (1.0), the program will normalize the frequency distribution and show this to you in an output table. As many as 20 quantities can be entered. The initial entries scroll off the screen as you near the bottom of the screen. In the error correction input summary, each of the quantity/frequency entry lines is numbered to make modification easier to handle. All quantity/frequency entries will appear on one screen (in columns, 12 entries to a column as necessary).

Figure 13.1 shows a sample entry for the discrete demand model.

**Figure 13.1**
Sample Discrete
Demand Entry

DISCRETE DEMAND MODEL

MEAN DEMAND PER DAY ?   36

LEAD TIME (DAYS) ?   5

STOCKOUT COST PER UNIT PER PERIOD ?   30

CARRYING COST PER UNIT PER YEAR ?   4.75

NUMBER OF ORDERS PLACED PER YEAR ?   7

NUMBER OF DIFFERENT QUANTITIES USED DURING REORDER
PERIODS ?   5

| QUANTITY | FREQUENCY |
|---|---|
| 140 | 6 |
| 160 | 6 |
| 180 | 4 |
| 200 | 2 |
| 220 | 2 |

**Output and Solution**

The output for this model is presented in one or two tables:

1. A normalized frequency distribution. If the frequency distribution entered did not sum to 1.00, the output will include the normalized frequency distribution. Note that this output identifies an "AVERAGE DEMAND DURING LEAD TIME." This figure is calculated as mean demand × lead time, *not* from the distribution shown (they should, but may not be, the same). Safety stock values are calculated beginning at this average demand figure.

2. The solution values, which include:
   a. A summary of total costs at various safety stock levels (costs are rounded to the nearest dollar).
   b. Identification of both the optimal amount of safety stock and the optimal reorder point.

Figures 13.2 and 13.3 (p. 272) show sample output.

**Figure 13.2**
Sample
Normalized
Frequency

| QUANTITY | PROBABILITY |
|----------|-------------|
| 140 | 0.300 |
| 160 | 0.300 |
| 180 | 0.200 |
| 200 | 0.100 |
| 220 | 0.100 |

AVERAGE DEMAND DURING LEAD TIME =   180   UNITS

Press any key to continue.

**Figure 13.3**
Sample Optimum
Safety Stock and
Reorder Point
Output

SUMMARY OF TOTAL COSTS AT VARIOUS SAFETY STOCK LEVELS:

| SAFETY STOCK | CARRYING COST | STOCKOUT COST | TOTAL COSTS |
|--------------|---------------|---------------|-------------|
| 0 | $0 | $1260 | $1260 |
| 20 | $95 | $420 | $515 |
| 40 | $190 | $0 | $190 |

OPTIMAL SAFETY STOCK =   40   UNITS

OPTIMAL REORDER POINT =   220   UNITS

Press any key to continue.

## Example 1: ROP Determination with Discrete Demand Distribution

Dennco has determined that its mean daily demand is 12 units. Carrying cost is $4.50 per unit per year and stockout cost is $15 per unit per stockout. Lead time is 7 days. The company places 8 orders a year. After examining their inventory records for the last year, they discovered the following probability distribution for demand during the reorder period:

| Number of Units | Probability |
|-----------------|-------------|
| 70 | 0.3 |
| 80 | 0.3 |
| 90 | 0.2 |
| 100 | 0.1 |
| 110 | 0.1 |

How much safety stock should be kept on hand? What is the optimal reorder point?

Figure 13.4 shows the input (the input summary for the error correction routine is not shown). Figure 13.5 shows the output summary for this problem. Note that there is no need to show a normalized distribution since the probabilities are given in decimal values that add to 1.0.

```
                          DISCRETE DEMAND MODEL


MEAN DEMAND PER DAY ? 12

LEAD TIME (DAYS)? 7

STOCKOUT COST PER UNIT PER PERIOD? 15

CARRYING COST PER UNIT PER YEAR ? 4.5

NUMBER OF ORDERS PLACED PER YEAR ? 8

NUMBER OF DIFFERENT QUANTITIES USED DURING REORDER PERIODS ? 5
        QUANTITY      FREQUENCY
        --------      ---------
           70            .3
           80            .3
           90            .2
          100            .1
          110            .1
```

**Figure 13.4**      Example 1: Discrete Demand Input

```
SUMMARY OF TOTAL COSTS AT VARIOUS SAFETY STOCK LEVELS:

          SAFETY        CARRYING        STOCKOUT        TOTAL
          STOCK           COST            COST          COSTS
          ------        --------        --------        -----
            0             $0             $648           $648
            6             $27            $360           $387
           16             $72            $120           $192
           26             $117            $0            $117

OPTIMAL SAFETY STOCK =  26   UNITS

OPTIMAL REORDER POINT =   110  UNITS

            Press any key to continue.
```

**Figure 13.5**      Example 1: Discrete Demand Output/Solution

As you can see from this output, the solution to the problem is clearly defined. The optimal safety stock to have on hand is 26 units, making the optimal reorder point 110 units.

Another example will demonstrate how to use the model when reorder point or average demand during the reorder period is used instead of daily demand and lead time.

### Example 2: ROP Determination with Discrete Demand Distribution Given Average Demand or Reorder Point

L&T Gifts sells one item with an average demand during lead time of 250. They place 4 orders a year for this item. Stockout costs are $55 per unit and carrying costs are $15. The following quantities and frequencies have been used during the reorder period:

```
                        DISCRETE DEMAND MODEL


MEAN DEMAND PER DAY ? 250

LEAD TIME (DAYS)? 1

STOCKOUT COST PER UNIT PER PERIOD? 55

CARRYING COST PER UNIT PER YEAR ? 15

NUMBER OF ORDERS PLACED PER YEAR ? 4

NUMBER OF DIFFERENT QUANTITIES USED DURING REORDER PERIODS ? 6
         QUANTITY      FREQUENCY
         --------      ---------
            150           12
            200           17
            250           44
            300           17
            350           6
            400           4
```

**Figure 13.6**     Example 2: Discrete Demand Input

| Quantity | Frequency |
|----------|-----------|
| 150 | 12 |
| 200 | 17 |
| 250 | 44 |
| 300 | 17 |
| 350 | 6 |
| 400 | 4 |

Find the optimal safety stock level and the optimal reorder point.

Figure 13.6 shows the input, 13.7a shows the normalized distribution (needed for this problem), and 13.7b shows the solution for this problem.

**Figure 13.7a**
Example 2: Discrete Demand— Normalized Distribution

```
   QUANTITY      PROBABILITY
   --------      -----------
     150           0.120
     200           0.170
     250           0.440
     300           0.170
     350           0.060
     400           0.040


   AVERAGE DEMAND DURING LEAD TIME =   250   UNITS


             Press any key to continue.
```

```
SUMMARY OF TOTAL COSTS AT VARIOUS SAFETY STOCK LEVELS:

        SAFETY       CARRYING      STOCKOUT        TOTAL
        STOCK          COST          COST          COSTS
        ------       --------      --------        -----
          0            $0           $4510          $4510
         50           $750          $1540          $2290
        100          $1500          $440           $1940
        150          $2250          $0             $2250

OPTIMAL SAFETY STOCK =   100   UNITS

OPTIMAL REORDER POINT =   350   UNITS

             Press any key to continue.
```

**Figure 13.7b**    Example 2: Discrete Demand Output/Solution

The optimal safety stock is identified as 100 units and the reorder point is 350 units. You can also see that the cost associated with this level of safety stock is $1,940. Note both the way average demand is handled and how frequency is entered. The average demand is entered under mean demand per day and the lead time is entered as 1. Frequency of use in this case is just that, the number of times this quantity was used.

## 13.4 Continuous Demand Distribution—Mean and Standard Deviation of Use Known

With this model you have a choice of determining either the service level achieved at a certain reorder point (the probability of meeting demand with that particular reorder point), or the optimal safety stock level and reorder point required to achieve a desired service level.

### Data Entry

This program requires that you be aware of what it is you are trying to determine, service level or reorder point and safety stock. As prompted:

1.  Indicate (by menu selection) whether you are trying to determine service level or reorder point and safety stock. Select "SERVICE LEVEL" if you are considering a certain reorder point and want to know the probability of there being no stockouts at that reorder point. Select "REORDER POINT AND SAFETY STOCK" if you want to know what safety stock (SS) and reorder point will ensure a desired service level.

2.  Enter mean demand and standard deviation of demand.

Input is then dependent upon what is being determined:

1.  For service level option, enter the desired reorder point. Figure 13.8 shows a sample entry for the service level option.

2.  For safety stock and reorder point option, enter the service level desired. Most firms can establish a probability of being out of stock that they can live with, that is, they determine the number of stockouts they are willing to live with during a reorder period and define it as the percent of orders/period. Here you are entering not that number (known as stockout risk), which will probably be relatively small, but the stockout risk (percentage) subtracted from 1, that is, the percentage of orders that will not have a stockout (known as the service level). If you are willing to be out of stock 5 percent of the time, enter 95. Do not use the percent sign. Figure 13.9 shows a sample entry for determining ROP and safety stock.

**Figure 13.8**
Sample
Service Level
Determination
Input

```
CONTINUOUS DEMAND MODEL

DO YOU WANT TO DETERMINE:
    SERVICE LEVEL
    REORDER POINT AND SAFETY STOCK
SELECT AN OPTION   ( SERVICE LEVEL /REORDER POINT)

WHAT IS THE MEAN DEMAND DURING THE REORDER PERIOD ?   150

WHAT IS THE STANDARD DEVIATION OF DEMAND ?   7

WHAT REORDER POINT IS BEING CONSIDERED ?   162
```

**Figure 13.9**
Sample ROP and
Safety Stock
Determination
Input

```
CONTINUOUS DEMAND MODEL

DO YOU WANT TO DETERMINE:
    SERVICE LEVEL
    REORDER POINT AND SAFETY STOCK
SELECT AN OPTION   (SERVICE LEVEL/ REORDER POINT )

WHAT IS THE MEAN DEMAND DURING THE REORDER PERIOD ?   65

WHAT IS THE STANDARD DEVIATION OF DEMAND ?   8

WHAT IS THE SERVICE LEVEL DESIRED ?   97.5
```

**Output and Solution**

Output depends upon what is being determined, service level or ROP and safety stock:

1.  Output for service level determination is simply the calculated Z value and the probability as determined from the Standard Normal Table. Figure 13.10 (p. 278) shows a sample output.

2.  Output for ROP and safety stock determination identifies both the safety stock level and the reorder point. Whenever a firm cannot order a part unit, it will be necessary for you to round up to the next whole number to achieve the desired service level (to merely round to the nearest whole number could occasionally result in a slight underachievement of the desired service level). The output sample is shown in Figure 13.11.

**Figure 13.10**
Sample Service
Level Solution

```
THE Z VALUE IS =  1.714

CALCULATING—PLEASE WAIT

THE SERVICE LEVEL   = 95.7   %

Press any key to continue
```

**Figure 13.11**
Sample Reorder
Point and Safety
Stock Solution

```
THE SAFETY STOCK IS 15.68    UNITS
THE REORDER POINT IS 80.68 UNITS

Press any key to continue
```

As usual, it is possible to change the data and run the problem again, using the Ending Menu.

### Example 3:  Continuous Demand Distribution Determining Service Level

In the previous chapter, we determined that S&R Beverage Company has a ROP of 81 cases. If we now assume that demand during lead time is not constant, that 81 is the average usage during lead time, and that analysis of inventory records shows a standard deviation of 8, determine the probability of being out of stock if S&R decides to use a ROP of 89 cases.

Figure 13.12 shows the input for this problem (not including the error

```
CONTINUOUS DEMAND MODEL

DO YOU WANT TO DETERMINE:
    SERVICE LEVEL
    REORDER POINT WITH SAFETY STOCK
SELECT AN OPTION    (SERVICE LEVEL/REORDER POINT)

WHAT IS THE MEAN DEMAND DURING THE REORDER PERIOD ? 81

WHAT IS THE STANDARD DEVIATION OF DEMAND ? 8

WHAT REORDER POINT IS BEING CONSIDERED ? 89
```

**Figure 13.12**     Example 3: Service Level Input

correction input summary). Figure 13.13 shows the output/solution to this problem. Since we will use the same data (with a slight modification) in the next example, we have included the Ending Menu with the "Modify Data and Run Again" option selected.

As you can see, with a reorder point of 89 cases, S&R achieves a service level of 84.1 percent. That means that 15.9 percent of the time, they will have a stockout during the reorder period. Note the Ending Menu selection.

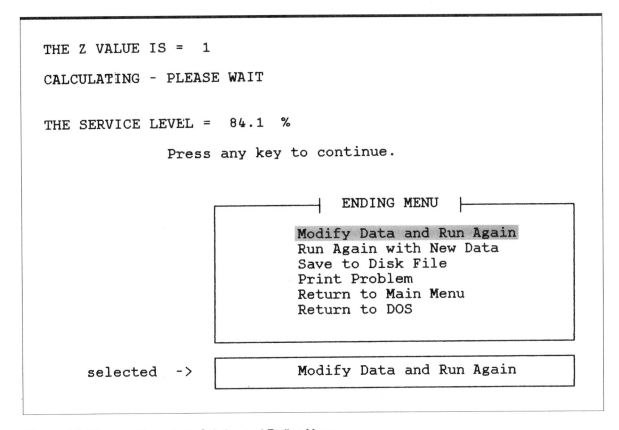

```
THE Z VALUE IS =  1

CALCULATING - PLEASE WAIT


THE SERVICE LEVEL =  84.1  %

          Press any key to continue.

                        ┤ ENDING MENU ├
                    ┌──────────────────────────────┐
                    │  Modify Data and Run Again     │
                    │  Run Again with New Data       │
                    │  Save to Disk File             │
                    │  Print Problem                 │
                    │  Return to Main Menu           │
                    │  Return to DOS                 │
                    └──────────────────────────────┘

   selected  ->     ┌──────────────────────────────┐
                    │    Modify Data and Run Again   │
                    └──────────────────────────────┘
```

**Figure 13.13**      Example 3: Solution and Ending Menu

### Example 4: Continuous Demand Distribution Determining Safety Stock Level

Supposing S&R decides that this probability of a stockout is too great. They would like a service level of 97 percent. Using the mean and standard deviation given previously, find the optimal safety stock level and reorder point.

Figure 13.14 (p. 280) shows the change being made in the data (we are now seeking to determine ROP and safety stock), and the new output/solution.

**Figure 13.14**
Example 4:
Determining ROP
and Safety Stock
Changing the Data
and the New
Solution

```
HERE IS WHAT YOU ENTERED:

   (1)   FIND SERVICE LEVEL
   (2)   MEAN DEMAND        =   81
   (3)   STANDARD DEVIATION  =   8
   (4)   DESIRED REORDER POINT =   89

DO YOU WISH TO MODIFY THE DATA ?   (YES/NO)

WHICH LINE DO YOU WISH TO CHANGE ? 1

WHAT IS THE SERVICE LEVEL DESIRED ? 97


CALCULATING - PLEASE WAIT


THE SAFETY STOCK IS   15.04   UNITS

THE REORDER POINT IS   96.04   UNITS

               Press any key to continue.
```

As you can see from the output, S&R would achieve its desired service
level with a 15.04 (rounded up to 16) unit safety stock. The resulting reorder point is 96.04 cases.

One more example of this model will clear up any misunderstanding
of the use of a desired service level to determine the best safety stock to
have on hand.

### Example 5: Continuous Demand Distribution—Determining Safety Stock Level

Glenco carries an inventory item whose demand during lead time is not
constant, but is normally distributed. If the mean demand is 450 and the
standard deviation is 10, find the level of safety stock that should be maintained so that stockouts occur only 5 percent of the time. What reorder
point does this require?

Figures 13.15 and 13.16 show the input and output for this problem.
Notice that the problem states a policy resulting in stockouts only 5 percent of the time. We enter this as a service level of 95. No error correction
summary is shown this time.

```
CONTINUOUS DEMAND MODEL

DO YOU WANT TO DETERMINE:
    SERVICE LEVEL
    REORDER POINT WITH SAFETY STOCK
SELECT AN OPTION    (SERVICE LEVEL/REORDER POINT)

WHAT IS THE MEAN DEMAND DURING THE REORDER PERIOD ? 450

WHAT IS THE STANDARD DEVIATION OF DEMAND ? 10

WHAT IS THE SERVICE LEVEL DESIRED ? 95
```

**Figure 13.15**    Example 5: Determining ROP/Safety Stock Input

**Figure 13.16**
Example 5:
Determining
ROP/Safety
Stock Solution

```
CALCULATING - PLEASE WAIT


THE SAFETY STOCK IS  16.5  UNITS

THE REORDER POINT IS  466.5  UNITS

              Press any key to continue.
```

As you can see the safety stock is 16.5 units and the reorder point is 466.5 units. As explained earlier, you may wish to round up to the next whole number to achieve the desired service level.

## 13.5 Single Period Model—Marginal Analysis

This model will identify the stocking level, that is, the order quantity, that maximizes expected profits by using marginal analysis. It will also determine expected profit at the identified stocking level. Normally, this model will be used to handle seasonal or perishable items with a limited useful life that cannot be carried in inventory and sold in future periods, such as newspapers or fresh flowers. Usually one order is placed for the product, but exact demand is not known. The objective of the model is to identify the stocking level that will minimize long run excess (original cost per unit − salvage value per unit) and shortage costs (unrealized profit per unit), thus maximizing profit. The model is looking at the probability of selling at least one additional unit (the marginal unit). It is comparing the marginal profit made if the unit is sold, with the marginal loss incurred when the unit is not sold.

### Data Entry

You are prompted to enter:

1. Marginal profit on the item—selling price − cost on each item sold.
2. Marginal loss on unsold items. This is cost − salvage value on each item not sold.
3. The number of different sales levels and their frequency of occurrence. This is a two-part response. Enter the number of sales levels (up to 20) that have been observed or recorded. Then, as prompted, enter the recorded sales levels and the number of times each occurred or the probability that each would occur (pressing ⟨RET⟩ after each entry to complete it). Demand figures must be entered in ascending order.

DEMAND   FREQUENCY

Figure 13.17 shows a sample input for this model.

**Figure 13.17**
Sample Single
Period Input

```
SINGLE PERIOD MODEL

WHAT IS THE MARGINAL PROFIT ON THIS ITEM (PRICE − COST) ?   17

WHAT IS THE MARGINAL LOSS ON UNSOLD ITEMS (COST − SALVAGE
VALUE) ?   11

HOW MANY DIFFERENT DEMAND LEVELS ARE THERE ?   4
                        DEMAND      FREQUENCY
                          12           .2
                          15           .3
                          18           .3
                          21           .2
```

### Output and Solution

As shown in the sample output in Figure 13.18, output for the single period model identifies the optimum quantity to stock and the expected profit at the stocking level.

**Figure 13.18**
Sample Single
Period
Output/Solution

THE OPTIMUM QUANTITY TO STOCK IS    18    UNITS

EXPECTED PROFIT AT THIS STOCKING LEVEL = $ 247.20

Press any key to continue.

**Example 6: Single Period**

A particular item in Dennco's inventory sells for $8. This item costs $4, and unsold items can be returned to the supplier, who will refund the cost less a handling charge of $2 per item. Dennco has recorded the following demand levels.

| Demand | Frequency |
|--------|-----------|
| 6 | 3 |
| 8 | 4 |
| 9 | 2 |
| 10 | 1 |

What is the optimal stocking level for this item? Figure 13.19 shows the input for this problem and Figure 13.20 (p. 284) shows the output.

```
SINGLE PERIOD MODEL


WHAT IS THE MARGINAL PROFIT ON THIS ITEM (PRICE - COST) ? 4

WHAT IS THE MARGINAL LOSS ON UNSOLD ITEMS (COST - SALVAGE VALUE) ? 2

HOW MANY DIFFERENT DEMAND LEVELS ARE THERE ? 4
          DEMAND          FREQUENCY
          ------          ---------
            6                3
            8                4
            9                2
           10                1
```

**Figure 13.19**     Example 6: Single Period Input

As you can see, the optimal stocking level is 8 units and the expected profit (contribution) at this level is $28.40.

```
THE OPTIMUM QUANTITY TO STOCK IS   8   UNITS

EXPECTED PROFIT AT THIS STOCKING LEVEL =          $28.40

                   Press any key to continue.
```

**Figure 13.20**     Example 6: Single Period Solution

## 13.6

**Summary Notes** for the Probabilistic Inventory Programs

1. After each prompted entry the ⟨RET⟩ key has to be pressed to complete the entry.

2. When entering values, enter numbers only (no commas, $ or % characters). You may enter costs as whole dollar amounts without a decimal, for example, 10 instead of 10.00.

3. Discrete demand model: The time frame used for demand and lead time must be consistent (it is not necessary that daily figures be used). Use a lead time of 1 for average demand during lead time.

4. Discrete demand model: You can enter frequency as either a whole number or as a probability of occurrence (decimal), but must be consistent throughout the problem. Probabilities do not have to add to one (1.00). The program will normalize.

5. Discrete demand model and single period model: Quantities and demand levels (which must be listed when prompted) are limited to *20* entries, and must be entered in *ascending* order.

6. Continuous demand model—ROP/safety stock option: The service level desired is for the particular reorder period. The service level that you enter is the stockout risk (the percentage of orders per period) subtracted from 1. This is the percentage of orders that will not have a stockout, for instance, if you are willing to be out of stock 10 percent of the time (a stockout risk of 10 percent), enter 90.

## 13.7

**Problems**

1. Given the following information

| | |
|---|---|
| Mean daily demand | = 14 units |
| Lead time | = 7 units |
| Carrying cost | = $5/unit/yr. |
| Stockout cost | = $25/unit/stockout |
| Optimal no. orders/yr. | = 6 |

and this probability distribution for demand during the reorder period,

| Number of Units | Probability |
|:---:|:---:|
| 81 | .1 |
| 91 | .2 |
| 98 | .4 |
| 105 | .2 |
| 115 | .1 |

determine the safety stock level to keep on hand and the optimal reorder point.

2. L&T Gifts sells a gift item with an average demand during lead time of 400. They place 6 orders per year for this item. Stockout costs are $65 per unit and carrying costs are $14 per unit. The following quantities and frequencies have been used during the reorder period:

| Quantity | Frequency |
|:---:|:---:|
| 380 | 15 |
| 390 | 26 |
| 400 | 40 |
| 420 | 10 |
| 440 | 9 |

Find the optimal safety stock and ROP. What costs are associated with this ROP level?

3. If L&T Gifts (Problem 2) discovers that they made a mistake and carrying costs are really $38, does this change the safety stock level? What is the new cost associated with this safety stock?

4. Rochester Supply Company carries an inventory item with a lead time average demand of 100 units and a standard deviation of 20 units. Inventory records show that demand during lead time is normally distributed. If RSC decides to use an ROP of 110 units, what is the probability of a stockout on that item?

5. What amount of safety stock should be maintained by RSC in Problem 4, if they want to maintain a service level of 96 percent?

6. Dennco carries an item with an annual demand of approximately 1,500 units. Carrying costs are $12/unit and ordering costs are $36. Demand during lead time shows some variability, but analysis shows an average demand of 50 units with a standard deviation of 10 units. What are the reorder point and safety stock level if the firm desires a 2 percent probability of a stockout on any given order cycle? If a manager sets the ROP at 68 units, what is the probability of a stockout on any given order cycle? If this ROP is used, how many times would you expect to stockout during the year?

7. Matt's Music Store carries a guitar with an annual demand of 600, a recommended economic order quantity of 75, and a normal lead time demand distribution with an average demand of 36 and standard deviation of 7.5.
   a. What is the ROP if the firm is willing to tolerate 2 stockouts per year?
   b. What is the ROP if they decide they can tolerate only a 1 percent probability of a stockout?
   c. If carrying costs are $15 per unit per year, what are the safety stock levels and annual safety stock costs for the ROPs found in a and b?

8. A local theater arts group is planning to build a new theater. Based on attendance records at the current location, attendance averages 500 per performance with a standard deviation of 20. If they wish to accommodate ticket sales at a 97 percent service level, what seating capacity should they build into the new theater?

9. Peter's Farm Market sells homemade apple pies for $3.50. The pies cost $1.50 to make, and any unsold pies are sold to a local supermarket chain as day-old items at $1.25. Peter's has recorded the following demand levels.

| Pies Sold | Number of Days |
|-----------|----------------|
| 7         | 20             |
| 8         | 30             |
| 10        | 40             |
| 12        | 10             |

What is the optimal stocking level for apple pies?

10. Peter's also sells apple cider in the fall and early winter. The cider is pressed on premises once a week, with no preservatives added. Once the cider starts to go bad it cannot be sold. The cider sells for $2.25 per gallon and costs $.75 per gallon to make. At the end of the week, unsold cider is disposed of. Peter's recorded the following sales figures from the previous year:

| Gallons Sold | Weeks |
|--------------|-------|
| 300          | 3     |
| 350          | 5     |
| 400          | 6     |
| 450          | 2     |

What is the optimal stocking level for this item?

Chapter **14**

# Decision Theory

**D**ecision theory, or decision analysis, offers a rational approach for identifying the best alternative from among several possibilities, given an uncertain future. It provides a logical process for making decisions. For the manager, decision-making involves situations in which several choices exist, and he or she must select the one that will optimize some objective (as we have seen in all the preceding chapters). Most of these decisions must be made with less than complete or perfect information, that is, under conditions of uncertainty. Under such situations, decision theory methodology can be used to determine the optimal strategy.

To use this logical, step-by-step process the user must first: identify all of the alternatives (decisions) to be considered; identify the possible future events, that is, the states of nature for the problem, including everything that might happen, but defined in such a way that all events are mutually exclusive; and determine the conditional payoff associated with each combination of decision alternative and state of nature. Once this has been done, the procedures in decision analysis can be used to solve any problems that have a limited number of alternatives and a finite number of possible future occurrences or states of nature.

## 14.1 The Decision Theory Program

The objective of the various models in this program is to select the best decision from among the alternatives, given an uncertain future. Decision-making situations are categorized (in decision theory and by this program) by the decision environments. They are dependent upon the degree of certainty the decision maker has about future events and by the amount of knowledge the user has concerning the states of nature.

The models in this program solve problems in situations of uncertainty in which probabilities cannot be assigned to future occurrences and in situations where probabilities can be assigned (sometimes referred to as a condition of risk). When probabilities cannot be assigned, the program offers the user a choice of maximin, maximax, minimax regret, and equal likelihood as decision criteria, realizing that different criteria can lead to different recommendations. Each of these will identify the optimal alternative. Where probabilities can be assigned, the program uses expected value as the decision criterion. This model also provides the user with the expected opportunity loss and thus, the expected value of perfect information (EVPI). In addition, the program gives the user the option of using a Bayesian procedure to develop posterior probabilities from those probabilities previously assigned. It also determines an optimal decision strategy for the problem, provides the expected value of sample information (EVSI), and measures the efficiency of sample information.

All of the decision-making criteria used by this program are based on monetary value—on the potential payoffs of the decision alternatives. Of course, there are certain decision-making situations in which decisions are not based on payoff but on some more subjective criterion (often called utility). Although an attempt is sometimes made to assign a value (measured in something called utiles) to utility, it is an extremely subjective measure that is difficult to assess. While it is possible for you to assign a utility value and use these models to select a decision based on expected utility instead of monetary value, we are not attempting to measure utility, make decisions based on utility or, in any way, discuss utility theory.

Before entering the data for this program, it is a good idea to analyze the decision situation. Dependent upon the nature of the decision to be made, you might want to set up a decision tree, payoff table, or decision matrix. These tools offer useful techniques for analyzing the specific decision situation and provide both an illustration of the decision-making process and a means of visualizing the problem. They certainly make it easier to enter the data in an error-free manner.

## 14.2 Data Entry

Data entry begins with the selection of the model you wish to run. The decision theory models from which you can select are shown in menu form here:

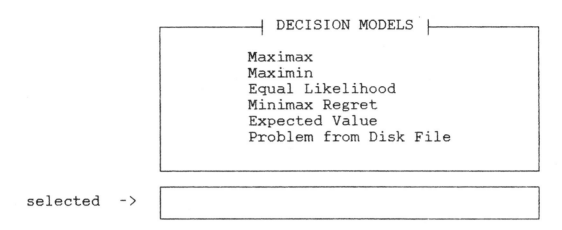

```
                 ─┤ DECISION MODELS ├──────────

                    Maximax
                    Maximin
                    Equal Likelihood
                    Minimax Regret
                    Expected Value
                    Problem from Disk File


selected   ->
```

Note that there are two distinct kinds of decision models included in these choices. Maximax, maximin, equal likelihood, and minimax regret are used to solve problems in which probabilities cannot be assigned to future occurrences. Expected value (and expected value with Bayes posterior probabilities, which can also be solved with this model) are used to solve problems in which probabilities can be assigned. It is important to understand the difference and recognize when to use each one. Data entry is from prompted input to describe the matrix (number of decisions and states of nature) and from a tabular fill-in-the-decision-matrix input (conditional outcomes, probabilities of occurrence, etc.). While the data entry technique is the same for both types of models, for clarity, we will present each type separately in detail.

Error correction is in tabular format. Every entry in the decision matrix can be modified, using the designated cursor movement keys to move through the table in order to retype an entry, and various function keys to change the type of problem and the size of the matrix. The designated keys are defined on screen. For review of this procedure check Chapter one.

Once again, because we attempt to have the output appear similar to the way it is displayed in your textbook, we have to limit the size of the decision matrix because of screen width. You are therefore limited to a problem with 20 alternatives and 20 states of nature (although matrices with more than 10 columns require more than one screen width for display). Moreover, each cell in the matrix can display only a seven-digit number (scaling, scientific notation, etc. are discussed in Chapter one).

## 14.3 Models with No Probability Assigned
Maximax, Maximin, Equal Likelihood, Minimax Regret

Since the criterion selected for making the decision determines which alternative will be chosen as optimal, it is very important to select the most appropriate criterion or criteria. These criteria reflect different decision-making philosophies (or the degree of optimism the decision maker has about the future). Different criteria will more than likely lead to different recommendations. While these decision criteria seek to maximize the expected measure of benefit, usually a monetary value like profit, these models can also be used for a minimization objective.

### Data Entry

For each of these models you must first describe the matrix and then fill it in.

As prompted:

1.  Enter the number of decisions (alternatives) in the problem (limit 20).

2.  Enter the states of nature (possible outcomes or future events) in the problem (limit 20).

3.  Enter the conditional outcomes (payoffs or costs) in the cells in the matrix, which has been set up from the first two entries. You have described the matrix as so many rows (decisions—D1, D2, etc.) by so many columns (states of nature—S1, S2, etc.). Cell values are limited to seven-digit numbers. Note that if you are solving a minimization problem, enter the negative of the value, that is, multiply all outcomes (costs) by −1. Use the cursor movement keys as designated on screen to move through the table and then type your entries in the proper cells.

Figure 14.1 shows a sample entry for a maximax problem with 4 decision alternatives and 3 possible outcomes.

### Output and Solution

The output for these four models includes:

1.  The decision matrix, with a results column added. Note that with minimax regret this table is called a regret table. The optimal decision is indicated with an asterisk (*).

2.  The optimal decision for the given criterion.

3.  The optimal value.

**Figure 14.1**
Sample Maximax
Input

HOW MANY DECISIONS (ALTERNATIVES) ?   4

HOW MANY STATES OF NATURE (OUTCOMES) ?   3

[MAXIMAX] ENTER THE CONDITIONAL PAYOFF VALUES:

|    | S1  | S2  | S3  |
|----|-----|-----|-----|
| D1 | −40 | 280 | 95  |
| D2 | 70  | 190 | 150 |
| D3 | 20  | 200 | 180 |
| D4 | 90  | 160 | 100 |

Use Arrow keys, [Home], [End], [PgUp], [PgDn] to make entries.
[F3] Changes Model,    [F9] Delete Row,    [F6] Add Row
[F9] Accepts Entries    [F7] Delete State,    [F8] Add State

**Figure 14.2**
Sample Maximax
Problem Output

|    | S1  | S2  | S3  | RESULTS |   |
|----|-----|-----|-----|---------|---|
| D1 | −40 | 280 | 95  | 280     | * |
| D2 | 70  | 190 | 150 | 190     |   |
| D3 | 20  | 200 | 180 | 200     |   |
| D4 | 90  | 160 | 100 | 160     |   |

OPTIMAL MAXIMAX DECISION =>   D1

OPTIMAL VALUE =   280

Press any key to continue.

Figure 14.2 shows the solution for our sample maximax problem.

Recall that the "Modify Data" option of the Ending Menu (which comes up when you press any key, as instructed) is very useful with these four no probability models, because it allows you to compare the optimal solutions using different criteria without having to reenter all of the data. We will demonstrate this in the following problems.

### Example 1: Problem without Probability Assignment—Solved Using Different Criteria

Dennco Manufacturing, which produces widgets, is considering a move into the production of wadgets, a totally new concept in machine parts. To do so would require them to acquire new machinery. They can purchase or lease a new machine or they can rebuild some old ones. The future market for wadgets is unknown, but they can assume either a favorable or an unfavorable market. Management at Dennco is generally optimistic about the future. The expected net profits (in thousands) are given in the table below.

|  | Unfavorable | Favorable |
|---|---|---|
| **Purchase** | −20 | 140 |
| **Lease** | 35 | 95 |
| **Rebuild** | 5 | 100 |

What should Dennco do? Compare the solutions using three criteria, maximax, equal likelihood, and minimax regret.

Figure 14.3 shows the input to the problem. Note that we first choose the maximax decision criterion to arrive at a decision. Figure 14.4 shows this first solution. We will then select the "Modify Data and Run Again" option from the Ending Menu, shown in Figure 14.5.

```
HOW MANY DECISIONS (ALTERNATIVES) ? 3

HOW MANY STATES OF NATURE (OUTCOMES) ? 2


[MAXIMAX]    ENTER THE CONDITIONAL PAYOFF VALUES:



        S1        S2

   D1  -20       140
   D2  35        95
   D3  5         100



Use Arrow keys, [Home], [End], [PgUp], [PgDn] to make entries.
 [F3] Changes Model,          [F5] Delete Row,        [F6] Add Row
 [F9] Accepts entries,        [F7] Delete State,      [F8] Add State
```

**Figure 14.3**     Example 1: Maximax Input

**Figure 14.4**
Example 1:
Maximax
Output/Solution

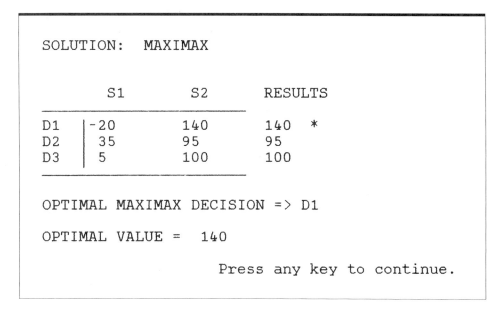

```
SOLUTION:   MAXIMAX


           S1          S2        RESULTS

D1    | -20         140        140    *
D2    |  35          95         95
D3    |   5         100        100


OPTIMAL MAXIMAX DECISION => D1

OPTIMAL VALUE =   140

                        Press any key to continue.
```

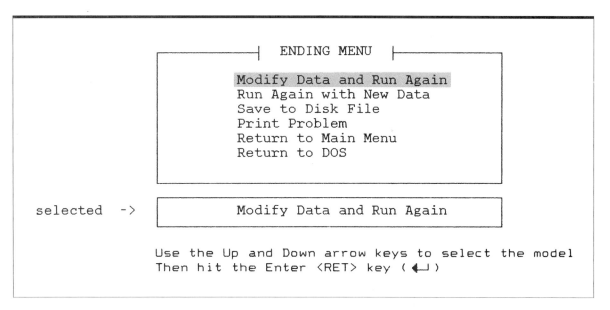

```
                 ┤  ENDING MENU  ├

              Modify Data and Run Again
              Run Again with New Data
              Save to Disk File
              Print Problem
              Return to Main Menu
              Return to DOS



selected  ->    Modify Data and Run Again


      Use the Up and Down arrow keys to select the model
      Then hit the Enter <RET> key ( ⏎ )
```

**Figure 14.5**    Ending Menu—Modify Data Option Selected

Next, we will solve the problem using the equal likelihood criterion. To do so requires pressing the [F3] function key to change the model, as directed on screen. Note that the [F3] key must be pressed twice since the models are changed in a given sequence and maximin follows maximax (the sequence is in the order given on the model selection menu). Figure 14.6 (p. 294) shows the original matrix, the change to equal likelihood, and the new solution. Note that the model being used is shown in brackets above the matrix. When we have the solution, we will use the ''Modify Data'' option once again to solve the problem using the minimax regret criterion. The Ending Menu is not shown again.

```
[MAXIMAX]      HERE IS WHAT YOU ENTERED:


         S1        S2

   D1  | -20      140
   D2  |  35       95
   D3  |   5      100


Use Arrow keys, [Home], [End], [PgUp], [PgDn] to make entries.
[F3] Changes Model,        [F5] Delete Row,       [F6] Add Row
[F9] Accepts entries,      [F7] Delete State,     [F8] Add State


[EQUAL LIKELIHOOD]    HERE IS WHAT YOU ENTERED:


         S1        S2

   D1  | -20      140
   D2  |  35       95
   D3  |   5      100


SOLUTION:  EQUAL LIKELIHOOD

         S1        S2        RESULTS

   D1  | -20      140        60
   D2  |  35       95        65   *
   D3  |   5      100        52.5


OPTIMAL EQUAL LIKELIHOOD DECISION => D2

OPTIMAL VALUE =   65

               Press any key to continue.
```

**Figure 14.6**     Example 1: Model Change to Equal Likelihood and Solution

Figure 14.7 shows the problem solution using the minimax criterion. It includes the data summary for equal likelihood, the change to the minimax regret model, having used the [F3] key to change the model, and finally the solution.

```
[EQUAL LIKELIHOOD]      HERE IS WHAT YOU ENTERED:


            S1        S2
        ┌─────────────────
   D1   │ -20       140
   D2   │  35        95
   D3   │   5       100
        │


Use Arrow keys, [Home], [End], [PgUp], [PgDn] to make entries.
[F3] Changes Model,          [F5] Delete Row,        [F6] Add Row
[F9] Accepts entries,        [F7] Delete State,      [F8] Add State


[MINIMAX REGRET]    HERE IS WHAT YOU ENTERED:


            S1        S2
        ┌─────────────────
   D1   │ -20       140
   D2   │  35        95
   D3   │   5       100
        │



REGRET TABLE
SOLUTION:  MINIMAX REGRET


            S1        S2       RESULTS
        ┌───────────────────────────────
   D1   │  55         0         55
   D2   │   0        45         45
   D3   │  30        40         40   *



OPTIMAL MINIMAX REGRET DECISION => D3

OPTIMAL VALUE =  40

             Press any key to continue.
```

**Figure 14.7**      Example 1: Minimax Regret Changes and Solution

After all this, we are ready to consider a decision for Dennco's problem. Using maximax we would choose decision 1 (purchase), with a value of 140 ($140,000). With equal likelihood the decision changes to D2 (lease) with a value of 65 ($65,000). The minimax regret criterion results in choosing decision 3 (rebuild), which has a regret value of 40 ($40,000). As you can see, the decision depends upon the decision criterion used.

## 14.4 Models with Probability Assigned
Expected Value
Expected Value with Bayes Posterior Probabilities

The expected value model computes the expected value (the average payoff if this particular decision situation occurred a number of times) for each alternative and then selects the decision with the best expected value. The expected value with Bayes posterior probabilities allows you to enter the number of possible outcomes and the conditional probabilities for each outcome, and it uses this input to revise the probabilities. It can be run only after an expected value solution has been achieved. However, in the special event that you wish only to revise probabilities using Bayes, you can do so as described in Section 14.5.

### Expected Value Data Entry

Data entry is essentially the same as for the previous no probabilities models. You must first describe the size of the matrix (as prompted) and then enter the conditional payoff values in the decision matrix. The opportunity to do posterior probabilities comes within the program output.
   As prompted:

1. Enter the number of decisions (alternatives) in the problem (limit 20).

2. Enter the states of nature (possible outcomes or future events) in the problem (limit 20).

3. Enter the conditional outcomes (payoffs or costs) and the probability of occurrence for each outcome (state of nature) in the matrix cells. Enter the probabilities as decimal values ($0<=P<=1$). The sum of the probabilities of the states of nature must $= 1$.

   Remember, cell values are limited to seven-digit numbers. If you are solving a minimization problem, enter the negative of the value, that is, multiply all outcomes (costs) by $-1$. Use the cursor movement keys as designated on screen to move through the table and enter the values in the matrix cells.

Note that if you are changing from a nonprobabilistic model to the expected value model (using the "Modify Data" option), the probabilities row will be added to the matrix. You then make the entries as usual.

Figure 14.8 shows a sample of this entry.

**Figure 14.8**
Sample Expected
Value Input

```
HOW MANY DECISIONS (ALTERNATIVES) ?   3

HOW MANY STATES OF NATURE (OUTCOMES) ?   3

[EXPECTED VALUE]        ENTER THE CONDITIONAL PAYOFF VALUES:


                       S1      S2      S3

        D1            150     150     150
        D2             70     200     200
        D3           -100     300     500
        PROB           .5      .3      .2


Use Arrow keys, [Home], [End], [PgUp], [PgDn] to make entries.
[F3] Changes Model,     [F9] Delete Row,     [F6] Add Row
[F9] Accepts Entries    [F7] Delete State    [F8] Add State
```

**Expected Value Output and Solution**

The output for the expected value model includes:

1. The decision matrix with the calculations included as a final results column; the decision is marked by an asterisk (*).

2. The optimal expected value decision.

3. The optimal value.

4. An opportunity loss table and the optimal decision and value from these calculations.

5. EVPI.

6. The opportunity to develop posterior probabilities. If your response to this is YES, you must enter additional data. This will be discussed in the next section of the chapter.

Figure 14.9 (p. 298) shows a sample output for an expected value problem without Bayes revisions.

**Figure 14.9**
Sample Expected
Value Output

|     | S1   | S2  | S3  | RESULTS |
| --- | ---- | --- | --- | ------- |
| D1  | 150  | 150 | 150 | 150  *  |
| D2  | 70   | 200 | 200 | 135     |
| D3  | −100 | 300 | 500 | 140     |
| PROB | .5  | .3  | .2  |         |

OPTIMAL EXPECTED VALUE DECISION =>  D1

OPTIMAL VALUE =>  150

Press any key to continue.

OPPORTUNITY LOSS TABLE

|     | S1  | S2  | S3  | RESULTS |
| --- | --- | --- | --- | ------- |
| D1  | 0   | 150 | 350 | 115  *  |
| D2  | 80  | 100 | 300 | 130     |
| D3  | 250 | 0   | 0   | 125     |
| PROB | .5 | .3  | .2  |         |

OPTIMAL EXPECTED VALUE DECISION => D1

OPTIMAL VALUE => 115

EVPI = 115

DO YOU WANT TO DEVELOP POSTERIOR PROBABILITIES ? (YES/ NO )

## Expected Value with Bayes Posterior Probabilities Data Entry

If you choose to develop posterior probabilities, you will have to enter additional data:

1. The number of possible outcomes (a prompted response).
2. The conditional probabilities for each possible outcome for each state of nature—P(outcome or result|state of nature). These are the conditional probabilities of the results or outcomes given the states of nature, such as P(I1|S1). Enter the value in decimal form such that $0<=P<=1$ and the sum of each column is 1 (when there is more than one row). This is another tabular entry.

The program will then develop a decision strategy for the problem by developing posterior probabilities (the prior or original probabilities entered into the program will be revised) using the conditional probabilities. In other words, the program gives you the opportunity to make the decision based upon additional information by combining the new information (called an indicator or sample information) with the prior probabilities using a Bayesian technique.

### Expected Value Output

The outcome for a Bayes revision includes:

1.  For each outcome:
    a.  A table showing the computation of the posterior probabilities $P(S|I)$.
    b.  A new expected value decision table.
    c.  A statement of the decision strategy given that outcome.
2.  The EVSI.
3.  The efficiency of sample information.

**Figure 14.10**
Bayes Revision
Input and Output

```
BAYES ANALYSIS

HOW MANY POSSIBLE OUTCOMES ARE THERE ?   2

[EXPECTED VALUE WITH BAYES REVISIONS]      ENTER CONDITIONAL
PROBABILITIES:

                          S1    S2    S3

               I1         .2    .6    .7
               I2         .8    .4    .3

Use Arrow keys, [Home], [End], [PgUp], [PgDn] to make entries.
[F3] Changes Model,    [F9] Delete Row,    [F6] Add Row
[F9] Accepts Entries   [F7] Delete State   [F8] Add State

FOR OUTCOME   1

        S          P(S)        P(I|S)       P(I,S)      P(S|I)

        S1          .5           .2         0.100       0.238
        S2          .3           .6         0.180       0.429
        S3          .2           .7         0.140       0.333

                                            0.420
```

**Figure 14.10**
(*continued*)

Press any key to continue.

|     | S1   | S2  | S3  | RESULTS |
| --- | ---- | --- | --- | ------- |
| D1  | 150  | 150 | 150 | 150     |
| D2  | 70   | 200 | 200 | 169.06  |
| D3  | −100 | 300 | 500 | 271.4 * |
| PROB | .238 | .429 | .333 | |

IF OUTCOME I1 OCCURS THEN DECISION D3 IS OPTIMAL

VALUE OF THIS DECISION GIVEN OUTCOME = 271.4

Press any key to continue.

FOR OUTCOME   2

| S   | P(S) | P(I\|S) | P(I,S) | P(S\|I) |
| --- | ---- | ------- | ------ | ------- |
| S1  | .5   | .8      | 0.400  | 0.690   |
| S2  | .3   | .4      | 0.120  | 0.207   |
| S3  | .2   | .3      | 0.060  | 0.103   |
|     |      |         | 0.580  |         |

Press any key to continue.

|     | S1   | S2  | S3  | RESULTS |
| --- | ---- | --- | --- | ------- |
| D1  | 150  | 150 | 150 | 150 *   |
| D2  | 70   | 200 | 200 | 110.3   |
| D3  | −100 | 300 | 500 | 44.6    |
| PROB | .690 | .207 | .103 | |

IF OUTCOME I2 OCCURS THEN DECISION D1 IS OPTIMAL

VALUE OF THIS DECISION GIVEN OUTCOME = 150

Press any key to continue.

THE EXPECTED VALUE FOR THIS PROBLEM USING THE BAYESIAN VALUES 200.99

EXPECTED VALUE OF SAMPLE INFORMATION = 50.99

EFFICIENCY OF SAMPLE INFORMATION =   44.3 %

Press any key to continue.

Figure 14.10 shows the additional entries and output for the sample problem.

### Example 2: Expected Value

Baxter Building Company is considering the construction of condominiums along the shore of Lake Erie. Because of the design, Baxter finds it most economical to build in blocks of 30 units. They feel they currently have the resources to build 30, 60, or 90 units. The sales manager feels the sale of these units will be a function of the regional economy, which can be categorized as poor, moderate, or boom. The accounting department has produced the following profit figures based upon the construction costs and sales estimates (figures in thousands of dollars).

| Build | | (S1) Poor | (S2) Moderate | (S3) Boom |
|---|---|---|---|---|
| D1 | 30 | 70 | 70 | 70 |
| D2 | 60 | 10 | 210 | 210 |
| D3 | 90 | −50 | 150 | 350 |

```
HOW MANY DECISIONS (ALTERNATIVES) ? 3

HOW MANY STATES OF NATURE (OUTCOMES) ? 3

[EXPECTED VALUE]     ENTER THE CONDITIONAL PAYOFF VALUES AND PROBABILITIES:


        S1       S2       S3

 D1  │ 70       70       70
 D2  │ 10      210      210
 D3  │ -50     150      350
 PROB│ .5       .3       .2


Use Arrow keys, [Home], [End], [PgUp], [PgDn] to make entries.
[F3] Changes Model,        [F5] Delete Row,        [F6] Add Row
[F9] Accepts entries,      [F7] Delete State,      [F8] Add State
```

**Figure 14.11**    Example 2: Expected Value Input

Initial economic estimates indicate a .5 chance the economy will be poor, .3 it will be moderate, and .2 it will boom. How many units should Baxter build?

Figure 14.11 shows the input using expected value. Figure 14.12 shows the output. (Note that the answer to "DO YOU WANT TO DEVELOP POSTERIOR PROBABILITIES?" is YES.)

```
SOLUTION:   EXPECTED VALUE


          S1          S2          S3        RESULTS
      _____
D1    |   70          70          70         70
D2    |   10         210         210        110     *
D3    |  -50         150         350         90
      _____

PROB     .5          .3          .2

OPTIMAL EXPECTED VALUE DECISION => D2

OPTIMAL VALUE =   110

                    Press any key to continue.


OPPORTUNITY LOSS TABLE


          S1          S2          S3        RESULTS
      _____
D1    |   0          140         280         98
D2    |  60            0         140         58     *
D3    |  120          60           0         78
      _____

PROB     .5          .3          .2

OPTIMAL EXPECTED VALUE DECISION => D2

OPTIMAL VALUE =   58

EVPI =   58

DO YOU WANT TO DEVELOP POSTERIOR PROBABILITIES ? (YES/NO)
```

**Figure 14.12**     Example 2: Expected Value Output/Solution

The program gives this solution to the problem. We are told that decision 2, building 60 units, is optimal. However, now we wish to determine whether it is worth it to purchase additional information. We will work from the same data entered, and indicate that we want to do a Bayesian revision. Example 3 shows this.

### Example 3: Expected Value with Bayes Revised Probabilities

Baxter has found it can commission a special study of the regional economy for $15,000. Researchers indicate the study would give a favorable or unfavorable economic indication. The following table shows the conditional probabilities of the study results given the actual state of nature.

|                  | Poor(S1) | Moderate(S2) | Boom(S3) |
|------------------|----------|--------------|----------|
| Favorable (I1)   | .1       | .6           | .8       |
| Unfavorable (I2) | .9       | .4           | .2       |

What is the new expected value for this problem, what decision strategy is recommended, what is the EVSI, and what is the efficiency of this sample information?

The rather lengthy input and solution to this problem are shown in Figure 14.13, which includes the entries required to develop the posterior probabilities. Note that the solution to this problem begins in the previous example with the answer YES to "DO YOU WANT TO DEVELOP POSTERIOR PROBABILITIES ?".

```
BAYES ANALYSIS

HOW MANY POSSIBLE OUTCOMES ARE THERE ? 2

[EXPECTED VALUE WITH BAYES REVISIONS]      ENTER CONDITIONAL PROBABILITIES:


       |   S1      S2      S3
    ___|_____
       |
    I1 |  .1      .6      .8
    I2 |  .9      .4      .2
    ___|_____



Use Arrow keys, [Home], [End], [PgUp], [PgDn] to make entries.
  [F3] Changes Model,         [F5] Delete Row,       [F6] Add Row
  [F9] Accepts entries,       [F7] Delete State,     [F8] Add State

                                                       (continued)
```

**Figure 14.13**    Example 3: Expected Value with Bayes Revision Input and Solution

```
FOR OUTCOME   1

     S        P(S)     P(I|S)     P(I,S)     P(S|I)
   ─────────────────────────────────────────────────
     S1        .5        .1       0.050      0.128
     S2        .3        .6       0.180      0.462
     S3        .2        .8       0.160      0.410
   ─────────────────────────────────────────────────
                                  0.390

              Press any key to continue.


          S1        S2        S3      RESULTS
   ─────────────────────────────────────────────
   D1 |   70        70        70      70
   D2 |   10       210       210      184.4
   D3 |  -50       150       350      206.4   *
   ─────────────────────────────────────────────
   PROB  .128      .462      .41


IF OUTCOME I1 OCCURS THEN DECISION D3 IS OPTIMAL

VALUE OF THIS DECISION GIVEN OUTCOME =   206.4

              Press any key to continue.


FOR OUTCOME   2

     S        P(S)     P(I|S)     P(I,S)     P(S|I)
   ─────────────────────────────────────────────────
     S1        .5        .9       0.450      0.738
     S2        .3        .4       0.120      0.197
     S3        .2        .2       0.040      0.066
   ─────────────────────────────────────────────────
                                  0.610

              Press any key to continue.


          S1        S2        S3      RESULTS
   ─────────────────────────────────────────────
   D1 |   70        70        70      70.07   *
   D2 |   10       210       210      62.61
   D3 |  -50       150       350      15.75
   ─────────────────────────────────────────────
   PROB  .738      .197      .066


IF OUTCOME I2 OCCURS THEN DECISION D1 IS OPTIMAL

VALUE OF THIS DECISION GIVEN OUTCOME =   70.07

              Press any key to continue.


THE EXPECTED VALUE FOR THIS PROBLEM USING THE BAYESIAN VALUES =   123.24

EXPECTED VALUE OF SAMPLE INFORMATION =   13.24

EFFICIENCY OF SAMPLE INFORMATION =   22.8 %

              Press any key to continue.
```

**Figure 14.13**      (continued)

As you can see, we are told that if the outcome is favorable we should choose alternative 3 and build 90 units. If the outcome is not favorable, we should select decision 1 to build 30 units. The expected value using the Bayesian values is 123.24 ($123,240), the EVSI is 13.24 ($13,240), and the efficiency of the sample information is 22.8 percent. Obviously, Baxter should not spend $15,000 for a study that is worth only $13,420.

## 14.5  Using Bayes to Revise Probabilities—A Special Situation

In cerVain cases, for instance some homework problems, you may just want to calculate posterior probability without expected value calculations. In this case, just follow these few steps:

1.  Select the expected value model.
2.  Enter a zero (0) in response to the number of decisions prompt.
3.  Respond to the states of nature prompt from your problem.
4.  Enter the probabilities in the table and accept with [F9].
5.  Answer YES to "DO YOU WANT TO DEVELOP POSTERIOR PROBABILITIES ?"
6.  Answer the Bayes input prompt for number of outcomes.
7.  Enter the conditional probabilities in the table and accept with [F9].

You will be given the table showing the calculations of posterior probabilities (P(S|I)) for each outcome. The following example demonstrates how this works.

### Example 4: Bayes Probability Revision

The Langford Baking Company has determined that at any given time, there is a 50 percent chance their oven will be at the right temperature, a 30 percent chance it will be too hot, and a 20 percent chance it will be too cool. The Tempervac Control Company has installed a warning device which sounds an alarm if the temperature is out of range. The following table gives the conditional probabilities that the alarm will sound.

|  | Temp OK | Too hot | Too cool |
|---|---|---|---|
| **Alarm sounds** | .1 | .4 | .7 |

What is the probability the alarm will sound? If the alarm just sounded, what is the probability the oven temperature is actually correct?

Figure 14.14 shows the input and solution to this problem.

```
HOW MANY DECISIONS (ALTERNATIVES) ? 0

HOW MANY STATES OF NATURE (OUTCOMES) ? 3


[EXPECTED VALUE]    ENTER THE CONDITIONAL PAYOFF VALUES AND PROBABILITIES:



            S1       S2       S3

     PROB   .5       .3       .2



Use Arrow keys, [Home], [End], [PgUp], [PgDn] to make entries.
[F3] Changes Model,           [F5] Delete Row,          [F6] Add Row
[F9] Accepts entries,         [F7] Delete State,        [F8] Add State



DO YOU WANT TO DEVELOP POSTERIOR PROBABILITIES ? (YES/NO)

BAYES ANALYSIS

HOW MANY POSSIBLE OUTCOMES ARE THERE ? 1


[EXPECTED VALUE WITH BAYES REVISIONS]    ENTER CONDITIONAL PROBABILITIES:



            S1       S2       S3

     I1     .1       .4       .7



Use Arrow keys, [Home], [End], [PgUp], [PgDn] to make entries.
[F3] Changes Model,           [F5] Delete Row,          [F6] Add Row
[F9] Accepts entries,         [F7] Delete State,        [F8] Add State



      S       P(S)    P(I|S)    P(I,S)    P(S|I)

      S1       .5       .1      0.050     0.161
      S2       .3       .4      0.120     0.387
      S3       .2       .7      0.140     0.452

                               0.310

            Press any key to continue.
```

**Figure 14.14**    Example 4: Bayes Revision of Probabilities Input and Solution

The probability that the oven temperature is correct, given that the alarm just sounded, is 16.1 percent. The probability that the alarm will sound at all is 31 percent.

## 14.6

**Summary Notes**
for the Decision Theory Programs

1. Size: the decision matrices are limited to 20 (decisions) by 20 (states of nature); cell entries are limited to 7-digit numbers

2. If you are solving a minimization problem, enter the negative of the value, that is, multiply all outcomes (costs) by $-1$.

3. Enter probabilities as decimal values ($0<=P<=1$). The sum of the probabilities of the states of nature must $= 1$.

4. Enter conditional probabilities, for example, $P(I1|S1)$ in decimal form such that $0<=P<=1$ and the sum of each column is 1 (when there is more than one row).

5. To use Bayes to calculate posterior probability without decision alternatives, simply enter a zero (0) in response to the number of decisions prompt and proceed as usual, following on-screen directions.

6. Moving around the table: Arrow keys move cursor right, left, up, down; [HOME] moves cursor to left-hand edge of line; [END] moves cursor to right-hand edge of line; [PgUp] moves cursor to first row of the matrix; [PgDn] moves cursor to last row of the matrix.

7. Function keys in entering data: [F3] changes the model; [F5] deletes a row (used to eliminate a decision); [F6] adds a row (used to add a decision); [F7] deletes a state; [F8] adds a state; [F9] accepts the entries. The [F9] key must be pressed to continue the program and achieve a solution.

8. Error correction is of the tabular input type. All entries in the matrix can be modified using the cursor movement keys and function keys just described.

## 14.7

**Problems**

1. The Alpantos Company is trying to decide whether or not to add a new product line. The success of this venture will depend upon economic conditions, which can be good or poor. The following table shows the payoffs associated with each outcome.

|  | Good Economic Conditions | Poor Economic Conditions |
|---|---|---|
| New Pdt Line | 48,000 | 12,500 |
| Existing Line | 35,700 | 18,000 |

Select the best decision using:
a.  Maximax
b.  Maximin
c.  Equal likelihood
d.  Minimax regret

2. Given the following payoff table:

|  | S1 | S2 | S3 | S4 | S5 | S6 |
|---|---|---|---|---|---|---|
| D1 | 7 | 9 | 6 | 4 | 10 | 8 |
| D2 | 10 | 5 | 7 | 5 | 8 | 4 |
| D3 | 4 | 6 | 11 | 9 | 10 | 7 |
| D4 | 9 | 4 | 6 | 12 | 9 | 5 |
| D5 | 6 | 8 | 5 | 4 | 11 | 9 |
| D6 | 10 | 7 | 8 | 10 | 6 | 6 |

Select the best decision using:
a.  Maximax
b.  Maximin
c.  Equal likelihood
d.  Minimax regret

3. If the probabilities associated with the states of nature in Problem 2 are .05, .10, .20, .30, .25, and .10, what decision would you recommend based upon an expected value criterion?

4. An investor is trying to decide whether to place his money into one of two real estate investments or into bonds. The return on the real estate investments will depend upon the results of a rezoning hearing. The possible outcomes are shown below:

|  | Rezoning Approved | Rezoning Denied |
|---|---|---|
| Real Estate A | 155,000 | 35,000 |
| Real Estate B | 135,000 | 85,000 |
| Bonds | 100,000 | 100,000 |

Determine the best decision using:
a.  Maximax
b.  Maximin
c.  Equal likelihood
d.  Minimax regret

5. If the investor in Problem 4 feels there is a 30 percent chance that the zoning board will approve the rezoning, what should his decision be, using

expected value as his criterion? What would the expected value of perfect information (EVPI) be?

6. The Big Plow plowing service is considering three alternatives: 1. purchasing a new truck and plow; 2. purchasing a new plow blade for an existing truck; or 3. no additional investment (status quo). The payoff from this investment will depend upon the weather conditions. Possible payoffs are shown below:

|  | Snowfall | | |
|---|---|---|---|
|  | **Light** | **Moderate** | **Heavy** |
| **Truck** | −16,000 | 8,000 | 32,000 |
| **Blade** | −2,000 | 9,000 | 24,000 |
| **Status** | 3,000 | 10,000 | 18,000 |

If the forecast probabilities for snowfall for the coming season are .4 (light), .35 (moderate), and .25 (heavy), what decision should Big Plow make on an expected value basis? What is the EVPI?

7. A professor at a local university has done studies relating the length of fur on the rare blue-woolly caterpillar with the snowfall during the winter. Given the following conditional probabilities, how much would it be worth for Big Plow to hire this professor to locate a blue-woolly and measure its fur?

|  | **Light** | **Moderate** | **Heavy** |
|---|---|---|---|
| **Long fur** | .10 | .40 | .85 |
| **Short fur** | .90 | .60 | .15 |

What would Big Plow's optimal decision strategy be based upon the professor's findings?

8. Big Jake's is considering an investment with two possible outcomes, one favorable, one not. The probability of a favorable outcome is 32 percent. Based upon an expected value analysis, Big Jake's has decided the investment is not worthwhile. A study can be undertaken, however, which might clarify the possible outcomes. The probability that the study will yield positive results given conditions for a favorable outcome is 72 percent, and positive results given conditions for an unfavorable outcome will occur only 11 percent of the time.
   a. What is the probability the study will yield favorable results?
   b. What is the probability of a favorable outcome if the study was conducted and did yield positive results?

9. The Burke Company is considering the introduction of a new product. They know from past data that 50 percent of all new products in this area fail to break even, 30 percent just break even, and 20 percent produce a reasonable return. One option open to Burke is to test market this product before making a final decision. In the past, good test market results have been achieved with products which fail to break even only 5 percent of the time, with products which break even 30 percent of the time, and with products which yield a reasonable return 78 percent of the time. If Burke test markets this product and the results are good, what is the probability the product will yield a reasonable return?

**10.** The Panhandle Investment Company is considering an investment in a new broadway show. They can invest in a drama, a comedy, or a musical. Once the show opens, it will be a smash hit, a moderate success, or a bomb. The payoffs from each of these outcomes (in thousands of dollars) are shown in the following table.

|  | Hit | Moderate Success | Bomb |
|---|---|---|---|
| **Drama** | 160 | 140 | −50 |
| **Comedy** | 200 | 100 | −20 |
| **Musical** | 380 | 45 | −150 |

If the probability of a hit is 15 percent and a moderate success is 25 percent, what should Panhandle do?

The three investments Panhandle is considering are all scheduled for pre-Broadway openings in Peoria, Ill. In the past, audiences in Peoria have reacted wildly (I1), warmly (I2), coolly (I3), or walked out (I4). The conditional probabilities for later Broadway success are shown below:

|  | Hit(S1) | Success(S2) | Bomb(S3) |
|---|---|---|---|
| **I1** | .6 | .4 | .1 |
| **I2** | .2 | .3 | .1 |
| **I3** | .1 | .2 | .2 |
| **I4** | .1 | .1 | .6 |

a. Without a trial opening in Peoria, what should Panhandle do?
b. What is the expected value of perfect information?
c. With the trial opening in Peoria, what is the optimal decision strategy for Panhandle?
d. If it will cost Panhandle an extra $10,000 to let the plays open in Peoria before making any decision, what should the company do?
e. What is the efficiency of the information gained by opening in Peoria?

# Chapter 15

# Queuing

**W**aiting in line is a fact of life. However, time is a valuable resource; the reduction of waiting time is an important issue for managers. Queuing theory, encompassing a large number of quantitative models relating to different types of queuing situations, offers managers a way of analyzing waiting lines. These models can help managers make decisions about the operation of their specific waiting line situation.

The goal of queuing analysis is to balance desirable service levels with service costs, by minimizing the sum of customer waiting costs and service costs. However, these models do not really solve waiting line problems in the sense of giving an optimal solution or an actual recommended decision. Many of the parameters of a queuing problem are not known with certainty but are based on averages and probabilities. Thus, the model is descriptive. Optimization occurs when the user varies the parameters, obtaining new operating characteristics and then compares the results. The final decision based on this analysis is made by the manager, using his experience and needs. This decision may reflect a tradeoff of these two costs, or since it is difficult to establish a cost for customer waiting time, the decision may be a policy variable (achieving an acceptable level of waiting time).

There are many queuing models from which to choose. It is essential that the right model—the model that closely approximates the specific problem—be chosen. The choice, of course, depends upon the nature of the system, including the following parameters: 1. nature or source of the calling population; 2. the queue discipline (the order in which customers are served); 3. the number of servers or channels; 4. the arrival pattern or rate (assumed to conform to some probability distribution); 5. the service pattern (also a random variable and also assumed to conform to some probability distribution).

Queuing models will, in general, have the following operating characteristics: the average number of units (customers) in line and in the system; the average time each unit spends in the line and in the system; the probability of a specific number of units being in the system; the probability that the service facility is idle, that is, a utilization measurement.

A reading of many management science textbooks reveals some disagreement on terminology, nomenclature, and formulas used for queuing theory and queuing models. Note that we have chosen to use operating characteristics to describe the queue, that is, the conditions in the queue after it has been analyzed by the model, not to describe the queue parameters, for example, arrival rate, discipline and calling population.

## 15.1  The Queuing Program

This program offers the user a choice of models:

1.  Single server (channel), with an infinite source (calling population), a random arrival pattern described by a Poisson distribution, a random service-time pattern described by a negative exponential distribution, and always enough room in the queue (infinite queue).

2.  Multiple server, single waiting line, infinite source, Poisson arrival, exponential service, infinite queue.

3.  Single server, infinite source, Poisson arrival, variable service, infinite queue.

4.  Single server, infinite source, Poisson arrival, exponential service, finite queue.

5.  Single server, finite source, Poisson arrival, exponential service, infinite queue.

6.  Multiple server, single waiting line, infinite source, Poisson arrival, exponential service, finite queue length.

The models assume that the customers or units arrive individually and randomly, that no balking or reneging occurs (except in the case of finite queues), and that the queue discipline is first come, first served (FIFO).

The objective of these models is to help the user analyze the queuing situation and to help determine the ideal level of service, that is, the level that will balance the cost of providing service with the cost of customers waiting for that service. With each of these models, the user can determine the average number of customers waiting either in line or in the system (both in line and being serviced), the average time a unit waits (again both in line or in the system), and system utilization, that is, the probability that the server is busy or that a customer will have to wait. In some cases the model will determine the probability that a specified number of customers are waiting. Since one evaluation criterion is total expected cost, the program will also calculate this total cost (sum of waiting costs and service costs) to allow the user to make an economic evaluation.

These models require very little in the way of advance preparation by the user. However, before using them, it is important for the user to analyze the specific queuing problem in order to select the correct model.

## 15.2  Data Entry

The first step in data entry for this program is the selection, from the menu shown here, of the model to be run. Select the model, using the arrow keys to highlight your choice, and then press ⟨RET⟩ to complete the entry.

```
              ┤ QUEUING MODELS ├
      ┌─────────────────────────────────────┐
      │                                     │
      │    Single Server (SS)               │
      │    Multiple Servers (MS)            │
      │    SS, Variable Service Time        │
      │    SS, Finite Queue Length          │
      │    SS, Finite Population            │
      │    MS, Finite Population            │
      │    Problem from Disk File           │
      │                                     │
      │                                     │
      └─────────────────────────────────────┘

selected  ->  ┌─────────────────────────────────────┐
              │                                     │
              └─────────────────────────────────────┘

      Use the Up and Down arrow keys to select the model
      Then hit the Enter <RET> key ( ◀┘ )
```

Data entry for these models is from prompted input. This means that you must respond to a series of questions. These questions and responses describe the problem and provide the program with the data necessary for solution of the problem. All of the queuing models require you to enter (in response to prompts) the mean arrival rate and mean service rate. Other prompts are model or problem specific, which means they provide a more detailed description of a specific type of queuing problem. All models allow you to do an economic analysis of the problem if desired. This necessitates entering the service cost and waiting cost.

Once the data is entered and a solution determined, several of the models offer the opportunity to calculate the probability of there being a specified number of units in the system. However, this is treated as part of the output rather than input.

We will first describe data entry that is common to all models, and then discuss the problem specific entries. Note that the common entries are, in fact, the entries needed to solve a single server queuing problem (the simplest case). Recall that with prompted input, the ⟨RET⟩ key completes the entry.

For all queuing problems, you are required to enter:

1.  Mean arrival rate. How many units or customers arrive or are expected to arrive in a given time? These numbers are steady-state averages (the average level that a system realizes over a period of time, ignoring phenomena such as early morning rush).

2.  The mean service rate. What is the average length of time it takes to service a customer? This rate must be compatible with the arrival rate, that is, they must both be stated in the same time units, for example, per day or per hour. Since the service rate for multiple servers is assumed to be the same for each server, enter the rate per server, that is, rate of one server. The service rate must be greater than the arrival rate. For multiple servers, total service rate (mean service rate multiplied by the number of servers) must be greater than the mean arrival rate.

3.  A response (YES or NO) to the opportunity to do economic analysis. Economic analysis determines a total cost figure for the given situation. To see this figure, select YES in response to the question

    DO YOU WANT TO DO ECONOMIC ANALYSIS ? (YES/NO)

    and then in response to the prompts, enter
    a.  The cost of service. Give this figure for the same time period as arrival and service rate, stated as so much per unit of time (for example, $25 per hour). Do not enter dollar ($) signs.
    b.  The cost of waiting. As difficult as it sometimes is to estimate waiting costs, you still must enter a per customer waiting cost.

Figure 15.1 shows a sample entry for a **single server** problem.

**Figure 15.1**
Sample Single Server Problem Entry (These entries are common to all queuing problems)

WHAT IS THE MEAN ARRIVAL RATE ?   9

WHAT IS THE MEAN SERVICE RATE ?   12

DO YOU WANT TO DO ECONOMIC ANALYSIS ? ( YES /NO)

WHAT IS THE COST OF SERVICE ?   63

WHAT IS THE COST OF WAITING ?   160

**Problem Specific Prompts**

1. Problems with **multiple servers** (model 2, multiple server and model 6, multiple server, finite population).

   Enter the number of servers. Servers means channels (not individuals). For instance, a team of five may make up one channel; in which case two teams of five each would be two channels.

2. Problems with **variable service time** (model 3, single server, variable service time).

   Enter the standard deviation of the service rate as given in the problem. Answering 0 makes it a single server, constant service time model.

3. Problems with a **finite queue length** (model 4, single server, finite queue length). A finite queue is a line of specific or restricted length, such as the line for drive-up service when the line cannot extend beyond a fixed boundary, or a check-out line when studies have indicated that customers will not wait if there are more than a given number in line.

   Enter the maximum queue length as given in the problem. It should be an integer.

4. Problems with a finite population (model 5, single server, finite population and model 6, multiple servers, finite population). A finite population means there is a limited number of customers (usually a relatively small number). The arrival rate is dependent on the number of units already in line. Because the source is limited, the greater the number in line, the lower the arrival rate will be (there are fewer of the population available to get in line).

   Enter the size of the population.

## 15.3 Output and Solution

In general, output includes:

1. Average number of units in the system.
2. Average number of units in the queue.
3. Average time in the system.
4. Average time in the queue.
5. Utilization rate (given as a percentage).
6. The probability of the server (service facility) being idle.

Note that the word "average" is not used in the output. You are expected to realize that these are averages.

If you chose to do an economic analysis, the output will also include:

1. Service cost.

2. Waiting cost.

3. Total costs.

You are also asked if you wish to calculate the probability of finding a given number of customers in the system.

Calculate probability of n customers in system ? (YES/NO)

If the answer is YES, you must indicate the number (n) you want to use.

WHAT n DO YOU WANT TO USE ?

Output then shows the probability that there will be this many customers in the system. Since this question is repeated until you answer no, you are able to determine a probability distribution. Figure 15.2 shows a sample output for a Single Server Queuing problem.

**Figure 15.2**
Sample Single
Server Output

```
NUMBER OF UNITS IN SYSTEM =   3
NUMBER OF UNITS IN QUEUE =   2.25
TIME IN SYSTEM =   .3333
TIME IN QUEUE =   .25
UTILIZATION RATE =   75 %
PROBABILITY SERVICE FACILITY IS IDLE =   25 %
PROBABILITY AN ARRIVING UNIT WILL HAVE TO WAIT =   75 %
SERVICE COST =   $ 63
WAITING COST =   $ 480
TOTAL COST =   $ 543

CALCULATE PROBABILITY OF n CUSTOMERS IN SYSTEM ? ( YES /NO)

WHAT n DO YOU WANT TO USE ?   10
P( 10 ) = .014        ( 1.4 % )

CALCULATE PROBABILITY OF n CUSTOMERS IN SYSTEM ? (YES/ NO )
```

The following examples will demonstrate the specific input required and the output generated for each of the 6 queuing models. We will also use the data modification and error correction features to make you more familiar with their usefulness and increase your comfort level with the models.

## 15.4   Examples

### Example 1:  Model 1—Single Server

The Petrilli Trucking Company currently has one loading dock at its Philadelphia warehouse. Trucks are loaded and unloaded by a 3-person team. The trucks arrive every 20 minutes on the average (Poisson distribution). The time required to unload a truck is exponentially distributed. A team can load or unload an average of four trucks per hour. The team is paid $21 per hour ($7 per person) and Petrilli estimates the cost of having the truck off the road at $58 per hour.

a.  What are the operating characteristics and costs per hour associated with the current system?

b.  What is the probability there will be 2 or fewer trucks at the facility?

c.  If the team is increased to 4, it will be able to service 4.5 trucks per hour. Is the additional $7 per hour cost justified?

d.  What is the probability of 2 or fewer trucks at the facility with the 4-person team?

Figure 15.3 shows the input for this problem (we are not including the error correction input summary). Notice that you must answer YES to "DO YOU WANT TO DO ECONOMIC ANALYSIS ?". Figure 15.4 shows the initial output for this problem. In response to "CALCULATE PROBABILITY OF n CUSTOMERS IN SYSTEM ?", we answer YES in order to determine the answer to part b of the problem. When we answer YES, we get the following question.

WHAT n DO YOU WANT TO USE ?

**Figure 15.3**
Example 1: Single
Server Input

```
WHAT IS THE MEAN ARRIVAL RATE ? 3

WHAT IS THE MEAN SERVICE RATE ? 4

DO YOU WANT TO DO ECONOMIC ANALYSIS ?    (YES/NO)

WHAT IS THE COST OF SERVICE ? 21

WHAT IS THE COST OF WAITING ? 58
```

```
    ***   SINGLE SERVER   ***

NUMBER OF UNITS IN SYSTEM =  3

NUMBER OF UNITS IN QUEUE =  2.25

TIME IN SYSTEM =  1

TIME IN QUEUE =  .75

UTILIZATION RATE =  75 %

PROBABILITY SERVICE FACILITY IS IDLE = 25 %

PROBABILITY AN ARRIVING UNIT WILL HAVE TO WAIT = 75 %

SERVICE COST = $ 21

WAITING COST = $ 174

TOTAL COST = $ 195

CALCULATE PROBABILITY OF n CUSTOMERS IN SYSTEM ?   (YES/NO)

WHAT n DO YOU WANT TO USE ? 1

P( 1 ) =  .188         ( 18.8 % )

CALCULATE PROBABILITY OF n CUSTOMERS IN SYSTEM ?   (YES/NO)

WHAT n DO YOU WANT TO USE ? 2

P( 2 ) =  .141         ( 14.1 % )

CALCULATE PROBABILITY OF n CUSTOMERS IN SYSTEM ?   (YES/NO)
```

**Figure 15.4**     Example 1: Single Server Output

Since we are asked for the probability that 2 or fewer trucks are in the system, we must answer this for both 2 trucks and 1 truck (but not for 0 trucks since that probability is equal to the probability the facility is idle, P(0)).

In order to determine questions c and d, we must use the "Modify Data" option in the Ending Menu. Note that we go through the error correction twice to make all the necessary changes (both service rate and cost of service changed). Figure 15.5 shows the change in the data and Figure 15.6 shows the solution to these questions.

**Figure 15.5**
Example 1: Single
Server Data
Change

```
HERE IS WHAT YOU ENTERED:

    (1)   SINGLE SERVER
    (2)   MEAN ARRIVAL RATE =   3
    (3)   MEAN SERVICE RATE =   4
    (4)   ECONOMIC ANALYSIS:   YES
    (5)   COST OF SERVICE = $ 21
    (6)   COST OF WAITING = $ 58

DID YOU MAKE ANY MISTAKES ? (YES/NO)

WHICH LINE DO YOU WISH TO CHANGE ? 3

WHAT IS THE MEAN SERVICE RATE ? 4.5


HERE IS WHAT YOU ENTERED:

    (1)   SINGLE SERVER
    (2)   MEAN ARRIVAL RATE =   3
    (3)   MEAN SERVICE RATE =   4.5
    (4)   ECONOMIC ANALYSIS:   YES
    (5)   COST OF SERVICE = $ 21
    (6)   COST OF WAITING = $ 58

DID YOU MAKE ANY MISTAKES ? (YES/NO)

WHICH LINE DO YOU WISH TO CHANGE ? 5

WHAT IS THE COST OF SERVICE ? 28


HERE IS WHAT YOU ENTERED:

    (1)   SINGLE SERVER
    (2)   MEAN ARRIVAL RATE =   3
    (3)   MEAN SERVICE RATE =   4.5
    (4)   ECONOMIC ANALYSIS:   YES
    (5)   COST OF SERVICE = $ 28
    (6)   COST OF WAITING = $ 58

DID YOU MAKE ANY MISTAKES ? (YES/NO)
```

```
      ***   SINGLE SERVER    ***

NUMBER OF UNITS IN SYSTEM =   2

NUMBER OF UNITS IN QUEUE =   1.3333

TIME IN SYSTEM =  .6667

TIME IN QUEUE =   .4444

UTILIZATION RATE =  66.70001 %

PROBABILITY SERVICE FACILITY IS IDLE =   33.33 %

PROBABILITY AN ARRIVING UNIT WILL HAVE TO WAIT =   66.67 %

SERVICE COST = $ 28

WAITING COST = $ 116

TOTAL COST = $ 144

CALCULATE PROBABILITY OF n CUSTOMERS IN SYSTEM ?   (YES/NO)


WHAT n DO YOU WANT TO USE ? 1

P( 1 ) =  .222          ( 22.2 % )

CALCULATE PROBABILITY OF n CUSTOMERS IN SYSTEM ?   (YES/NO)

WHAT n DO YOU WANT TO USE ? 2

P( 2 ) =  .148          ( 14.8 % )

CALCULATE PROBABILITY OF n CUSTOMERS IN SYSTEM ?   (YES/NO)
```

**Figure 15.6**     Example 1: Single Server Solution

The answer to question a can be read directly from the output. There are, on average, 3 units in the system and 2.25 in the queue. Each unit averages 1 hour in the system and ¾ hour in the queue, with a facility utilization rate of 75 percent and a probability of 25 percent that the facility is idle. Using this .25 and the probabilities determined by the program that 2 trucks and 1 truck would be in the system (.141 and .188 respectively), we can determine the probability that there would be 2 or fewer trucks waiting (.25 + .188 + .141) at .579 (57.9 percent). Adding the fourth person reduced the total cost from $195 to $144. It would seem worthwhile to add another person. The probability that there would be 2 or fewer trucks in line with the fourth man added changes to .703 (70.3 percent).

### Example 2: Model 2—Multiple Servers

The Petrilli Trucking Company (Example 1) is considering the addition of a second loading dock at its Philadelphia facility (arrival = 3 per hour; waiting cost = $58 per hour).

a.  Assuming each dock will be manned by a 3-person team (service rate = 4 per hour; service cost = $21 per hour), what are the operating characteristics and costs associated with this new 2-server system?

b.  What is the probability that 2 or fewer trucks will be at the facility with the new system?

c.  Should Petrilli consider 4-person teams (service rate = 4.50 per hour; service cost = $28 per hour) for each dock?

At the conclusion of the problem in Example 1 (at the Ending Menu), we could have chosen the "Modify Data" option and made the changes in the data necessary to solve this problem. However, we choose instead to solve this as a new problem and to reenter the data ("Run Again with New Data"). Again we will be calculating the probability of a certain number (2 or fewer) of units being in the system. We will be using the "Modify Data" option in the Ending Menu to make a cost comparison (3-person versus 4-person teams). Figure 15.7 shows the input, Figure 15.8 the initial solution, and Figure 15.9 the data changing for comparison and the answer to question c. The initial error correction input summary is omitted.

```
WHAT IS THE MEAN ARRIVAL RATE ? 3

WHAT IS THE MEAN SERVICE RATE ? 4

HOW MANY SERVERS ARE THERE ? 2

DO YOU WANT TO DO ECONOMIC ANALYSIS ?   (YES/NO)

WHAT IS THE COST OF SERVICE ? 21

WHAT IS THE COST OF WAITING ? 58
```

**Figure 15.7**    Example 2: Multiple Servers Input

```
   ***   MULTIPLE SERVERS   ***

NUMBER OF UNITS IN SYSTEM =  .8729

NUMBER OF UNITS IN QUEUE =  .1229

TIME IN SYSTEM =  .291

TIME IN QUEUE =  .041

UTILIZATION RATE =  37.5 %

PROBABILITY SERVICE FACILITY IS IDLE =  45.5 %

PROBABILITY AN ARRIVING UNIT WILL HAVE TO WAIT =  20.48 %

SERVICE COST = $ 42

WAITING COST = $ 50.63

TOTAL COST = $ 92.63

CALCULATE PROBABILITY OF n CUSTOMERS IN SYSTEM ?   (YES/NO)


WHAT n DO YOU WANT TO USE ? 1

P( 1 ) =  .341          ( 34.1 % )

CALCULATE PROBABILITY OF n CUSTOMERS IN SYSTEM ?   (YES/NO)

WHAT n DO YOU WANT TO USE ? 2

P( 2 ) =  .128          ( 12.8 % )

CALCULATE PROBABILITY OF n CUSTOMERS IN SYSTEM ?   (YES/NO)
```

**Figure 15.8**    Example 2: Multiple Servers Output/Solution

Once again you can read the characteristics directly from the output in Figure 15.9. Total hourly cost with two channels is $92.63, much lower than the total cost determined in Example 1 for a single channel with a four-person team. Of course this does not consider the cost of adding the second loading dock. The probability of there being two or fewer trucks in the system (P(0) + P(1) + P(2)) is .924 (.455+.341+.128). If Petrilli adds a fourth person to each team of servers, the total hourly cost increases to $99.50, still less than the four-person team of the one-channel model, but higher than the two-channel, three-person teams.

```
HERE IS WHAT YOU ENTERED:

    (1)    MULTIPLE SERVERS
    (2)    MEAN ARRIVAL RATE =   3
    (3)    MEAN SERVICE RATE =   4
    (4)    NUMBER OF SERVERS =   2
    (5)    ECONOMIC ANALYSIS:   YES
    (6)    COST OF SERVICE = $ 21
    (7)    COST OF WAITING = $ 58

DID YOU MAKE ANY MISTAKES ? (YES/NO)

WHICH LINE DO YOU WISH TO CHANGE ? 3

WHAT IS THE MEAN SERVICE RATE ? 4.5


HERE IS WHAT YOU ENTERED:

    (1)    MULTIPLE SERVERS
    (2)    MEAN ARRIVAL RATE =   3
    (3)    MEAN SERVICE RATE =   4.5
    (4)    NUMBER OF SERVERS =   2
    (5)    ECONOMIC ANALYSIS:   YES
    (6)    COST OF SERVICE = $ 21
    (7)    COST OF WAITING = $ 58

DID YOU MAKE ANY MISTAKES ? (YES/NO)

WHICH LINE DO YOU WISH TO CHANGE ? 6

WHAT IS THE COST OF SERVICE ? 28


HERE IS WHAT YOU ENTERED:

    (1)    MULTIPLE SERVERS
    (2)    MEAN ARRIVAL RATE =   3
    (3)    MEAN SERVICE RATE =   4.5
    (4)    NUMBER OF SERVERS =   2
    (5)    ECONOMIC ANALYSIS:   YES
    (6)    COST OF SERVICE = $ 28
    (7)    COST OF WAITING = $ 58

DID YOU MAKE ANY MISTAKES ? (YES/NO)
```

**Figure 15.9**     Example 2: Multiple Servers Data Change and Solution

```
    ***   MULTIPLE SERVERS   ***

NUMBER OF UNITS IN SYSTEM =  .75

NUMBER OF UNITS IN QUEUE =   .0833

TIME IN SYSTEM =  .25

TIME IN QUEUE =  .0278

UTILIZATION RATE =  33.3 %

PROBABILITY SERVICE FACILITY IS IDLE =  50 %

PROBABILITY AN ARRIVING UNIT WILL HAVE TO WAIT =  16.67 %

SERVICE COST = $ 56

WAITING COST = $ 43.5

TOTAL COST = $ 99.5

CALCULATE PROBABILITY OF n CUSTOMERS IN SYSTEM ?   (YES/NO)
```

**Figure 15.9**      (continued)


### Example 3: Model 3—Variable Service Time

One person arrives at the candy machine in the snackbar every minute on
the average. The machine takes 20 seconds to dispense a candy bar (a constant time). Assuming a Poisson arrival rate, how many people will be
waiting at the machine? How long will they be at the machine? What is the
probability no one will be at the machine?

Figures 15.10 and 15.11 show the input (with no economic analysis)
and output for this problem.

```
WHAT IS THE MEAN ARRIVAL RATE ? 1

WHAT IS THE MEAN SERVICE RATE ? 3

WHAT IS THE STANDARD DEVIATION OF THE SERVICE RATE ?

DO YOU WANT TO DO ECONOMIC ANALYSIS ?   (YES/NO)
```

**Figure 15.10**      Example 3: Constant Service Time Input

```
   ***   SINGLE SERVER, VARIABLE SERVICE TIME   ***

NUMBER OF UNITS IN SYSTEM =  .4167

NUMBER OF UNITS IN QUEUE =  .0833

TIME IN SYSTEM =  .4167

TIME IN QUEUE =  .0833

UTILIZATION RATE =  33.3 %

PROBABILITY SERVICE FACILITY IS IDLE =  66.67 %


             Press any key to continue.
```

**Figure 15.11**    Example 3: Constant Service Time Output

### Example 4: Model 3—Variable Service Time

Students arrive at a counselor's office every 30 minutes on the average. The counselor can see four students every hour, but studies show this service rate is not exponentially distributed. It is estimated that the standard deviation of service is .2 hour. If arrivals approximate a Poisson distribution, what are the operating characteristics of this system?

Figures 15.12 and 15.13 show the entries and output for this problem.

```
WHAT IS THE MEAN ARRIVAL RATE ? 2

WHAT IS THE MEAN SERVICE RATE ? 4

WHAT IS THE STANDARD DEVIATION OF THE SERVICE RATE ? .2

DO YOU WANT TO DO ECONOMIC ANALYSIS ?   (YES/NO)
```

**Figure 15.12**    Example 4: Variable Service Time Input

```
    ***   SINGLE SERVER, VARIABLE SERVICE TIME   ***

NUMBER OF UNITS IN SYSTEM =  .91

NUMBER OF UNITS IN QUEUE =  .41

TIME IN SYSTEM =  .455

TIME IN QUEUE =  .205

UTILIZATION RATE =  50 %

PROBABILITY SERVICE FACILITY IS IDLE =  50 %


                  Press any key to continue.
```

**Figure 15.13**    Example 4: Variable Service Time Output/Solution

### Example 5: Model 4—Finite Queue Length

The Jayhawk Diner has a drive-up window. Statistics show that 16 customers arrive per hour and the clerk can serve 22 customers per hour. Unfortunately, there is room in the drive-up lane for only 4 cars, including the one being served. Because the street is highly congested, customers unable to enter the drive-up lane must pass by. What are the operating characteristics of this system? How many customers will drive by because the lane is full? If Jayhawk estimates it loses $6.00 in sales each time a car must drive by, how much do they lose in sales per hour?

The input and output for this problem are shown in Figures 15.14 and 15.15. Note that the output for this model also includes a determination of a balking rate, that is, the percentage of people who will leave without service.

```
WHAT IS THE MEAN ARRIVAL RATE ? 16

WHAT IS THE MEAN SERVICE RATE ? 22

WHAT IS THE MAXIMUM QUEUE LENGTH ? 4

DO YOU WANT TO DO ECONOMIC ANALYSIS ?   (YES/NO)
```

**Figure 15.14**    Example 5: SS, Finite Queue Length Input

```
     ***   SINGLE SERVER, FINITE QUEUE LENGTH   ***

 NUMBER OF UNITS IN SYSTEM =  1.6246

 NUMBER OF UNITS IN QUEUE =  .9447

 TIME IN SYSTEM =  .1086

 TIME IN QUEUE =  .0632

 PROBABILITY SERVICE FACILITY IS IDLE =  32.01 %

 BALKING RATE =  6.51 %

 CALCULATE PROBABILITY OF n CUSTOMERS IN SYSTEM ?   (YES/NO)
```

**Figure 15.15**     Example 5: SS, Finite Queue Length Output/Solution

To discover the lost sales, we must multiply the balking rate (6.51 percent) times the mean arrival rate times the $6.00 per lost sale. The result is $6.2496 or $6.25 lost sales per hour.

### Example 6: Model 5—Single Server, Finite Population

The Denneco Company has 5 large machines, each of which breaks down an average (Poisson) of once a day. The repair person hired to service these machines can repair a machine in 2 hours on average (exponentially distributed).

a. If the repair person is paid $22 per hour and the machine time is worth $50 per hour, what is the total cost associated with repairs?

b. If a two-person repair team can repair machines in 1.6 hours, would Denneco be economically justified in hiring another repair person?

Figure 15.16 shows both the initial input and solution for the problem. Figure 15.17 shows the data change and solution for the second part of this problem.

With one repair person, the total cost (salary of repair person plus lost machine time) is $111.81 per hour. Making it a two-person repair team increases the total cost to $115.22 per hour.

```
WHAT IS THE MEAN ARRIVAL RATE ? 1

WHAT IS THE MEAN SERVICE RATE ? 4

WHAT IS THE SIZE OF THE POPULATION ? 5

DO YOU WANT TO DO ECONOMIC ANALYSIS ?  (YES/NO)

WHAT IS THE COST OF SERVICE ? 22

WHAT IS THE COST OF WAITING ? 50


   ***   SINGLE SERVER, FINITE POPULATION   ***

NUMBER OF UNITS IN SYSTEM =  1.7963

NUMBER OF UNITS IN QUEUE =  .9953

TIME IN SYSTEM =  .5607

TIME IN QUEUE =  .3107

PROBABILITY SERVICE FACILITY IS IDLE =  19.91 %

SERVICE COST = $ 22

WAITING COST = $ 89.81

TOTAL COST = $ 111.81


                    Press any key to continue.
```

**Figure 15.16**      Example 6: SS, Finite Population Input and Solution

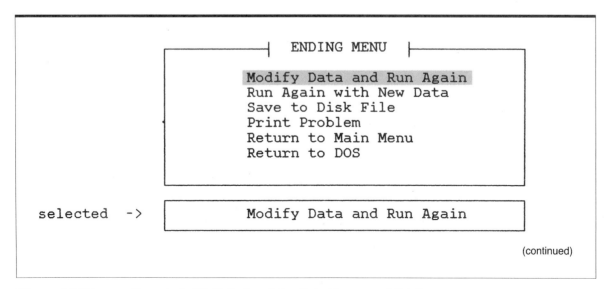

**Figure 15.17**      Example 6: SS, Finite Population Data Change and Solution

```
HERE IS WHAT YOU ENTERED:

    (1)    SINGLE SERVER, FINITE POPULATION
    (2)    MEAN ARRIVAL RATE =  1
    (3)    MEAN SERVICE RATE =  4
    (4)    POPULATION SIZE =  5
    (5)    ECONOMIC ANALYSIS:  YES
    (6)    COST OF SERVICE = $ 22
    (7)    COST OF WAITING = $ 50

DID YOU MAKE ANY MISTAKES ? (YES/NO)

WHICH LINE DO YOU WISH TO CHANGE ? 3

WHAT IS THE MEAN SERVICE RATE ? 5


HERE IS WHAT YOU ENTERED:

    (1)    SINGLE SERVER, FINITE POPULATION
    (2)    MEAN ARRIVAL RATE =  1
    (3)    MEAN SERVICE RATE =  5
    (4)    POPULATION SIZE =  5
    (5)    ECONOMIC ANALYSIS:  YES
    (6)    COST OF SERVICE = $ 22
    (7)    COST OF WAITING = $ 50

DID YOU MAKE ANY MISTAKES ? (YES/NO)

WHICH LINE DO YOU WISH TO CHANGE ? 6

WHAT IS THE COST OF SERVICE ? 44



HERE IS WHAT YOU ENTERED:

    (1)    SINGLE SERVER, FINITE POPULATION
    (2)    MEAN ARRIVAL RATE =  1
    (3)    MEAN SERVICE RATE =  5
    (4)    POPULATION SIZE =  5
    (5)    ECONOMIC ANALYSIS:  YES
    (6)    COST OF SERVICE = $ 44
    (7)    COST OF WAITING = $ 50

DID YOU MAKE ANY MISTAKES ? (YES/NO)
```

(continued)

**Figure 15.17**    (continued)

```
     ***   SINGLE SERVER, FINITE POPULATION   ***

NUMBER OF UNITS IN SYSTEM =  1.4243

NUMBER OF UNITS IN QUEUE =   .7092

TIME IN SYSTEM =  .3983

TIME IN QUEUE =  .1983

PROBABILITY SERVICE FACILITY IS IDLE =  28.49 %

SERVICE COST = $ 44

WAITING COST = $ 71.22

TOTAL COST = $ 115.22


                 Press any key to continue.
```

**Figure 15.17**    (continued)

### Example 7: Model 6—Multiple Servers, Finite Population

The Densmore Manufacturing Company has 4 machines. Each machine needs adjusting twice in an eight-hour day (Poisson distribution). Densmore's has 2 mechanics. Each requires 6 hours to readjust a machine (exponential distribution). What is the probability that all 4 machines are properly adjusted? What is the probability that half of the machines will be out of adjustment? What is the probability that all the machines will be out of adjustment? How do the above probabilities change if Densmore adds a third mechanic?

Figure 15.18 shows the initial input for this problem. Figure 15.19 shows the output for the problem, giving the probability that the service facility is idle (all four machines properly adjusted), and then calculating the probability of first 2 and then 4 units being in the system (half the machines and all the machines out of adjustment). Figure 15.20 shows the data change, using the "Modify Data" option in the Ending Menu and the error correction to add the server. Figure 15.21 shows the solution with the revised data.

**Figure 15.18**
Example 7: MS,
Finite Population
Input

```
WHAT IS THE MEAN ARRIVAL RATE ? 2

WHAT IS THE MEAN SERVICE RATE ? 1.33

HOW MANY SERVERS ARE THERE ? 2

WHAT IS THE SIZE OF THE POPULATION ? 4

DO YOU WANT TO DO ECONOMIC ANALYSIS ?  (YES/NO)
```

```
    ***   MULTIPLE SERVER, FINITE POPULATION   ***

NUMBER OF UNITS IN SYSTEM =  2.7646

NUMBER OF UNITS IN QUEUE =  .9069

TIME IN SYSTEM =  1.1189

TIME IN QUEUE =  .3671

PROBABILITY SERVICE FACILITY IS IDLE =  1.78 %

CALCULATE PROBABILITY OF n CUSTOMERS IN SYSTEM ?  (YES/NO)

WHAT n DO YOU WANT TO USE ? 2

P( 2 ) =  .241        ( 24.1 % )

CALCULATE PROBABILITY OF n CUSTOMERS IN SYSTEM ?  (YES/NO)

WHAT n DO YOU WANT TO USE ? 4

P( 4 ) =  .272        ( 27.2 % )

CALCULATE PROBABILITY OF n CUSTOMERS IN SYSTEM ?  (YES/NO)
```

**Figure 15.19**    Example 7: MS, Finite Population Solution

**Figure 15.20**
Example 7: MS,
Finite Population
Data Change

```
HERE IS WHAT YOU ENTERED:

    (1)   MULTIPLE SERVER, FINITE POPULATION
    (2)   MEAN ARRIVAL RATE =   2
    (3)   MEAN SERVICE RATE =   1.33
    (4)   NUMBER OF SERVERS =   2
    (5)   POPULATION SIZE =   4
    (6)   ECONOMIC ANALYSIS:   NO

DID YOU MAKE ANY MISTAKES ?  (YES/NO)

WHICH LINE DO YOU WISH TO CHANGE ?  4

HOW MANY SERVERS ARE THERE ?  3
```

```
    ***   MULTIPLE SERVER, FINITE POPULATION   ***

NUMBER OF UNITS IN SYSTEM =   2.4688

NUMBER OF UNITS IN QUEUE =   .1663

TIME IN SYSTEM =   .8062

TIME IN QUEUE =   .0543

PROBABILITY SERVICE FACILITY IS IDLE =   2.44 %

CALCULATE PROBABILITY OF n CUSTOMERS IN SYSTEM ?   (YES/NO)

WHAT n DO YOU WANT TO USE ?  2

P( 2 ) =   .331          ( 33.1 % )

CALCULATE PROBABILITY OF n CUSTOMERS IN SYSTEM ?   (YES/NO)

WHAT n DO YOU WANT TO USE ?  4

P( 4 ) =   .166          ( 16.6 % )

CALCULATE PROBABILITY OF n CUSTOMERS IN SYSTEM ?   (YES/NO)
```

**Figure 15.21**     Example 7: MS, Finite Population Output/Solution

With 2 mechanics (servers), the probability that all four machines are properly adjusted is 1.78 percent; the probability that half of the machines are out of adjustment is 24.1 percent; the probability that all of the machines are out of adjustment is 27.2 percent. Adding the third server changes these probability figures. The probability that all four machines are properly adjusted becomes 2.44 percent; that half are out of adjustment changes to 33.1 percent; that all are out of adjustment becomes 16.6 percent.

## 15.5

**Summary Notes**
for the Queuing Programs

1. Do not use dollar signs ($) or commas (,) in any of the entries.

2. Mean arrival rate (the average level that a system realizes over a period of time), mean service rate (the average length of time it takes to service a customer), service cost, and waiting cost must be given for the same time units, for example, per hour or per day.

3. Number of servers refers to number of service channels and must be an integer.

4. Maximum queue length for a finite queue and size of the finite population are integers.

5. You can edit the entries by using the backspace/erase key if you discover the errors before the entry is completed. Erase the incorrect entry and type in the correct entry.

6. The error correction routine for the queuing models is of the "HERE IS WHAT YOU ENTERED" input summary type, discussed fully in Chapter one.

## 15.6

**Problems**

For the following problems, assume a Poisson distribution for the arrivals and an exponential distribution for the service times (unless otherwise stated in the problem).

1. Given a single server system with an arrival rate of 25 per hour and a service rate of 30 per hour, determine the system utilization rate. What is the average time a unit is in the system? What is the probability of there being more than 2 units in the system?

2. If the situation in Problem 1 is changed to a multiple channel system with 2 servers, how are the operating characteristics affected?

3. Given a multiple channel system with 4 servers, an arrival rate of 175 per hour, and a service rate per server of 50 per hour, determine the operating

characteristics of the system. Each server is paid $5.75 per hour and waiting costs are estimated at $75 per hour. Is it economically justifiable to add a fifth server (channel)?

4. The information directory of the public library is computerized. The computer answers each query at a constant rate of 30 seconds (2 per minute). Users arrive at an average rate of 75 per hour. How long will each person spend at the machine?

5. The Merrick Company has a tool crib where machinists check out specialized equipment. Machinists arrive at the tool crib every 6 minutes. The tool crib attendant can serve 12 machinists per hour. If the attendant is paid $6.00 per hour and the machinists $18.00 per hour, determine the operating characteristics of the tool crib and the costs associated with this situation.

6. The Merrick Company is considering the addition of a second attendant at the tool crib in Problem 5, making it, in effect, a 2-channel system. How will this change the answers found in Problem 5?

7. The machinists in Problems 5 and 6 always use their trip to the tool crib as an excuse for a side trip to the coffee machine. This machine brews each cup of coffee individually, taking a constant 2 minutes to do so. How long will each machinist spend at the coffee machine? What does this cost the company in lost time (the value of the coffee machine's time may be considered $0.00).

8. If the coffee machine in Problem 7 serves 30 cups of coffee per hour with a standard deviation of 0.004 hour, how does this affect the answer to Problem 7?

9. The Milk House sells milk to shoppers in a hurry. Eighty customers arrive every hour. The clerk can serve 90 customers per hour. Because customers are in a hurry, however, they will not wait if more than 3 people are at the check-out counter. How many customers does the Milk House lose each eight-hour day?

10. Four junior executives report to a branch manager. The junior executives have questions for the manager every 15 minutes. If it takes the manager ten minutes to answer a question, how long will the junior executives spend waiting to talk to the branch manager? How often will the branch manager have some time to himself?

11. Three service men service 7 machines. If the machines run out of raw material once an hour and it takes a service person 40 minutes to refill and restart a machine, how many machines will be out of production on the average? If the service men are paid $5.00 per hour and machine time is valued at $26 per hour, would it be worthwhile for the company to add a fourth service person?

# Chapter **16**

# Markov Analysis

**M**arkov analysis is a decision technique used to predict movement within a system over time, given a knowledge of the rate of change. It is used to predict future events given current events. Markov processes are useful for studying the changes or evolution, over repeated trials (periods), of a system in which the outcome in any particular time period cannot be determined with certainty. Transition probabilities are used to describe the way the system changes from one period to the next. Thus, Markov analysis is a probabilistic technique, involving sequential events. Moreover, it is a descriptive rather than an optimization technique, in that it does not provide a recommended decision, but provides probabilistic information about a situation that will aid in the decision-making.

The fundamental Markovian assumption is that the present status of the process under study depends only upon its status in the immediately previous period. In other words, the probability that the system under study will be in a particular state (condition) after a specified time period depends only upon its current state. In addition, for this discussion it is assumed: there is a finite number of states; the transition probabilities for a given beginning state of the system sum to 1.0; the transition probabilities remain constant over time; the probabilities apply to all participants in the system; no new participants can enter, and no participants can leave the system; and the events or states are independent over time. These assumptions refer to a specific Markovian process, Markov chains with stationary transition probabilities.

Although realistic applications of Markov analysis may be somewhat limited (because of the difficulty of finding situations that meet all the necessary properties), there are a variety of decision situations in which the Markov technique has been successfully used. Its greatest use has been in marketing to measure such things as brand loyalty and market share. Moreover, it has been used in such diverse situations as analyzing accounts receivable behavior, measuring the life of newspaper subscriptions, predicting university enrollments, and determining future operation of machinery.

## 16.1  The Markov Program

The primary goal of this program is to obtain information about the future status of a given system—the probabilities associated with each state in a given future period or periods and the steady state probabilities. This program will determine the transitional probabilities for a given period or periods, the probability or quantity in the resulting vector in that period, and the steady state probabilities and quantities. The program will display each transition matrix, if desired by the user. In the situation where absorbing states exist, it provides the fundamental matrix.

The program requires no advance preparation by the user. However, it is important that the problem be analyzed and the user know the initial vector and transition probabilities.

## 16.2  Data Entry

This program, actually requiring very little input, is very easy to use. However, you are expected to be familiar with the Markov technique and terminology (as described in your management science textbook). To begin using Markov, it is necessary to first select the data entry method from the menu shown below:

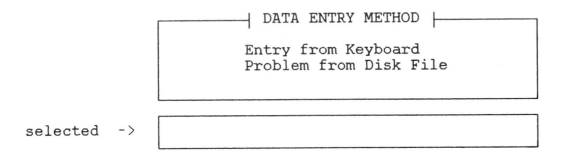

```
                    ┤ DATA ENTRY METHOD ├
              
                    Entry from Keyboard
                    Problem from Disk File



selected  ->   ┌─────────────────────────────────┐
               │                                 │
               └─────────────────────────────────┘
```

Recall that entry from keyboard and from disk file have been discussed in Chapter one.

Data entry requires both responding to prompts and filling in one or more blank tables (matrix).

1. Enter (in response to the prompt) the number of states in the transition matrix. The program accepts only integers between 2 and 12. This includes any absorbing states. Remember to press ⟨RET⟩ to complete the entry.

2. Enter the transition probabilities in the fill-in-the-blank matrix. The matrix has been set up by the program in accordance with your response to the initial prompt. Enter probabilities as decimal values, for example, 15 percent as .15. The probabilities in each row must sum to 1.0. Use the cursor movement keys to move through the table, typing each entry. The [F7] key deletes a state; [F8] adds a state. When all entries have been made and verified, accept the entries with the [F9] key. Figure 16.1 shows a sample matrix.

**Figure 16.1**
Sample Matrix
Input

ENTER THE TABLEAU VALUES:

| STATE | 1 | 2 | 3 |
|-------|-----|-----|-----|
| 1 | .7 | .2 | .1 |
| 2 | .2 | .6 | .2 |
| 3 | .1 | .1 | .8 |

3. Decide whether you wish to do transition analysis and respond to the prompt. If you do not wish to do transition analysis, answer NO. The program will then determine only steady state probabilities for this problem. If you choose to do market share analysis you will have two additional steps in the data entry process:
   a. As prompted, enter the number of trials or periods (integers only) or repeat occurrences to be analyzed.
   b. Fill in the table with the beginning vector or matrix values. These values can be given as decimals (percentage values), or as whole numbers. For example, in a system with 500 customers, the beginning vector can be entered as the number of customers (300 and 200), or as a percentage of the total customers available (.6 and .4). Figure 16.2 (p. 338) shows a sample entry.

**Figure 16.2**
Sample Beginning
Vector Values
Entry

ENTER BEGINNING VECTOR OR MATRIX VALUES:

| STATE | 1 | 2 | 3 |
|-------|-----|-----|-----|
| 1 | 100 | 60 | 20 |

## 16.3  Output and Solution

Before the solution appears on screen, the program requires one more decision from you. You must decide whether you want to see the transitional matrix after each period (for the number of periods entered previously) or only after the final period. Output depends upon whether or not you selected transition analysis. If you did not want transition analysis, output shows only steady state probabilities. When transition analysis is done, output includes:

1. Transition matrices (each transition matrix or only the final one, as you desire) and the resulting vector
2. The steady state probabilities and steady state distribution (if you entered vector values that were not initial percentages).

Figure 16.3 shows a sample output for a problem with transition analysis and beginning vector values that represent units and not percentages of total units. Only the final matrix is shown.

**Figure 16.3**
Sample Markov
Output

DO YOU WANT TO SEE:
      EACH TRANSITION MATRIX    or
      THE FINAL MATRIX ONLY
Your choice —> (EACH/ FINAL )

TRANSITION MATRIX AFTER 3 TRIALS (PERIODS)

|   | 1 | 2 | 3 |
|---|------|------|------|
| 1 | .451 | .289 | .260 |
| 2 | .310 | .338 | .352 |
| 3 | .218 | .197 | .585 |

(continued)

**Figure 16.3**
(continued)

RESULTING VECTOR (MATRIX)—AFTER 3 PERIODS

68.06    53.12    58.82

  Press any key to continue.

STEADY STATE PROBABILITIES:

|     | 1    | 2    | 3    |
| --- | ---- | ---- | ---- |
|     | .316 | .263 | .421 |

STEADY STATE DISTRIBUTION:

56.84    47.37    75.79

  Press any key to continue

## 16.4  Examples

The following examples will demonstrate how this program works.

### Example 1: Markov Analysis

The Discount Dollar Car Rental Company rents cars in Miami, Orlando, and Tampa, Florida. Cars are rented locally (returned to the same city) or one-way (returned to one of the other cities.) Discount Dollar has collected data which reveal the following weekly transition probabilities:

|         | Miami | Orlando | Tampa |
| ------- | ----- | ------- | ----- |
| **Miami**   | .6 | .3 | .1 |
| **Orlando** | .1 | .8 | .1 |
| **Tampa**   | .2 | .3 | .5 |

If Discount Dollar currently has 200 cars in Miami, 100 in Orlando, and 150 in Tampa:

1.  How many cars would be expected to be in each city after 3 weeks time?

2.  What are the steady state probabilities?

Figure 16.4 shows the input for this problem. Figure 16.5 shows the output/solution with only the final transition matrix being asked for and displayed.

```
HOW MANY STATES ARE IN THE TRANSITION MATRIX? 3


     ENTER THE TABLEAU VALUES:


  ────────────────────────────────
  STATE │   1       2       3
  ────────────────────────────────
    1   │  .6      .3      .1
    2   │  .1      .8      .1
    3   │  .2      .3      .5
  ────────────────────────────────


Use Arrow keys, [Home], [End], [PgUp], [PgDn] to make entries.
[F9] Accepts entries         [F7] Delete State,        [F8] Add State


DO YOU WISH TO DO TRANSITION (MARKET SHARE) ANALYSIS ? (YES/NO)

NUMBER OF TRIALS OR PERIODS? 3


     ENTER BEGINNING VECTOR OR MATRIX VALUES:


  ────────────────────────────────
  STATE │   1       2       3
  ────────────────────────────────
    1   │  200     100     150
  ────────────────────────────────


Use Arrow keys, [Home], [End], [PgUp], [PgDn] to make entries.
[F9] Accepts entries
```

**Figure 16.4**    Example 1: Markov Input

After 3 weeks, Discount Dollar can expect to have approximately 121 (121.45) cars in Miami, 249 (248.75) in Orlando, and 80 (79.8) in Tampa. Steady state probabilities are .233 for Miami, .6 for Orlando, and .167 for Tampa.

**Figure 16.5**
Example 1: Markov
Output/Solution

```
DO YOU WANT TO SEE:
  EACH TRANSITION MATRIX  or
  THE FINAL MATRIX ONLY
Your choice -> (EACH/FINAL)


TRANSITION MATRIX AFTER  3 TRIALS (PERIODS)

             1      2      3
         ┌─────────────────────
       1 │  .319   .525   .156
       2 │  .194   .65    .156
       3 │  .255   .525   .22
         └─────────────────────


RESULTING VECTOR (MATRIX) - AFTER  3  PERIODS:

  121.45        248.75        79.8

                  Press any key to continue.


STEADY STATE PROBABILITIES:

             1      2      3
         ─────────────────────
           .233   .6     .167
         ─────────────────────


STEADY STATE DISTRIBUTION:

   105         270          75

                  Press any key to continue.
```

## Example 2: Absorbing States

If a problem has one or more absorbing states (states which retain 100 percent of their population from period to period), we are usually interested in determining the fundamental matrix, which illustrates the percentage of a state's beginning vector that will move into a particular absorbing state over time. The following problem illustrates this.

Fairport Technical Junior College has developed the following transition probabilities for its freshmen and sophomores:

|  | Freshmen | Sophomores | Graduates | Early Leaves |
|---|---|---|---|---|
| **Freshmen** | .2 | .6 | 0 | .2 |
| **Sophomores** | 0 | .1 | .7 | .2 |
| **Graduates** | 0 | 0 | 1 | 0 |
| **Early Leaves** | 0 | 0 | 0 | 1 |

What portion of the current freshman class will finally graduate? What portion will be early leaves? What are the graduation and early leave percentages for sophomores?

Figure 16.6 shows the input (no transition analysis) for this problem. Note the presence of absorbing states (all students either leave early or graduate). The program requires no special entry for these absorbing states. Figure 16.7 shows the output/solution. It calls your attention to the absorbing states with the statement "2 ABSORBING STATES EXIST IN THIS MATRIX" and then shows the fundamental matrix and the probability of absorption.

```
HOW MANY STATES ARE IN THE TRANSITION MATRIX? 4


     ENTER THE TABLEAU VALUES:



  STATE |   1        2        3        4

    1   | .2       .6       0       .2
    2   | 0        .1       .7      .2
    3   | 0        0        1        0
    4   | 0        0        0        1



Use Arrow keys, [Home], [End], [PgUp], [PgDn] to make entries.
[F9] Accepts entries          [F7] Delete State,        [F8] Add State




DO YOU WISH TO DO TRANSITION (MARKET SHARE) ANALYSIS ? (YES/NO)
```

**Figure 16.6**    Example 2: Absorbing States Input

**Figure 16.7**
Example 2:
Absorbing States
Output/Solution

```
           2 ABSORBING STATES EXIST IN THIS MATRIX
           FUNDAMENTAL MATRIX:

                         3      4

                  1  ┌ 1.25   .83 ┐
                  2  │ 0      1.11 │
                     └             ┘
                              Press any key to continue.

           PROBABILITY OF ABSORPTION

                         3      4

                  1  ┌ .58    .42 ┐
                  2  │ .78    .22 │
                     └             ┘
                              Press any key to continue.
```

From this new matrix, we see that 58 percent of the current freshmen will graduate and 42 percent will leave early. Of the sophomores, 78 percent will graduate and 22 percent will leave early. Again, the row numbers show the state the students are moving from, for example, 1 = freshmen and 2 = sophomores. The column numbers indicate the absorbing states, for example, 3 = graduation and 4 = early leaves.

# 16.5

**Summary
Notes**
for the Markov
Program

1. Size: from 2 to 12 states (integer only). Anything over 10 will scroll as entries reach bottom of screen.

2. Transition probabilities: decimal values; each row must add to 1.0.

3. Number of trials: integers only.

4. Beginning vector or matrix values: can be decimals (percentage values) or whole numbers.

5. Moving around the table: arrow keys move cursor right, left, up, down; [HOME] moves cursor to left-hand edge of line; [END] moves cursor to right-hand edge of line; [PgUp] moves cursor to first row of the matrix; [PgDn] moves cursor to the last row.

6. Function keys in entering and changing data: [F7] deletes a state; [F8] adds a state.

7. To edit or correct errors and accept the entries: table or matrix entries should be edited or corrected, and problem modifications made *before the [F9] key is pressed to accept the entries.* Entries are changed by typing over an incorrect entry (the entry you wish to change), using the cursor movement keys to move throughout the table. Also, recall that

the Ending Menu offers you the opportunity to modify the data and run again.

## 16.6

**Problems**

1. Small City has two major department stores, Anderson's and Bell's. Studies have shown that when a customer shops at one of the stores, he or she tends to shop there again. The transition probabilities are shown in the table below:

|  | Anderson's | Bell's |
|---|---|---|
| Anderson's | .7 | .3 |
| Bell's | .4 | .6 |

   a. Assuming a customer shops only once a week, if a customer shopped at Anderson's today, what is the probability he/she will shop there next week, in two weeks, and in three weeks?
   b. If Small City has 15,000 customers, what is the steady state number of customers each store can expect to have?

2. A market research firm has gathered the following statistics on brand switching among four major brands of toothpaste as well as a composite "all others."

|  | Brand | | | | |
|---|---|---|---|---|---|
|  | A | B | C | D | O |
| A | .5 | .2 | 0 | .2 | .1 |
| B | .1 | .45 | .2 | .1 | .15 |
| C | .2 | 0 | .6 | .05 | .15 |
| D | 0 | .2 | .1 | .65 | .05 |
| O | .15 | .2 | .1 | .1 | .45 |

   a. What will the transition probabilities look like after two periods and after four periods?
   b. What will be toothpaste A's market share over the long run?

3. Lawrence has three fast-food restaurants, MacDougall's, Big Bob's, and Kentucky Fried Burgers. The probability of a customer eating at a restaurant on any given day is dependent upon the restaurant he or she ate at the previous day. These probabilities are shown below:

|  | MD | BB | KFB |
|---|---|---|---|
| MD | .6 | .2 | .2 |
| BB | .1 | .7 | .2 |
| KFB | .3 | .1 | .6 |

   a. If a customer just ate at MacDougall's, what is the probability he or she will eat there the next three times?
   b. What percent of the customers in Lawrence can Kentucky Fried Burgers expect to get in the long run?

4. MacDougall's restaurant in Problem 3 is considering a new menu item, the Big Hog. It is estimated that with the introduction of this new item, the transition probabilities will change to the following.

|       | MD  | BB  | KFB |
|-------|-----|-----|-----|
| **MD**  | .8  | .15 | .05 |
| **BB**  | .15 | .65 | .2  |
| **KFB** | .4  | .1  | .5  |

MacDougall's estimates this introduction will be worthwhile only if they can increase their overall market share by at least 5 percent. Should they go ahead with the introduction?

5. The Mason Company has three levels of accountants, I, II, and III. Their records show the following annual promotion probabilities. (Level S represents separations—voluntary and involuntary.)

|       | I  | II | III | S   |
|-------|----|----|-----|-----|
| **I**   | .4 | .3 | 0   | .3  |
| **II**  | 0  | .6 | .2  | .2  |
| **III** | 0  | 0  | .9  | .1  |
| **S**   | 0  | 0  | 0   | 1.0 |

  a. If Mason has 100 level I accountants, how many of them will reach level III in 2 years?
  b. If Mason has 300 level I accountants, 200 level II's, and 100 level III's, what will the distribution look like after 3 years (assuming no new hires)?

6. The Denneco Company finds its machines can be categorized into one of four conditions: excellent, good, fair, and down. Machines that are down are repaired immediately, placing them back in the excellent category. The transition probabilities between categories are shown below:

|            | Excellent | Good | Fair | Down |
|------------|-----------|------|------|------|
| **Excellent** | .3        | .5   | .2   | 0    |
| **Good**      | 0         | .6   | .3   | .1   |
| **Fair**      | 0         | 0    | .5   | .5   |
| **Down**      | 1.0       | 0    | 0    | 0    |

The company currently has 150 machines. Machines which are down cost the company $300 in lost production before they are fixed. Machines in fair condition cost the company $80 in lost production.
  a. How much is lost, on the average, due to machines being in fair condition or down?
  b. The company is considering a preventative maintenance program which would call for the mechanics to repair all machines found to be in fair condition. Would this action save Denneco any money? (Assume no additional costs for repairs.)

7. The Best Buy Department Store has done an analysis of its accounts receivable and finds they fall into one of 4 categories: paid-in-full, 30 days,

60 days, and bad debt. The table below shows the probability of change in the accounts from month to month:

|  | PIF | 30 | 60 | BD |
|---|---|---|---|---|
| **PIF** | .9 | .1 | 0 | 0 |
| **30** | .7 | 0 | .3 | 0 |
| **60** | .98 | 0 | 0 | .02 |
| **BD** | 0 | 0 | 0 | 1.0 |

   a.  Out of 1,000 PIF accounts this month, what distribution of accounts can Best Buy assume after 3 months, after 5 months?
   b.  Can you see any long run problems for Best Buy if they consider a 3 percent bad debt rate to be acceptable?

8.  Wayco Products carries a variety of mail-order products. When Wayco receives an order, it may find that product on-hand, discontinued, on-order, or replaced with a new, improved product. The transition probabilities showing movement between categories are as follows.

|  | On-hand | Discontinued | On-order | Replaced |
|---|---|---|---|---|
| **On-hand** | .5 | .1 | .3 | .1 |
| **Discontinued** | 0 | 1.0 | 0 | 0 |
| **On-order** | .3 | .25 | .25 | .2 |
| **Replaced** | 0 | 0 | 0 | 1.0 |

   a.  Over time, what percent of on-hand products will be discontinued? What percent will be replaced?
   b.  What percent of on-order products will be discontinued? What percent will be replaced?

# Appendix A

# Problem Solutions

Some answers may be rounded. Others may require additional calculations.

## Chapter 3—Linear Programming

1. X1 = 4, X2 = 4, X3 = 0, Z = 32

2. X1 = 10, X2 = 10, X3 = 55, Z = 235

3. X1 = 16.364, X2 = 14.182, X3 = 6.545, Z = 88.364

4. a) X1 = 0, X2 = 20, X3 = 90, Z = 600
   b) B, because it has the largest shadow price
   c) 1.33
   d) no
   e) 60 units

5. a) X1 = 180, X2 = 90, X3 = 0, Z = 1,800
   b) 3.33 < C1 < 8.5
      6.5 < C2 < 15
      NO LIMIT < C3 < 10
   c) 360 < b1 < 540
      300 < b2 < 450
      90 < b3 < NO LIMIT

6. Chain—500, Specialty—300, Discount—200 ($9,900)

7. TB = 140, IB = 280, RE = 280, NSI = 0 ($ 000's), Z = 81,200

8. A = 5.71 oz, B = 10.29 oz, cost = 94.9 cents/box

9. a) 33.778 figure skates, 7.111 hockey skates, $469.33
   b) the blade department
   c) make 48 figure skates and no hockey skates. 37.33 of the figure skates will be

made on regular time in the blade department and 10.67 on overtime

10. A = 110, B = 70, cost = $199.10

## Chapter 4—Integer Programming

1. X1 = 12, X2 = 14, Z = 178

2. X1 = 1, X2 = 1, X3 = 8, Z = 89

3. A = 27, B = 0, C = 46, Z = 73

4. A = 1, B = 3, C = 2, Z = 21

5. A = 29, B = 13, Z = 197

6. X = 0, Y = 18, Z = 304

7. X = 0.75, Y = 18, Z = 303

8. X1 = 9, X2 = 0, X3 = 1.7, Z = 185.8

9. Buy machines A, D and E. $21(000)

10. Buy 1 Catamaran, 7 Wind Surfers and 6 Buggies for an hourly rental income of $180.

11. Buy no shares of stock A, 5,882 shares of stock B, invest $150,015 in real estate, and buy 100 industrial bonds for an annual yield of $89,498.95.

## Chapter 5—Goal Programming

(The notation DnB will be used for negative deviations and DnA for positive deviations—deviations **B**elow and **A**bove.)

1. **a)** X1 = 0, X2 = 43.333, X3 = 20, D3B = 23.333, D4A = 106.667, Goal nonachievement = 130
   **b)** X1 = 25.455, X2 = 32.727, X3 = 7.273, D4A = 149.091, Goal nonachievement = 149.09

2. **a)** X1 = 0, X2 = 14, X3 = 0, D1B = 6, D2A = 26; all goals achieved.
   **b)** no change in the answer to part (a).

3. TB = 25,000; IB = 465,000; RE = 210,000; NS = 0; D3B = 175,000; D4A = 565,000 (rounded). Priority level 4 goals not achieved (565,000 deviation).

4. TB = 357,143; IB = 0; RE = 342,857; NS = 0; D2B = 132,857; D3B = 175,000; D4A = 100,000 (rounded). Priority level 2 and 3 goals are not achieved (P2 = 10,000 and P3 = 132,857).

5. A = 7.333; B = 8.667; D1B = 0.113; D2A = 0.053; D3B = 0.367. Goals not achieved (0.11 deviation).

6. A = 5.714; B = 10.286; D2A = 0.037; D3B = 0.334; D4A = 0.049. Goals not achieved (0.05 deviation).

7. TV = 10; R = 15; N = 15; D1B = 1,750; D3A = 7,500; D5B = 5. All goals achieved.

8. TV = 5.132; R = 20; N = 17.07; D3A = 3,174.344; D4B = 4.868; D6A = 2.007. Priority level 3 goals not achieved (2.01 deviation). Note, however, that fractional parts of ads are being placed. Thus, this answer would probably be rounded to TV = 5; R = 20 and N = 17 with larger deviations than those shown.

9. A = 200; B = 240; C = 220; D4A = 190. Priority level 3 goal not achieved (190 deviation).

10. A = 55; B = 60; D2A = 11; D4A = 3; D5A = 245. Priority level 2 and 4 goals are not achieved (P2 = 3 and P4 = 245).

11. A = 55; B = 60; D2A = 11; D4A = 3; D5A = 277. Priority level 2 and 4 goals are not achieved (P2 = 3 and P4 = 377).

## Chapter 6—Transportation

1. A–W 35, A–X 15, B–X 40, B–Z 40, C–W 40, D–Y 50, D–Z 40 (1,055)

2. 1–C 175, 1–D 125, 2–A 150, 2–D 50, 3–B 75, 3–C 150 (25,375)

3. 1–B 150, 2–C 200, 3–A 100, 3–C 50, 4–A 150, 4–B 150, 3–dummy 25 (2,160)

4. **a)** 1–A 50, 2–A 125, 3–E 25, 3–F 50, 4–D 100, 5–E 225, 6–B 50, 6–C 100, 6–D 50 (4,400)
   **b)** 1–A 50, 2–A 125, 3–D 25, 3–F 50, 4–D 75, 4–E 25, 5–E 225, 6–B 50, 6–C 100, 6–D 50 (4,500)

5. Roch–New 150, FW–Atl 175, Den–Atl 75, Den–Top 175, 50 units unfilled demand at Newark and Atlanta (4,625)

6. **a)** Roch–New 200, Roch–Atl 50, FW–Atl 175, Den–Atl 25, Den–Top 175, Den–Pho 150 (5,425)
   **b)** Roch–New 200, Roch–Atl 50, FW–Top 175, Den–Atl 200, Den–Pho 150 (5,425) (this is an alternate optimal solution)

7. A–X 10, A–Z 10, B–Y 30, B–Z 10, C–X 30, 15 units not shipped to center Z (280)

8. B–R 15, B–Ol 8, S–U 7, S–OF 5, A–P 10, A–U 5, 2 units not shipped from Buffalo and 8 not shipped from Syracuse (13.6)

9. **a)** Boston–B 700, Boston–C 2,800, Denver–A 3,700, Denver–B 1,300 (218,100)
   **b)** customer B's demand will be 2,200 units short

10. KC–StL 50, KC–O 15, D–C 15, D–O 35, D–SD 50, SLC–C 35 (16,805)

## Chapter 7—Assignment

1. Weinstein to 3, Garcia to 4, Krammeritsch to 2, and Biorn to 1; minimum cost = 156

2. **a)** 1 to A, 2 to B, 3 to C, 4 to F, 5 to E, and 6 to D; minimum cost = 79
   **b)** reassign 1 to C and 3 to A (all other assignments remain unchanged); minimum cost = 83

3. 1 to 1, 2 to 2, 3 unassigned, 4 to 3; minimum cost = 923

**4. a)** 1 to A, 3 to B, and 4 to C; minimum cost = 29

**b)** job 2 remains unassigned

**5. a)** Richards to 2, Santiago to 3, Murphy to 4, and Jancowski to 1; minimum time = 75

**b)** Yes. Richards to 1, Santiago to 4, Murphy to 2, and Jancowski to 3; minimum time = 77

**6.** Sara to Periodicals, Aaron to Media, and Sean to Books; minimum time = 6.5

**7. a)** Job 2 to M&M, Job 3 to S.S.&J., and Job 5 to D&B, Inc.; minimum cost = 30,900

**b)** Yes, Jobs 1 and 4 remain unassigned.

**8.** Office to Rockland to Hogshead to Big Flats to New City to Port City and back to the office; minimum distance = 570 miles

**9.** Home to Bagel shop to Bakery to Repair shop to Computer center and back home; minimum distance = 19 miles

## Chapter 8—Network Flow Models

**1.**

| Branch | Value | Path |
|---|---|---|
| 1–2 | 7 | 1–3–2 |
| 1–3 | 6 | 1–3 |
| 1–4 | 13 | 1–4 |
| 1–5 | 12 | 1–3–5 |
| 1–6 | 17 | 1–3–5–6 |
| 1–7 | 26 | 1–3–7 |

**2.**

| Branch | Value | Path |
|---|---|---|
| 1–2 | 20 | 1–2 |
| 1–3 | 33 | 1–4–3 |
| 1–4 | 25 | 1–4 |
| 1–5 | 18 | 1–5 |
| 1–6 | 32 | 1–5–6 |
| 1–7 | 45 | 1–4–7 |
| 1–8 | 55 | 1–4–7–8 |

**3.**

| Branch | Value | Path |
|---|---|---|
| 1–2 | 16 | 1–3–2 |
| 1–3 | 10 | 1–3 |
| 1–4 | 18 | 1–4 |
| 1–5 | 34 | 1–3–6–5 |
| 1–6 | 26 | 1–3–6 |

**4.**

| Branch | Value | Path |
|---|---|---|
| 1–2 | 20 | 1–2 |
| 1–3 | 32 | 1–2–3 |
| 1–4 | 30 | 1–4 |
| 1–5 | 45 | 1–2–5 |
| 1–6 | 48 | 1–4–6 |
| 1–7 | 64 | 1–2–5–7 |

Downtown should be able to make all deliveries with three trucks, although the last route will be twice as long as the first.

**5.**

| Branch | Flow | Flow | Paths: |
|---|---|---|---|
| 1–2 | 5 | 8 | 1–3–7 |
| 1–3 | 8 | 3 | 1–2–3–7 |
| 1–4 | 6 | 2 | 1–2–5–3–7 |
| 2–3 | 3 | 6 | 1–4–6–7 |
| 2–5 | 2 | | |
| 3–7 | 13 | | |
| 4–6 | 6 | | Maximal flow through |
| 5–3 | 2 | | network = 19 |
| 6–7 | 6 | | |

**6.** Maximal flow through the network = 49

**7.** Maximal flow through the network = 25

**8.**

| Branch | Branch Value |
|---|---|
| 1–3 | 3 |
| 3–2 | 4 |
| 2–5 | 6 |
| 5–6 | 3 |
| 6–8 | 6 |
| 8–7 | 2 |
| 7–4 | 3 |
| 8–9 | 6 |
| 9–10 | 4 |

Minimum total span = 37

**9.**

| Branch | Branch Value |
|---|---|
| 1–3 | 40 |
| 3–2 | 20 |
| 2–5 | 15 |
| 5–7 | 20 |
| 7–9 | 8 |
| 7–6 | 10 |
| 6–8 | 25 |
| 3–4 | 30 |
| 9–10 | 30 |
| 10–12 | 10 |
| 12–11 | 15 |

Minimum total span = 223

**10.**

| Branch | Branch Value |
|---|---|
| 1–2 | 1.5 |
| 1–4 | 2.5 |
| 4–3 | 2 |
| 2–5 | 3.6 |
| 5–6 | 1.8 |
| 6–7 | 1.9 |
| 6–8 | 3.7 |

Minimum total span = 17

## Chapter 9—Network Scheduling with PERT

1. Network completion time = 21, critical path = A–C–F–H, variance = 9.66

2. Project completion time = 18, critical path = B–D–F–J

3. **a)** Project completion time = 64
   **b)** This project has multiple critical paths. The critical paths are 1–2–5–7–8 and 1–4–3–6–7–8
   **c)** The project completion time will remain 64, but there will be only one critical path, 1–4–3–6–7–8
   **d)** Yes. The critical path will remain 1–4–3–6–7–8, but the project completion time will be cut to 55

4. The expected completion time is 26.5 days (path A–C–G–I). Probability of completion within 27 days = 57%. There are 2.3 days slack on activity F and none on G.

5. **a)** Network completion time = 22 (path 1–2–4–8–9)
   **b)** Approximately 13.6%

6. **a)** Network completion time = 23.33
   **b)** Critical path = 1–2–5–7–8
   **c)** Standard deviation on critical path = 2.25

7. **a)** Network completion time = 29.83 (weeks)
   **b)** Approximately 12.9%

8. **a)** Critical path = C–E–F–J–M–P
   **b)** Project completion time = 47

9. **a)** Critical path = 1–3–4–5–6–9–11
   **b)** Project completion time = 35
   **c)** Slack on activity 4–7 = 5
   Slack on activity 6–9 = 0
   **d)** Standard deviation on critical path = 2.05
   **e)** The probability the project will be completed within 34 weeks is approximately 31.2%. The probability it will be completed within 37 weeks is approximately 83.5%.

## Chapter 10—Forecasting

1. 19.33 with a MAD of 4.04

2. 18 with a MAD of 3.92

3. 19 with a MAD of 3.87. The weighted average seems to give a slightly better forecast in terms of accuracy.

4. 417.96

5. 509.2; alpha = 0.3, beta = 0.2 (adjusted forecast = 483.87)

6. 4,954.65 with a MAD of 434.155

7. 5,295.37 with a MAD of 319.783. This MAD is lower, suggesting the trend adjusted forecast is more accurate.

8. 60.63 with a MAD of 7.992. Yes, the search option suggests an alpha of 0.9 and a beta of 0.8, with a forecast of 65.08 and a MAD of 6.659.

9. $Y = -5.522 + .141 X$
   $r = .966$ ($r^2 = .933$)
   when $X = 145$, $Y = 14.939$—expect sales of 15 snowblowers

10. period 1—0.8485
    2—1.0000
    3—1.4815
    4—0.6667

11. $Y = -2.353 + .576 X$
    $S(e) = 1.231$
    Yes, there is a linear relationship. The correlation coefficient is .93.
    When $X = 17$, $Y = 7.447$. They should expect 7 or 8 loan applications.

## Chapter 11—Computer Simulation

1. 
| Value | Frequency |
| --- | --- |
| 150 | 2 |
| 160 | 8 |
| 170 | 7 |
| 180 | 7 |
| 190 | 4 |
| 200 | 2 |

2. This problem should be done using nonrepeatable sequences of random numbers and, therefore, answers will vary. Average figures must be calculated by hand—the program will not provide them.

3. This problem must be solved in two steps. The first step uses the probability someone is home and willing to buy—resulting in 76 purchases. Using 76 as the number of purchase simulations, the results are:

| Value | Frequency | Total Sales |
|---|---|---|
| 10000 | 10 | 100,000 |
| 20000 | 10 | 200,000 |
| 30000 | 20 | 600,000 |
| 40000 | 17 | 680,000 |
| 50000 | 6 | 300,000 |
| 60000 | 13 | 780,000 |
| | | 2,660,000 |

4. Carrying cost = 2,180.94
Ordering cost = 432.00
Stockout cost = 94,675.00
Total cost = 97,287.94

5. Carrying cost = 4,957.38
Ordering cost = 384.00
Stockout cost = 175.00
Total cost = 5,516.38

6. Carrying cost = 2,262.18
Ordering cost = 432.00
Stockout cost = 81,935.00
Total cost = 84,629.18
The average demand changes from 299.0 units to 298.2 units.

7. Answers will vary for this problem. A minimal cost solution should be less than $2,400 total cost.

8.

| | Total | Hourly Average | Percent |
|---|---|---|---|
| Total arrivals | 77 | 25.7 | |
| Number served | 48 | 16.0 | 62.3 % |
| Number balking | 0 | 0.0 | 0.0 % |
| Number in line | 29 | | 37.7 % |

Average length of service = 3.7 minutes
Average time spent waiting = 32.8 minutes
Average number in line = 13.9
Average interarrival time = 2.4 minutes

9.

| | Total | Hourly Average | Percent |
|---|---|---|---|
| Total arrivals | 71 | 23.7 | |
| Number served | 50 | 16.0 | 70.4 % |
| Number balking | 22 | 7.3 | 31.0 % |
| Number in line | 4 | | 5.6 % |

Average length of service = 3.5 minutes
Average time spent waiting = 12.2 minutes
Average number in line = 3.5
Average interarrival time = 2.5 minutes

10.

| | Total | Hourly Average | Percent |
|---|---|---|---|
| Total arrivals | 77 | 23.7 | |
| Number served | 50 | 16.7 | 70.4 % |
| Number balking | 22 | 7.3 | 31.0 % |
| Number in line | 2 | | 2.8 % |

Average length of service = 3.5 minutes
Average time spent waiting = 6.0 minutes
Average number in line = 1.6
Average interarrival time = 2.5 minutes

11.

| | Total | Hourly Average | Percent |
|---|---|---|---|
| Total arrivals | 70 | 23.3 | |
| Number served | 70 | 23.3 | 100.0 % |
| Number balking | 1 | 0.3 | 1.4 % |
| Number in line | 2 | | 2.9 % |

Average length of service = 2.1 minutes
Average time spent waiting = 2.6 minutes
Average number in line = 1.0
Average interarrival time = 2.6 minutes

## Chapter 12—Deterministic Inventory

1. EOQ = 1,000 units, ROP = 219 units, orders/year = 10

2. EOQ = 131 (131.45) units, cycle time = 9 days, total cost = $2,464.77

3. EOQ = 3,000 units, annual costs = $750, ROP = 2,019 units

4. PLS = 1,807 (1,807.39) units

5. PLS = 1,732 (1,732.05) units, production runs/year = 1 (1.44), ROP = 34 units

6. PLS = 11,296 (11,296.21) units, total inventory costs = $3,098.39, maximum inventory = 3,227 units

7. total cost = $3,302.18, EOQ with backorders = 240 (239.84) units, 66 units backordered

8. EOQ with backorders = 29 (28.98) units, total cost = $124.24, EOQ without backorders = 24 (24.49) units, total cost = $147

9. Take the discount (total cost = $13,707.50)

10. None, continue to purchase 150 units per order at $17.75 each.

11. Purchase quarterly (total cost = $194,870)

## Chapter 13—Probabilistic Inventory

1. Safety stock = 17 units, ROP = 115 units
2. Safety stock = 40 units, ROP = 440 units, cost = $560
3. Yes, safety stock = 20 units, ROP = 420 units, cost = $1,462
4. SL = 69.2%; probability of stockout = 30.8%
5. 35 units
6. ROP = 71 (70.6) units, SS = 21 (20.6) units
   At ROP of 68, probability of stockout = 3.6%
   Approximately 1 stockout per year
7. **a)** ROP = 42 (41.1) units
   **b)** ROP = 54 (53.475) units
   **c)** SS = 6 (5.1) units x $15 = $90 cost (SL = 75%)
   SS = 18 (17.475) units x $15 = $270 cost (SL = 99%)
8. 538 seats
9. Stock 10 apple pies
10. Stock 400 gallons of cider

## Chapter 14—Decision Theory

1. **a)** D1, new product line ($48,000)
   **b)** D2, existing line ($18,000)
   **c)** D1, new product line ($30,250)
   **d)** D1, new product line ($5,500)
2. **a)** D4 (12)
   **b)** D6 (6)
   **c)** D3 & D6 (7.833)
   **d)** D4 & D6 (5)
3. D3 (8.9)
4. **a)** D1 real estate A (155,000)
   **b)** D3 bonds (100,000)
   **c)** D2 real estate B (110,000)
   **d)** D2 real estate B (20,000)
5. D2 or D3 (real estate B or bonds) ($100,000)
   EVPI = $16,500
6. D3—no additional investment (status quo) ($9,200)
   EVPI = $3,500
7. If the blue-woolly has long fur, buy the new truck and plow (D1) with an expected value of $18,560. If it has short fur, make no additional investment (D3) with an expected value of $6,360.
8. **a)** 30.5%
   **b)** 75.5%
9. 57.6%
10. **a)** Panhandle should produce a comedy (D2) with an expected value of $43,000.
    **b)** EVPI = $37,000
    **c)** If the audience in Peoria reacts wildly (I1), choose the musical ($118,800); if it reacts warmly (I2), choose the comedy (D2) ($74,620); if it reacts coolly (I3), choose the comedy (D2) ($30,220); and if it walks out (I4), don't invest at all since the best decision (D2) will result in a $4,300 loss.
    **d)** Since the EVSI is only $2,880, don't wait for Peoria.
    **e)** 7.8%

## Chapter 15—Queuing

1. 83.3%
   0.2 hour or 12 minutes
   57.8%
2. Units in system = 1.0085, units in queue = .1752, time in system = .0403 hour, time in queue = .007 hour, and probability facility is idle = 41.2%
3. Units in system = 8.7522, units in queue = 5.2522, time in system = .05 hour, time in queue = .03 hour, and probability system is idle = 1.5%. Yes, adding a fifth server will reduce the total cost from $679.41 to $357.63.
4. .0153 hour or 55 seconds.
5. Units in system = 5, units in queue = 4.1667, time in system = .5 hour or 30 minutes, time in queue = .4167 hour, probability system is idle = 16.67%. Service cost = $6 per hour, waiting costs = $90 per hour, total cost = $96 per hour.
6. Units in system = 1.0085, units in queue = .1752, time in system = .1009 hour or 6 minutes, time in queue = .0175 hour, probability system is idle = 41.2%. Service cost = $12 per hour, waiting costs = $18.15 per hour, total cost = $30.15 per hour.

7. Each machinist will spend .0417 hour or 2.5 minutes at the coffee machine, at a cost of $7.50 per hour to the company.

8. Each machinist will spend .0537 hour or 3.2 minutes at the coffee machine, at a cost of $9.66 per hour to the company.

9. Balking rate = 15.59%. 15.59% of 80 = 12.47; 12.47 x 8 hours per day = 99.776 or 100 lost customers per 8 hour day.

10. .2836 hour or 17 minutes spent waiting. The branch manager will be idle 4.8% of the time.

11. 3.23 machines
Yes, it would reduce total cost from $99.17 to 95.47.

## Chapter 16—Markov Analysis

1. **a)** 70%, 61%, 58.3%
   **b)** Anderson's—8,571, Bell's—6,429

2. **a)** After two periods:

|   | A | B | C | D | E |
|---|---|---|---|---|---|
| A | .285 | .250 | .070 | .260 | .135 |
| B | .158 | .272 | .235 | .155 | .180 |
| C | .243 | .080 | .380 | .118 | .180 |
| D | .048 | .230 | .170 | .452 | .100 |
| E | .183 | .230 | .155 | .165 | .267 |

After four periods:

|   | A | B | C | D | E |
|---|---|---|---|---|---|
| A | .175 | .236 | .170 | .261 | .158 |
| B | .185 | .209 | .219 | .211 | .176 |
| C | .212 | .181 | .228 | .203 | .175 |
| D | .131 | .215 | .214 | .289 | .150 |
| E | .182 | .220 | .195 | .220 | .182 |

**b)** 17.5% of the market

3. **a)** 37.6%
   **b)** 33.3%

4. Yes, they will increase their steady state share from 33.3% to 54.9%

5. **a)** 6% or 6 level I accountants will reach level III in 2 years
   **b)** I—19, II—112, III—176

6. **a)** $11,055
   **b)** Yes, the new cost of machines being down would be $4,230

7. **a)**

| Distribution | PIF | 30 | 60 | BD |
|---|---|---|---|---|
| After 3 months | 884 | 88 | 27 | 1 |
| After 5 months | 883 | 88 | 27 | 2 |

**b)** Given the presence of an absorbing state, i.e., bad debts, all of Best Buy's accounts will eventually become bad debts over the "long-run." Since a rate of 3% is one-and-a-half times the current rate (2%), the movement towards absorption will be accelerated if they allow this transition to become 3%.

8. **a)** Over time, 52.6% of the on-hand products will be discontinued and 47.4% will be replaced.
   **b)** Over time, 54.4% of the on-order products will be discontinued and 45.6% will be replaced.

# Index

IMPORTANT: PLEASE READ BEFORE OPENING DISKETTE PACKAGE
THIS TEXT IS NOT RETURNABLE IF SEAL IS BROKEN.

West Services, Inc.
P.O. Box 64526
St. Paul, Minnesota 55164

## MICROCOMPUTER MODELS FOR MANAGEMENT DECISION MAKING
### SOFTWARE DISK LIMITED USE LICENSE

READ THE FOLLOWING TERMS AND CONDITIONS CAREFULLY BEFORE OPENING THIS DISKETTE PACKAGE. OPENING THE DISKETTE PACKAGE INDICATES YOUR AGREEMENT TO THE LICENSE TERMS. IF YOU DO NOT AGREE, PROMPTLY RETURN THIS PACKAGE UNOPENED TO WEST SERVICES FOR A FULL REFUND.

BY ACCEPTING THIS LICENSE, YOU HAVE THE RIGHT TO USE THE MICROCOMPUTER MODELS AND THE ACCOMPANYING DOCUMENTATION, BUT YOU DO NOT BECOME THE OWNER OF THESE MATERIALS.

THIS COPY OF THE MICROCOMPUTER MODELS IS LICENSED TO YOU FOR USE ONLY UNDER THE FOLLOWING CONDITIONS:

### 1. PERMITTED USES
You are granted a non-exclusive limited license to use the MICROCOMPUTER MODELS under the terms and conditions stated in this License. You may:
  a. Use the MICROCOMPUTER MODELS on a single computer.
  b. Transfer this copy of the MICROCOMPUTER MODELS and the License to another user if the other user agrees to accept the terms and conditions of this License. If you transfer this copy of the MICROCOMPUTER MODELS you must also transfer or destroy the backup copy you made. Transfer of this copy of the MICROCOMPUTER MODELS and the License automatically terminates this License as to you.

### 2. PROHIBITED USES
YOU MAY NOT USE, COPY, MODIFY, DISTRIBUTE OR TRANSFER THE MICROCOMPUTER MODELS OR ANY COPY, IN WHOLE OR IN PART, EXCEPT AS EXPRESSLY PERMITTED IN THIS LICENSE.

### 3. TERM
This License is effective when you open the diskette package and remains in effect until terminated. You may terminate this License at any time by ceasing all use of the MICROCOMPUTER MODELS and destroying this copy and any copy you have made. It will also terminate automatically if you fail to comply with the terms of this License. Upon termination, you agree to cease all use of the MICROCOMPUTER MODELS and destroy all copies.

### 4. DISCLAIMER OF WARRANTY
EXCEPT AS STATED HEREIN, THE MICROCOMPUTER MODELSARE LICENSED "AS IS" WITHOUT WARRANTY OF ANY KIND, EXPRESS OR IMPLIED, INCLUDING WARRANTIES OF MERCHANTABILITY OR FITNESS FOR A PARTICULAR PURPOSE. YOU ASSUME THE ENTIRE RISK AS TO THE QUALITY AND PERFORMANCE OF THE MICROCOMPUTER MODELS. YOU ARE RESPONSIBLE FOR THE SELECTION OF THE MICROCOMPUTER MODELS TO ACHIEVE YOUR INTENDED RESULTS AND FOR THE INSTALLATION, USE AND RESULTS OBTAINED FROM IT. WEST PUBLISHING AND WEST SERVICES DO NOT WARRANT THE PERFORMANCE OF NOR RESULTS THAT MAY BE OBTAINED WITH THE MICROCOMPUTER MODELS. West Services does warrant that the diskette(s) upon which the MICROCOMPUTER MODELS are provided will be free from defects in materials and workmanship under normal use for a period of 30 days from the date of delivery to you as evidenced by a receipt.

SOME STATES DO NOT ALLOW THE EXCLUSION OF IMPLIED WARRANTIES SO THE ABOVE EXCLUSION MAY NOT APPLY TO YOU. THIS WARRANTY GIVES YOU SPECIFIC LEGAL RIGHTS. YOU MAY ALSO HAVE OTHER RIGHTS WHICH VARY FROM STATE TO STATE.

### 5. LIMITATION OF LIABILITY
Your exclusive remedy for breach by West Services of its limited warranty shall be replacement of any defective diskette upon its return to West at the above address, together with a copy of the receipt, within the warranty period. If West Services is unable to provide you with a replacement diskette which is free of defects in material and workmanship, you may terminate this License by returning the MICROCOMPUTER MODELS, and the license fee paid hereunder will be refunded to you. In NO EVENT WILL WEST BE LIABLE FOR ANY LOST PROFITS OR OTHER DAMAGES INCLUDING DIRECT, INDIRECT, INCIDENTAL, SPECIAL, CONSEQUENTIAL OR ANY OTHER TYPE OF DAMAGES ARISING OUT OF THE USE OR INABILITY TO USE THE MICROCOMPUTER MODELS EVEN IF WEST SERVICES HAS BEEN ADVISED OF THE POSSIBILITY OF SUCH DAMAGES.

### 6. GOVERNING LAW
This Agreement will be governed by the laws of the State of Minnesota.

YOU ACKNOWLEDGE THAT YOU HAVE READ THIS LICENSE AND AGREE TO ITS TERMS AND CONDITIONS. YOU ALSO AGREE THAT THIS LICENSE IS THE ENTIRE AND EXCLUSIVE AGREEMENT BETWEEN YOU AND WEST AND SUPERSEDES ANY PRIOR UNDERSTANDING OR AGREEMENT, ORAL OR WRITTEN, RELATING TO THE SUBJECT MATTER OF THIS AGREEMENT.